Rhetorica in Motion

PITTSBURGH SERIES IN COMPOSITION,
LITERACY, AND CULTURE

David Bartholomae and Jean Ferguson Carr, Editors

Rhetorica in Motion

Feminist Rhetorical Methods & Methodologies

Edited by Eileen E. Schell and K. J. Rawson

With a Foreword by Kate Ronald

UNIVERSITY OF PITTSBURGH PRESS

Published by the University of Pittsburgh Press,
Pittsburgh, Pa., 15260
Copyright © 2010, University of Pittsburgh Press
All rights reserved
Manufactured in the United States of America
Printed on acid-free paper
10 9 8 7 6 5 4 3 2 1

LIBRARY OF CONGRESS
CATALOGING-IN-PUBLICATION DATA
Rhetorica in motion : feminist rhetorical methods
and methodologies / edited by Eileen E. Schell and
K. J. Rawson ; with a foreword by Kate Ronald.
p. cm. — (Pittsburgh series in composition, literacy,
and culture)
Includes bibliographical references and index.
ISBN-13: 978-0-8229-6056-0 (pbk. : alk. paper)
ISBN-10: 0-8229-6056-7 (pbk. : alk. paper)
1. Rhetoric—Research—Methodology.   2. English
language—Rhetoric—Research—Methodology.
3. Feminism—Research—Methodology.
4. Feminism and education.   I. Schell, Eileen E.
II. Rawson, K. J. (Kelly Jacob), 1981–
P301.R4716 2010
808'.0082—dc22

2009042709

To our feminist mentors

Contents

Foreword · *Kate Ronald*   ix

Acknowledgments   xiii

Introduction: Researching Feminist Rhetorical Methods   1
and Methodologies
Eileen E. Schell

ONE. THEORETICAL AND METHODOLOGICAL
CHALLENGES

Refiguring Rhetorica: Linking Feminist Rhetoric and   23
Disability Studies
Jay Dolmage and Cynthia Lewiecki-Wilson

Queering Feminist Rhetorical Canonization   39
K. J. Rawson

Cosmopolitanism and the Geopolitics of Feminist Rhetoric   53
Wendy S. Hesford

Growing Routes: Rhetoric as the Study and Practice   71
of Movement
Ilene Whitney Crawford

TWO. REFLECTIVE APPLICATIONS

Making Pathways: Inventing Textual Research Methods   89
in Feminist Rhetorical Studies
Kathleen J. Ryan

Rhetorics of Possibility: Challenging Textual Bias through   104
the Theory of the Flesh
Bernadette M. Calafell

Mining the Collective Unconscious: With Responses from   118
Ruth Ray and Gwen Gorzelsky
Frances J. Ranney

Researching Literacy as a Lived Experience   136
Joanne Addison

Rhetorica Online: Feminist Research Practices in Cyberspace   152
Heidi A. McKee and James E. Porter

THREE. PEDAGOGICAL POSTSCRIPT

Writing as Feminist Rhetorical Theory   173
Laura R. Micciche

Notes   189
References   199
List of Contributors   221
Index   225

Foreword · *Kate Ronald*

It's an honor and a pleasure to write the first words in this wonderful new collection that takes Rhetorica one step further from her static historical representation and moves her into new spaces with new tools. *Rhetorica in Motion* explores how all the work on feminist rhetorical theory and history leads to a revised and expanded feminist methodology—for research, teaching, and activism. Eileen Schell deftly and thoroughly explains the sites and perspectives of this methodology in her introduction. So I'll take the latitude that a foreword offers to speculate a bit about the figure of Rhetorica herself.

I'm delighted that Rhetorica appears again in a major title in our field. But my, how she has changed. She bolted into our consciousness on the cover of *Reclaiming Rhetorica: Women in the Rhetorical Tradition* in 1995. (That was a mere fourteen years ago! Think of the explosion of work since then—moving beyond reclamation toward use and consequence.) In the foreword to that volume, James Murphy describes the authors' work as a "glimmer of possibilities, an array of glances, an enthymeme" (Lunsford 1995, ix). And, in an almost eerily prescient last paragraph, Murphy directly addresses the readers of *Reclaiming Rhetorica*: "Let the reader of this book be warned, then, that these guides to partial knowledge offer a sort of enthymemic Newton's Third Law—that the reader's mind, once set in motion, may well stay in motion" (xi). I can't help but note the tentative nature of Murphy's praise: this movement may *well* stay in motion, and *well*, what might that movement lead to? The whole of the rhetorical enterprise might have to be reconceived and rewritten! Now, here, we have another landmark in that movement. *Rhetorica in Motion* certainly offers more than glimmers or glances; I would say that these authors explicitly explore the unstated warrants of their enthymemes as they chart the territories and tools of feminist methodology and offer sustained examinations of theoretical challenges, reflective applications, and pedagogical implications.

On the cover of *Reclaiming Rhetoric* stands Dame Rhetoric (as she is called in the collection) in a gown with a jeweled breastplate, wearing a crown and holding a sword in her right hand, with heralds and trumpets at her feet. As Schell notes, this figure appears as "Rhetorica XXIII" in *Die Tarocchi,* the tarot, attributed to the painter Mantegna. Sometimes, the sword has been interpreted to stand for rhetoric's defense of justice. However, we know little of the source of this tarot card. As Lisa Suter describes in her research on the "Iconography of Rhetoric," sketchy online sources might place it around 1450. Suter speculates that the sword represents power, authority, and the force of persuasion. The crown and the heralds indicate nobility, and the trumpets might mimic the sound of an orator—the ability to project to the back of an arena.[1] However little we may know historically about this Lady, however, in rhetoric and composition, we have clearly adopted her as our own.

Two of the most famous depictions of Dame Rhetorica provide more detailed sources for these images.[2] Around 410 CE, the Roman Martianus Capella wrote *The Marriage of Philosophy and Mercury*, a popular compendium with allegorical descriptions of the seven liberal arts as "learned ladies." As the story goes, Mercury has presented his bride with these seven handmaidens, and Lady Rhetorica appears with gifts. Capella describes her entrance with trumpets:

> In strode a woman of the tallest stature and abounding self-confidence, a woman of outstanding beauty; she wore a helmet, [. . .] in her hands the arms. . . she used either to defend herself or to wound her enemies. When she clashed weapons on entering, you would say that the broken booming of thunder was rolling forth with the shattering clash of a lightning cloud; indeed it was thought she could hurl thunderbolts like Jove. For like a queen with power over everything, she could drive a host of people where she wanted and draw them back where she wanted; she could sway them to tears and whip them to a frenzy, and change the countenance not only of cities but of armies in battle (Stahl, Johnson, and Burge 1977, 156).

Compare this image with the Lady Rhetoric as presented in the woodcut from the medieval encyclopedia *Margarita Philosophica* (1504). Again she has a sword, but now, more like the Rhetorica we know more familiarly through the history of rhetoric, she is seated, not striding, adorned, not helmeted, and offering gifts, not hurling thunderbolts. She is surrounded by learned men, including Aristotle, Seneca, Virgil, and Cicero. One scholar emphasizes her style, rendering the figure as traditionally feminine:

> By the sword and the lily which extend from her mouth she represents allegorically the two traditional functions of rhetoric: to attack and defend by verbal arguments and to embellish speech with verbal adornment. The beauty of her gown and the charm of her coiffure represent beauty of style as first taught by Gorgias. The words embroidered on the hem of her robe remind us of the *colores,* or figures of speech, and the enthymemes and exempla, types of deductive and inductive argument (Clark 1957, frontispiece).

In the afterword to *Reclaiming Rhetorica*, C. Jan Swearingen calls the Lady Rhetorica figure a "shapeshifter," and we can certainly see the changing stance of her shape over these one thousand years. Swearingen catalogs Rhetorica's shifting movements, "all different guises she's been given in past centuries and literatures, starting perhaps with Medusa, the Sirens . . . Cassandra . . . Diotima . . . and up through the many figures of lofty medieval iconography, on into the bawdy harlot of Erasmus's Praise of Folly." She continues the catalog right up to the "witch image" (1991, 331–32).[3] Lisa Suter would add the suffragists to this shapeshifting, since the cartoons and icons used to represent them are strikingly similar to the figures of Rhetorica. Swearingen concludes, "After she has done her shape shifting maybe she can resume as a real woman" (332).

Swearingen's comments open the section at the end of *Reclaiming Rhetorica* in which contributors to the volume were asked to imagine what the "reclaimed Dame" might say about the book. Most respondents strike a hopeful note about future research, especially about attention to the "sisters who are living the history and continuing to shape the world as rhetors and rhetoricians" (Redfern qtd. in Lunsford 1995, 332). I see those rhetors/rhetoricians at work in *Rhetorica in Motion*. If I could design the cover of this collection, I suggest a redrawn Rhetorica, or many Rhetoricas, perhaps on a plane, in a city and a village, and at a computer, and in a classroom, and in the archives, and as transgender, queer, disabled, wearing not a crown but perhaps a headscarf or a

Derby hat, not a helmet but perhaps safety goggles or sunshade. Instead of swords and lilies, she might have a tape recorder, a notebook, a passport, a document camera, a protest sign, a petition, a wiki, and a wallet. Instead of heralds, she might have students, teachers, collaborators, and a friend, and a family. Above all, she would not be seated in the center, but seeking the margins, always on the move.

Acknowledgments

This book has been many years in the making, and there are many people that have been involved along the way. First, we'd like to thank the members of the Feminist Rhetoric seminar from the fall of 2005: Tamika Carey, Carolyn Ostrander, Yu Lun, Pat Kohler, and Dianna Winslow. The idea for this book was germinated during the class and our conversations were very inspirational.

Thank you to Kristi Johnson and George Rhinehart for their meticulous copyediting and formatting work and to LouAnn Payne for her gracious administrative support. At University of Pittsburgh Press, we're grateful to Kelley Johovic, Deborah Meade, and Cynthia Miller for guiding us through this process. The two anonymous reviewers provided insightful critiques that really pushed us to rethink significant parts of the manuscript. Much credit is also due to the contributors to this volume—their thought-provoking chapters, timely revisions, and willingness to be a part of this project has made this book possible. We especially appreciate how they hung in there as this project went through revisions. A special thanks goes to Kate Ronald for being willing to write the foreword to our book; we are honored to have one of our leading feminist scholars introduce this volume.

Eileen would like to thank Lynn Worsham, her feminist mentor extraordinaire, who always pushed her to think about feminist methods and methodologies even when the way was not clear. Many thanks as well to feminist rhetoric and composition scholars over the years who have served as inspirations and guiding lights in the field: Andrea Lunsford, Patricia Bizzell, Elizabeth Flynn, Wendy Hesford, Gesa Kirsch, Shirley Logan, Gwen Pough, Susan Jarratt, Kate Ronald, Jacqueline Jones Royster, and Joy Ritchie. Feminist colleagues and friends across the country also have buoyed up Eileen's spirits in less than feminist times: Heather Bruce, Rebecca Dingo, Susan Lowry, Harriet Malinowitz, Laura Micciche, Jody Millward, Rachel Riedner, and Jen Wingard. Thanks especially to K. J. Rawson who put this project "in motion" and whose "can-do" spirit has kept Eileen going while she was juggling heavy administrative duties as a department chair. Eileen's partner Tom Kerr and daughter Autumn Kerr also deserve thanks for putting up with late-night writing sessions.

K. J. is grateful to Lois Agnew and Margaret Himley for their willingness to exchange ideas and read innumerable pages on this and many other projects. Thanks go to Scrog, Muffin, Jeff, Tol, Elisa, and especially Steph for all of their emotional support and love over the years. Finally, K. J. owes a special thank you to Eileen Schell for reading countless drafts and being willing to join forces in this venture.

Rhetorica in Motion

Introduction

Researching Feminist Rhetorical Methods and Methodologies

Eileen E. Schell

In titling this volume *Rhetorica in Motion*, we acknowledge the historical image of Rhetorica, a queen bearing a sword.[1] We also acknowledge the work set into motion by Andrea Lunsford and the members of Annette Kolodny's graduate seminar at Rensselaer Polytechnic Institute (RPI) who inspired the volume *Reclaiming Rhetorica* (1995), the first edited collection of women's rhetoric in the field of rhetoric and composition. Like *Reclaiming Rhetorica*, the inspiration for this book also began in a Feminist Rhetorics graduate seminar in upstate New York—this time in the fall of 2005 at Syracuse University, an hour away from Seneca Falls, the birthplace of the U.S. women's suffrage movement.

In that 2005 seminar, participants explored the burgeoning scholarship on feminist rhetorics, reading a wide variety of texts that exemplified feminist rhetorical research, particularly in a historical vein. Students raised many questions about the methods and methodologies that make up feminist rhetorical research—how do feminist researchers make decisions about what to study and under what conditions? How does one undertake the work of feminist rhetorical analysis? What counts as feminist rhetorics? How should feminist rhetoricians combine rhetorical methods, feminist methods, and methods from other disciplines? What difficult choices do feminist rhetoricians face as they navigate the uncertainties of working across disciplines or at the edges of multiple disciplines? How does one engage work that is truly interdisciplinary and at the same time maintain ties to a home discipline? What might constitute a productive attitude and practice toward questioning and being self-critical about one's own methods and methodologies?

Questions like these led me to remark at the end of the course that someone ought to edit a volume addressing a wide array of feminist rhetorical methods and methodologies—a collection where scholars model and reflect on their approaches to feminist rhetorical research. One of the students in the class, K. J. Rawson, internalized that offhand remark and approached me at the end of the term to volunteer for such a project; several months later, we issued a national call for contributions to *Rhetorica in Motion: Feminist Rhetorical Methods and Methodologies*.

The image of Rhetorica in motion also seemed a fitting one for a volume that comes a decade and a half after *Reclaiming Rhetorica* appeared in 1995. Since then, feminist scholars in rhetoric and composition have been on the move, establishing the Biennial International Feminism(s) and Rhetoric(s) Conference, a book series in feminisms and rhetorics at Southern Illinois University Press, a series of edited collections and anthologies on feminist rhetorics and women's rhetorics (see Lunsford and Ede 2006, 13–16), and several special issues of journals devoted to feminist rhetorics and feminist rhetorical historiography. The result, as Kate Ronald attests, is that feminist scholars have "recovered an amazing amount of rhetoric by women, reimagined our rhetorical heritage, and redefined rhetorical theory, creating a wholly new tradition, complete with new theories and . . . new practices of writing, reading, teaching, and feminist activism" (2008, 140). Feminist research, as many scholars have noted, has required a substantive rethinking of how we undertake rhetorical research, where and how we examine and analyze specific spaces, figures, communities, objects, and artifacts, and how we establish ethical—and where possible—participatory research practices.

In *Rhetorica in Motion*, contributors gather detailed explorations of research methods and methodologies that feminist rhetoricians make use of, negotiate, and create to fit particular research questions and projects. Following Sandra Harding's lead in *Feminism and Methodology*, we define research method as a "technique for (or way of proceeding in) gathering evidence" (1987, 2) and methodology as a "theory and analysis of how research does or should proceed" (3). Harding also introduces the term epistemology, meaning "a theory of knowledge," or how we come to know what we know and who is qualified to be a "knower" (3). In *Rhetorica in Motion*, we discuss all three, but with specific attention to feminist rhetorical methods and methodologies.

As we called for contributions to *Rhetorica in Motion*, K. J. and I wanted to explore what constitutes feminist rhetorical research and how it is undertaken. We wanted the volume to pull in two directions— to continue to map the terrain of well-defined areas of feminist inquiry such as archival research, literacy research, and online research and also to bring to the fore work in interdisciplinary areas of inquiry such as disability studies, gerontology/aging studies, Latina/o studies, queer and transgender studies, and transnational feminisms. We wanted the volume to represent a variety of spaces and locations of rhetorical study in the United States and in larger geopolitical contexts, thus connecting U.S. feminist rhetorics to the important work underway in transnational feminist rhetorics.[2]

In short, we wanted to create a volume that would demonstrate how feminist scholars develop, question, and modify their research methods and methodologies as they sustain scholarly work through various stages in their careers—whether as graduate students just beginning dissertations, assistant professors launching post-dissertation research, or tenured scholars continuing a current research project, launching a new line of work, or striving to bring to the field a new set of research questions and problems. We were interested in the *process* of doing feminist rhetorical research: how does a scholar unfold a research project over time, deepen a research inquiry, navigate and negotiate multiple fields of inquiry, address particular ethical challenges and struggles specific to feminist research, and possibly question the received wisdom of some of the field's ways of engaging research in feminist rhetorics? We hope this volume will provide some answers to these questions as well as potential models for undertaking a wide variety of feminist rhetorical research. At the same time, we know that a volume like this can only partially address the possible conversations, dilemmas, challenges, and sites for inquiry in feminist rhetorical research and that our project is part of an ongoing dialogue about what constitutes feminist rhetorical research.

Even as we cannot possibly do justice to the wide variety of approaches to feminist rhetorical research, *Rhetorica in Motion* reflects our commitment and our contributors' commitment to exercising the critical self-reflexivity and questioning that is a hallmark feature of feminist research. In part, this volume takes as its inspiration the insightful, self-aware, and self-reflexive approach of afrafeminist research methods and methodologies offered by Jacqueline Jones Royster in her book *Traces of a Stream*. Royster's thoughtful, searching exploration of Afrafeminist methods addresses what she calls "four sites of critical regard," including "careful analysis, acknowledgement of passionate attachments, attention to ethical action and commitment to social responsibility" (2000, 279). Her sites of critical regard have inspired me and a number of the contributors to think through our ethical, social, and political choices as feminist researchers In "Feminist Methods of Research in the History of Rhetoric: What Difference Do They Make," Patricia Bizzell observes that Royster's work—among other things–has inspired feminist rhetoricians to examine the role of caring, emotion, and attachment to one's research subjects (2003, 201; see also Kirsch and Rohan 2008). While feminist scholars are continuing work in the "rhetorical tradition," they are also adopting "radically new methods as well, methods which violate some of the most cherished conventions of academic research, most particularly in bringing the person of the research, her body, her emotions, and dare one say, her soul into the work" (Bizzell 2003, 204). In *Rhetorica in Motion*, a number of contributors are invested in exploring the roles that embodiment, emotion, and ethics play in examining and engaging one's research methods, methodologies, and relationships with research participants.

This volume also emerges, in part, from the challenges I faced—and many of us face—as feminist academics who work at the borders and edges of a number of interdisciplinary fields of inquiry; in my case, those fields are rhetoric and composition, women's studies/feminist studies, and labor studies. As a feminist graduate student in the late eighties and early nineties, I struggled to define my research methods and methodologies in feminist rhetorical studies and feminist composition studies—two relatively new areas of inquiry in the humanities. Like many graduate students working in a new area, I was continually confronted with the typical questions: What is your project? What is your method? And what is your methodology? These questions were often asked by colleagues skeptical of the validity of the fields of rhetoric, composition, and feminist studies, let alone attempts to bring all three together. Answering these questions proved to be difficult, yet worthwhile, and like many scholars in rhetoric and composition, I had to partially invent and combine methods and methodologies from across the disciplines to undertake my dissertation and my first book project. As Janice Lauer argued in "Composition Studies: Dappled Discipline," the scholarship many of us undertake in composition studies, and this is true of rhetorical studies as well, is multimodal: "From the start, then, this field has been marked by its multimodality and use of starting points from a variety of disciplines, all marshalled to investigate a unique and pressing set of problems" (1984, 22).

In 1991, when I was researching the working conditions of part-time women teachers of writing in the U.S., there was not a wide array of work on feminist composition or rhetorical studies that I could draw upon, although there was rich history of much earlier feminist communication scholarship.[3] Elizabeth Flynn's 1988 article "Composing as a Woman," the first direct article in composition studies on feminism, had only appeared three years earlier. A book chapter in 1991 by Susan Miller and an article by Sue Ellen Holbrook—and a handful of precursor articles on gender, pedagogy, and language (see Ritchie and Boardman 2003, 10–14)—referred to the idea that composition studies was a "feminized" field and explored gender, pedagogy, and the composing process.

Using those scholarly resources as a guide and inspiration, I worked across a range of disciplines to assemble a useful approach to my project, poring over the literature on feminisms and labor studies, studies of sex discrimination in higher education by feminist scholars, studies of part-time labor from a variety of disciplines, Marxist and social feminist theories on class and labor, the rhetoric of inquiry, the sociology of the emotions, and institutional histories of writing and writing instruction.[4] I often felt like a *bricoleur*, cobbling together bits and pieces from a variety of fields and working hard to structure and synthesize a coherent, if not complete, perspective. While my methods were often textually and rhetorically oriented, as I examined the common arguments and tropes about women's work as teachers in documents, labor statements, and studies of part-time labor, I also extended my methods to include qualitative research: interviews with part-time women faculty about their responses and reactions to their working conditions and the ways that gender factored into their thinking about their work. Thus, my research required that I be conversant in the work in my home discipline, but also in the ways that other disciplines might pose the question of gender and part-time labor.

The process of doing this research was not seamless or familiar, but often radically defamiliarizing as I came to terms with other disciplines'—and my own discipline's—research methods and methodologies. Having training in rhetorical theory was a benefit as it allowed me to analyze how different disciplines frame research questions, evaluate evidence, and make knowledge claims. As a feminist scholar trained to think about the politics of location (see Rich 1986) and power relations, I also thought about how disciplines frame their inquiries by establishing specific power relations and worldviews. Undergoing this process of working across disciplines was often painful, intimidating, and overwhelming, but it gave me an appreciation for the challenges of interdisciplinary research, and it helped me to develop the habit of being accountable and self-reflexive about my choices as a researcher.

The struggle I underwent to launch my work was hardly unique; in fact, one could call it a feminist rite of passage; numerous accounts of feminist research, including ones in this volume, tell a similar story of struggle, borrowing, invention, and adaptation. What seemed clear about my work as a feminist scholar—and that of my colleagues striving to do similar kinds of work—was that it required a mobility, flexibility, adaptability, and awareness of terms, concepts, and power relations— an awareness of the rhetorical nature of knowledge—that was both taxing and invigorating. The work I did as a feminist scholar also fed into my life as a feminist community member as I agitated for reproductive rights, for workplace equity, and for peace and social justice.

The idea of feminist rhetorical methods and methodologies as movement, as motion, and as action, then, inspires the title for this volume. As feminist researchers, we are often in motion between our various standpoints and positions, between our disciplinary locations in the academy, and between the specific texts, contexts, places, spaces, communities, and institutions we engage. Feminist rhetorical studies and interdisciplinary feminist studies as fields of inquiry are in constant motion as scholars debate and revise previously held notions of feminisms and rhetorics, introduce new subjects of research, new sites of inquiry, and engage methods, methodologies, and pedagogies in a variety of ways. Rhetorical studies is also in motion. As Ilene Crawford argues in this volume, rhetoric "can be a study and practice of our movement with/in rhetorics and with/in the world. Crawford asks us to consider our investments in our research methods and methodologies," and reminds us that our work as researchers involves movement not only across time and space, but also across disciplines, communities, and in, some cases, across the borders of the nation-state.

METHODS AND METHODOLOGIES IN FEMINIST RHETORICAL STUDIES

While *Rhetorica in Motion* offers important reflections and enactments of feminist rhetorical methods and methodologies, we must acknowledge our debt to the prior feminist work that has influenced and guided this edited collection. This volume has been enabled by over two decades of scholarship on feminist research methods and methodologies in rhetoric and composition studies and over three decades of research in feminist social sciences and in feminist communication studies. Across these fields, key questions have been raised about the work of conducting feminist research.

- What are the key principles of feminist research?
- How can feminist research come to terms with the complexity of gender and other categories of social difference and lived experience?
- What counts as evidence in feminist research and in feminist rhetoric, in particular? And why does feminist research matter—to paraphrase Patricia Bizzell: "What difference does it make?"

While feminist scholars across the social sciences and humanities have usually eschewed a unitary feminist method and methodology, they have often agreed upon a set of general principles that guide feminist research practices. Mary Fonow and Judith Cook summarize five main principles of feminist social science research:

- first, the necessity of continuously and reflexively attending to the significance of gender and gender asymmetry as a basic feature of all social life, including the conduct of research;

- second, the centrality of consciousness-raising or debunking as a specific methodological tool and as a general orientation or way of seeing;

- third, challenging the norm of objectivity that assumes that the subject and object of research can be separated from each other and that personal and/or grounded experiences are unscientific;

- fourth, concern for the ethical implications of feminist research and recognition of the exploitation of women as objects of knowledge;

- and, finally, emphasis on the empowerment of women and transformation of patriarchal social institutions through research and research results. (Fonow and Cook 2005, 2213)[5]

As Fonow and Cook argue, epistemology was and is a central framework in feminist studies, particularly feminist philosophical studies, through which to consider existing terminologies for discussing knowledge and research approaches, "including agency, cognitive authority, objectivity, methods of validation, fairness, standpoint, and context of discovery" (2005, 2212).

Yet even as they summarize these five areas, drawn from their earlier 1991 anthology *Beyond Methodology*, they argue that the "spectrum of epistemological and methodological positions among feminists is much broader" (Fonow and Cook 2005, 2213). They define newer trends, debates, and dilemmas in feminist research, including "the epistemic and ontological turn to the body," (2215), the conception and practice of "reflexivity" (2218), "the crisis in representation" brought on by postmodern theory, the implications of feminist research for "social action and policy" (2223), and new ways to deploy "quantitative methods" (2226).[6] They call for feminist researchers to "continue to critique, expand, and invent new ways of doing feminist research and theorizing about feminist critique" (2230)—a goal that K. J. and I share with the contributors to this volume.

Efforts to synthesize, present, and critique principles of feminist research also have a pronounced history in rhetoric and composition studies over the last decade and a half. Of particular importance is Gesa Kirsch's *Ethical Dilemmas in Feminist Research: The Politics of Location, Interpretation, and Publication*, a 1999 monograph that analyzes the "methodological and ethical implications of feminist research for composition studies" (x), especially with respect to qualitative inquiry. In her overview of feminist principles for research drawn from a wide swath of feminist literature on method and methodology across the disciplines, Kirsch identifies seven principles for feminist research; she characterizes these principles as specific commitments feminist scholars make to:

- ask research questions which acknowledge and validate women's experiences;
- collaborate with participants as much as possible so that growth and learning can be mutually beneficial, interactive and cooperative;
- analyze how social, historical, and cultural factors shape the research site as well as participants' goals, values, and experiences;
- analyze how the researchers' identity, experience, training and theoretical framework shape the research agenda, data analysis, and findings;
- correct androcentric norms by calling into question what has been considered 'normal' and what has been regarded as 'deviant'; *disability*
- take responsibility for the representations of others in research reports by assessing probable and actual effects on different audiences; and
- acknowledge the limitations of and contradictions inherent in research data as well as alternative interpretations of that data. (Kirsch 1999, 4–5)

While Kirsch's exploration of feminist principles of research and ethical dilemmas are applied specifically to composition studies, her work is significant for feminist rhetorical scholars. Indeed, she characterizes feminist research in rhetoric and composition as taking three major paths: "recovering the contributions of women rhetoricians"; "studying women's contributions to the history and development of writing studies"; and "studying how gender inequity effects women professionals in composition" (1999, 22). This overview parallels the view of feminist methodology offered by Patricia Sullivan in "Feminism and Methodology in Composition Studies," where she notes that "feminist scholarship in composition" has been "reactive" and "proactive":

it [feminist scholarship] focuses on received knowledge—as the existing studies, canons, discourses, theories, assumptions, and practices of our discipline—and reexamines them in light of feminist theory to uncover male biases and androcentrism; and it recuperates and constitutes distinctively feminine modes of thinking and expression by taking gender, and in particular women's experiences, perceptions, and meanings as the starting point of inquiry or as the key datum for analysis. (2003, 126)

While many feminist researchers have problematized the universal category of "woman" and the idea of uncovering "feminine modes of thinking and expression," Sullivan's concern is with theorizing how feminist research might proceed. To do this research, scholars have approached "two general strategies or approaches, one derived from the historical, critical, and interpretive practices of humanistic inquiry, the other from experimental and field-research models of the social sciences" (Sullivan 2003, 126).

The first branch of inquiry—"historical, critical and interpretive practices of humanistic inquiry"—has produced a rich network of "recovery and reclamation" scholarship in feminist literary studies and rhetorical studies. Second-wave feminist literary scholars were particularly engaged in a significant project of recovering the texts of women authors who were lost or neglected in literary history. This involved, in the words of eighteenth-century literary scholar Jean Marsden, the twin challenge of "unearthing forgotten literature," much of it out-of-print, and "uncovering as much information as possible about the women behind the texts." The goal of this work was threefold: "to bring long-lost women writers and their work to light, to bring them into scholarly discourse, and to make their work available to students and scholars" (2002, 657). This groundbreaking work indelibly altered the literary canon.

Scholars in feminist rhetorical studies have followed a similar trajectory as their counterparts in literary studies by undertaking a massive recovery project to bring women rhetors to light. Much of this important work in feminist rhetorical studies has addressed rhetorical recovery guided by feminist historiography in rhetoric. In "Sappho's Memory," Susan Jarratt divides the work in feminist historiography into two areas: "recovery of female rhetors and gendered analysis of both traditional and newly discovered sources" (2002, 11). Jarratt notes that these two areas of rhetorical research have led us to reconsider and reconfigure "traditional rhetorical categories, and along with them the relationships between past and present" (11). The intensive recovery efforts launched by feminist rhetoricians have produced a flurry of books and collections that uncover, collect, and analyze examples of women's

rhetorical practices and theories, thus contributing to the larger historical recovery project of feminist rhetorical histories. For instance, *Available Means: An Anthology of Women's Rhetoric,* edited by Joy Ritchie and
Kate Ronald (2001), provides a wonderful sourcebook of women's primary rhetorical texts and practices across the span of several centuries
and continents. Likewise, a series of edited collections have provided a
useful selection of essays assessing the contributions of various women
rhetoricians: Andrea Lunsford's *Reclaiming Rhetorica* (1995), mentioned
at the start of this introduction, Molly Meijer Wertheimer's *Listening to
Their Voices: Essays on the Rhetorical Activities of Historical Women* (1997),
and Christine Mason Sutherland and Rebecca Sutcliffe's *The Changing
Tradition: Women in the History of Rhetoric* (1999). Shirley Wilson Logan
offers groundbreaking work with the publication of the anthology *With
Pen and Voice: A Critical Anthology of Nineteenth-Century African American
Women* (1995), which provides a set of speeches and writings by African
American women rhetors, which she analyzes in further detail in her
single-authored book *"We Are Coming": The Persuasive Discourse of Nineteenth Century Black Women* (1999) (see also Royster 2000).[7] Kate Ronald
and Joy Ritchie's edited collection *Teaching Rhetorica* (2006) has framed
the ways that the reclamation of women's rhetorics has contributed to
new understandings of the ways we teach writing and rhetoric. As they
put it succinctly: "In other words, how are scholars teaching *Rhetorica*,
and what is *Rhetorica* teaching them?" (Ronald and Ritchie 2006, 2).

At the same time that the reclamation and recovery work in feminist rhetorics has been incredibly generative, it continues to be fraught
with particular challenges and debates over the potential normativizing
effects of scholarship based on the category of woman, over the most
productive approaches and bodies of evidence that can be gathered and
assessed about women's contributions, over the need to account for the
way gender intersects with race, class, nation, and culture, and over ethics and embodiment in feminist research.

Feminists working with poststructural theory, postcolonial theory,
postmodern theory, critical race theory, cultural studies, and ethnic
studies have challenged categories often taken for granted within feminist research—and feminist rhetorical research—such as the category of
woman, and constructions of the self, identity, and experience. As feminist disabilities scholar Rosemary Garland-Thomson argues:

Feminism questioned the coherence, boundaries, and exclusions of the term *woman*—the very category on which it seemed to depend. Conse-quently, it expanded its lexicon beyond gender differences to include the many inflections of identity that produce multiple subjectivities and sub-ject positions. Our most sophisticated feminist analyses illuminate how gender interlocks with race, ethnicity, sexuality and class systems. This focus on how identity operates prompted an interest in the relation be-tween bodies and identity. (2005, 1559)

The questioning of the category of woman sparked a lively and often intractable dialogue and debate in the 1980s and 1990s over the idea of "essentialism" in feminist scholarship.[8] In *Essentially Speaking*, Diana Fuss argued that essentialism is

> most commonly understood as a belief in the real, true essence of things, the invariable and fixed properties which define the 'whatness' of a given entity. . . . Importantly, essentialism is typically defined in opposition to difference. . . . The opposition is a helpful one in that it reminds us that a complex system of cultural, social, psychical, and historical differences, and not a set of pre-existent human essences, position and constitute the subject. However, the binary articulation of essentialism and difference can also be restrictive, even obfuscating, in that it allows us to ignore or deny the differences within essentialism. (1989, xi–xii).

In feminist rhetorical studies, a key example of the tensions that played out over essentialism and the category of "woman" in revisionary femi-nist rhetorical history can be found in the oft-cited debate between Kar-lyn Kohrs Campbell and Barbara Biesecker. That debate highlights the tensions between the two types of scholarship that Jarratt names the "recovery of female rhetors and gendered analysis of both traditional and newly discovered sources" (2002, 11).

Karlyn Kohrs Campbell's important two-volume work, *Man Cannot Speak for Her: A Critical Study of Early Feminist Rhetoric* (1989), recovered, and in some cases reprinted, the public addresses, essays, and treatises of the early feminists who advocated for women's suffrage. As Camp-bell's work demonstrates, women rhetors need to be considered on their own terms, rather than always in relation to a male-dominated rhe-torical tradition. In Barbara Biesecker's response (1992) to Campbell's work, she debates the assumed stability of the category of an individ-ual woman in history or "female tokenism" and asks if celebrating the achievement of exceptional female rhetors would result in neglecting the collective efforts of women to agitate, organize, and change their collective conditions (144). She contends that if feminist scholars want to "produce something more than the story of a battle over the right of individuals between men and women, we might begin by taking seriously post-structuralist objections to the model of human subjectivity that served as the cognitive starting point of our practices and our histories" (147). Instead of examining the rhetorical practices of individual women in history, what she calls the "affirmative action" approach (143), she wonders, as per Derrida's interrogation of human subjectivity, what it would be like to shift the question from "'who is speaking,' a question that confuses the subjects of history with the agents for history, to the question 'what play of forces made it possible for a particular speaking subject to emerge?'" (148). A "gender-sensitive history of Rhetoric" (156), she argues, would not rest on an "active/passive opposition" and man/woman focus, but it would account for the "formidable differences between and amongst women, and thus, address the real fact that different women, due to their various positions in the social structure, have available to them different rhetorical possibilities, and, similarly, are constrained by different rhetorical limits" (157).

Campbell's reply (1993) to Biesecker's critique points to, among other things, her engagement with writing histories of collective women (156). However, she maintains her right to focus on individual excellence and argues against Biesecker's construction of *techne* (154–58).

While the debate ended in a stalemate between the two scholars, it was generative for many of us seeking to understand how to engage poststructural and postmodern critiques of subjectivity in feminist rhetorics. Indeed, Michelle Ballif has argued that feminist rhetorical recovery efforts are problematic, as they rely on the patriarchal systems of canonization and the very traditions that excluded women in the first place (1992, 95). Drawing on poststructuralism and French feminism, Ballif urges readers to consider "alternative paradigms," examining how "Woman" can "un/speak in the unthought, not yet-thought non-spaces produced by alternative paradigms, by new idioms, by paralogical and paratactical and, thus, illegitimate discourses" (96). Ballif's critique asks us to consider how recovery projects can obscure just as much as they uncover and recover.

With the critique and destabilization of the category of "woman," and, in some cases, a questioning of the value of "figural histories that celebrate, indeed monumentalize individuals" (Biesecker 1992, 157), an emphasis on the intersectionality of race, gender, class, sexuality, and other categories of social difference began to take center stage in feminist rhetoric scholarship in the 1990s. This shift was prompted, in part, by earlier feminist scholars like Audre Lorde and contemporary feminist scholars such as Linda Alcoff, bell hooks, Chela Sandoval, Gayatri Spivak, Jacqui Alexander, and Chandra Mohanty, who began asking questions about race, colonization, and the epistemologies and methodologies of the oppressed: "Did oppressed people, by virtue of their knowledge of both the oppressor's views of reality and that of their own subjugated groups, have access to truer or better knowledge? Who is privileged in an epistemological sense—feminists, women of color, lesbians, working-class women, postcolonials? Who can speak for whom?" (Fonow and Cook 2005, 2212–13; see also Alcoff 1991–92). The epistemological and methodological perspectives offered by feminist and womanist scholars of color challenged existing feminist research methods and methodologies, pushed others in the field to work through the question of research ethics and gendered and raced power relations in the researcher/participant relationship. These perspectives also sparked further interrogation of the connections between "theory, method, and action" (Fonow and Cook 2005, 2213), and the connections and departure points between different categories of social difference.

The focus on both utilizing and interrogating intersectionality inspired many feminist scholars to begin asking how rhetors were not only gendered, but also raced and classed. Editors Jacqueline Jones Royster and Ann Marie Mann Simpkins provide a key example of intersectional analysis in rhetoric and composition in *Calling Cards: Theory and Practice in the Study of Race, Gender, and Culture* (2005). This productive series of essays accounts for the role of race, gender, and culture in rhetoric, literacy, and pedagogy work in the field. Contributors reflect on and examine their professional "calling cards," deploying the metaphor of the nineteenth-century calling card to examine how their foci on race, gender, and culture have shaped their methods, methodologies, and pedagogies. Inspired by Anna Julia Cooper, Royster asks readers to imagine "a world for rhetorical studies that is global, flexible, and specifically aware of its own complexity in the deploying of systems of domination and oppression" (2005, 13). This work of intersectional analyses of feminist rhetorics is ongoing and continues to be vigorously engaged in many articles, books, and edited collections, including this volume.

As Biesecker and Campbell have argued over how to approach feminist historical research, Xin Gale and feminist rhetorical historians Susan Jarratt and Cheryl Glenn have debated how to take up feminist rhetorical historiography and historical evidence. Gale presented her initial critique of Jarratt/Ong and Glenn's readings of the historical figure Aspasia at the 1997 Feminisms and Rhetorics Conference at Oregon State University. Both Jarratt and Glenn were present and responded vigorously to her critiques. In a trio of *College English* articles in 2000, Gale's critique of Jarratt/Ong (1995) and Glen's (1994) analyses of Aspasia sparked a wider discussion regarding the proper use of postmodern historical approaches, feminist histories, and the uses of historical evidence. Many feminist rhetorical scholars have returned to the Gale-Glenn-Jarratt debate as a way of puzzling through their own methods and methodological approaches to feminist historical research (Bizzell 2003; Wu 2000). The debate also has offered scholars an opportunity to reflect on the "role of emotion in feminist historiography" (Bizzell 2003, 198): How does feminist rhetorical research invoke a sense of solidarity and feminist community that does not appeal to those, like Gale, who may feel outside the boundaries of the real and imagined community of feminist rhetorical researchers? How does feminist rhetorical research persuade or fail to persuade a given audience (Bizzell 2003, 203–4)? Will the larger research community outside this specialized subfield find feminist rhetorical research to be persuasive and credible? What community norms are we operating under as we launch research projects and pitch them toward specific audiences (202)?

Beyond debating what can qualify as evidence and what considerations for audience must be taken into account in feminist research, feminist scholars must consider larger questions: What does feminist research do? What form does it take? Whose interests does it serve? In their introduction to *Teaching Rhetorica*, Kate Ronald and Joy Ritchie interrogate the meaning and purpose of feminist rhetorical research by asking the proverbial "So what?" question. They wonder "how rhetoric and composition will use this new area of study. How will this work make a difference in contexts beyond and alongside scholarship?" (2006, 3). One of the answers provided by Ronald, Ritchie, and the contributors to that volume is that feminist research has changed how we teach feminist rhetoric and redefined what counts as rhetoric and rhetorical theory. While their volume is concerned with the difference that feminist research has made for teaching rhetorical theory, pedagogy, and practice, their larger question and its related concerns hang in the air: "So what?" To what end does feminist rhetorical research continue? Who benefits? Who does not? And why? How can feminist rhetorical research make a difference, and not only for scholars taking up feminist rhetorics? How can feminist rhetorics be useful in addressing many of the pressing issues of our day, such as ongoing gender and racial discrimination and continued economic, social, and political injustices and inequities in a globalized world? These questions have not been fully answered in the scholarship in feminist rhetorical research, including this volume, yet they are important ones to ask and continue to address.

In this volume, we continue the discussion about feminist research by following well-laid tracks of feminist inquiry about research methods and methodologies, but we also seek to further the discussion about how feminist rhetorical research is currently being conducted on the ground by a range of scholars and a range of approaches. The contributors to this work demonstrate how feminist rhetorical methods and methodologies are themselves rhetorical, highly adaptive, moving, breathing and representative of a continuum of methodological approaches. At the same time, this volume questions the stated and unstated "norms" in feminist rhetorical research and the locations and approaches to feminist rhetorical research. Furthermore, we consider how our approaches to feminist rhetorical research can be revised to include rhetorical, political, and geographical locations that operate transnationally.

As a volume, *Rhetorica in Motion* is divided into three major areas. Part I, "Theoretical and Methodological Challenges," frames two major recent challenges in feminist rhetorical research: the challenge to normativity and the ideology of the normative body, and the challenge to conduct feminist rhetorical research that is global and transnational. A significant component of feminist rhetorical research, especially research in an historical vein, has involved the reclaiming of women rhetors who have been undervalued, lost, or forgotten. In the process of doing this important rhetorical reclamation work, how do we, as feminist rhetoricians, potentially reinscribe normalizing discourses about gender, race, sexuality, and the body? What are our responsibilities to conduct feminist rhetorical research that challenges normativity?

The chapters by Jay Dolmage and Cynthia Lewiecki-Wilson and K. J. Rawson answer these questions by examining how a critique of normativity shifts our approaches to feminist rhetorical research. While both chapters come at the question of normativity from different angles—disabilities studies and transgender theory respectively—they challenge "research that objectifies its subjects or is based on unacknowledged constructions of normalcy and deviancy" (Dolmage and Lewiecki-Wilson). Dolmage and Lewiecki-Wilson address how bringing feminism and disability studies together creates new possibilities for feminist methods in rhetorical scholarship, teaching, and service. Drawing on queer and transgender theories, K. J. Rawson offers strategies for engaging feminist rhetorical recovery and gendered analysis in ways that interrogate gender normativity and heteronormativity.

Contributions by Wendy S. Hesford and Ilene Crawford also question received norms, yet do so within the framework of transnational feminist theory, asking us to consider and question how the conceptions of rhetorics, in general, and feminist rhetorics, in particular, are conceived within the borders of the nation-state or within the imaginary of the West. Hesford argues that a transnational feminist rhetorical methodology—one that draws together transnational feminist studies and rhetorical studies through critiques of feminist cosmopolitanism—can help us interrogate feminist perspectives on location, situated knowledge, rhetorical identification, agency, and the public sphere. She theorizes the spatial and temporal as part of a transnational feminist rhetorical methodology and locates feminist cosmopolitanism and transnational feminisms on a methodological continuum. As Hesford offers a careful analysis of transnational representations of women across the globe, Ilene Crawford similarly asks questions about the methods and methodologies that will address literacy and rhetorical research in transnational contexts. Resisting the allure of cosmopolitanism described and critiqued by Hesford, Crawford analyzes how she arrived at feminist rhetorical methods of research and interaction that were workable for her research on women's literacy practices in Vietnam.

In Part II, "Reflective Applications," contributors continue to explore theoretical and methodological challenges, but they localize their inquiries in specific sites and research approaches: gender critique and textual research practices (Kathleen Ryan), feminist performance studies and theories of the flesh (Bernadette Calafell), archival research practices (Frances Ranney), experience sampling methods (Joanne Addison), and online research (Heidi McKee and James Porter). Across all of the essays, the authors in this section reflect on the particular methodological challenges and ethical dilemmas that unfolded as they conducted their research. Running across many of the essays are the concepts of invention, social context, imagination, and ethics, and the writers also offer a critical and self-reflexive stance toward their research, a hallmark feature of feminist research described by Kirsch in her synthesis of feminist research principles (1999, 4–5).

Kathleen Ryan engages feminist pragmatic rhetoric to address how feminist textual research can function as a form of scholarly invention and disciplinary invention. Challenging the focus on feminist rhetoric as textually oriented, Bernadette Calafell analyzes the connections and differences between theories of the flesh found in Chicana feminisms, African American feminisms, performance studies, and rhetorical studies. As she reflects on her struggles to find a methodological homeplace within rhetoric, performance studies, and Chicana and African American studies, she outlines an approach to rhetoric and performance studies grounded in a theory of the flesh.

Like Kathleen Ryan, Frances Ranney is interested in the question of invention—in this case, the invention process she engaged in as she researched "Fontia R.," an elderly female subject she encountered in her archival research on a foundation for seniors in need. Ranney invents the concept of "imagin-activation"—a concept drawn from Jungian psychoanalysis—to think through the ethics of imagining the life of Fontia R. and to critically account for her attachment to her. Respondents Ruth Ray and Gwen Gorzelsky further consider and reflect on the ethical research questions that Ranney raises. Shifting the conversation from considering textual research strategies and archival research practices, Joanne Addison focuses on feminist empiricism to understand literacy as a lived experience. Addison argues that feminist empiricism, when inflected by feminist standpoint theory, can help feminist researchers better understand the knowledge and insights of those outside the mainstream of society. Finally, Heidi McKee and James E. Porter examine the methodological and ethical issues feminist researchers face when conducting research in online environments. They use published cases and interviews with Internet researchers to address the complex ethical, political, and social problems feminist researchers must address as they undertake online research.

In "A Pedagogical Postscript," Laura Micciche models a method for engaging with feminist work that emphasizes writing as a conceptual and imaginative process of vital importance to feminist rhetorical theory. She explores a series of questions about the role that imagination—we can also think here of Ranney's notion of imagin-activation—and play can have in the writing classroom.

As the volume moves across the three areas of inquiry, we are aware that we do not offer easy answers or a pat formula for undertaking feminist research; rather we offer, as Fonow and Cook would say, a wide "spectrum of epistemological and methodological positions" that demonstrate the "vitality of feminist studies" (2005, 2213) in the field of feminist rhetorics. At the same time, we acknowledge that the vitality of feminist rhetorics is often challenged by a society in which many avoid the term "feminist" and many scholars seem to have developed what Gill Plain and Susan Sellers call cultural amnesia, where people act as if "the need to challenge patriarchal power or to analyse the complexities of gendered subjectivities had suddenly gone away, and as if texts were no longer the products of material realities in which bodies are shaped and categorised not only by gender, but by class, race, religion and sexuality" (2007, 1). The danger of this cultural amnesia, thus, is not only forgetting one's histories and origins, but the danger of acting in the contemporary world as if inequality and differential power relations are no longer an issue, thus allowing rollbacks of gains made for gender equity and the elimination of gender-based oppression. In an era when feminism has been declared dead by public commentators or, worse yet, by our colleagues, and in an era when students announce that they are no longer in need of feminism even while availing themselves of opportunities borne of feminism, it is difficult to maintain equanimity and, at times, a sense of optimism.

Yet as the scholars in this volume demonstrate, feminist rhetorical research is alive and well, multifaceted and in motion, reaching into continuing and new branches of inquiry, places, and spaces. And, as these scholars demonstrate, there is not one correct "feminist epistemology generating one correct feminist methodology for the interdisciplinary field of women's studies" (Fonow and Cook 2005, 2213) or for feminist rhetorical studies, for that matter. We, feminist scholars in rhetorical studies, are constantly in motion, "working within, against, and across" methods and methodologies, "combining elements from different perspectives" and different disciplines, addressing questions about the value and purpose of the work we do, and working to reconcile our methodological differences even as we realize that some of those differences cannot be reconciled (2213). We are *Rhetorica in Motion*.

One

Theoretical and Methodological Challenges

Refiguring Rhetorica

Linking Feminist Rhetoric and Disability Studies

Jay Dolmage and Cynthia Lewiecki-Wilson

Feminism and disability studies ought to be powerful allies. Feminist rhetorical methods provided a foundation for the emerging field of disability studies in the humanities in the late 1980s. And in the 1990s, disability studies theories and methods developed synergistically with feminism and other theories in directions that challenge and transform methods and theories across fields.

As feminists have argued, the received collection that we call rhetoric is made up of remnants of a classical past, layered over by accumulated practices from nearly three millennia in which the structures and values of patriarchy dominated, all wrapped up with over three centuries of Enlightenment logic. Within this messy collection of traditions, one constant was that female embodiment—because it deviated from male embodiment—was figured as dis-abled; to be a woman was to be disqualified from civic debate (see Crowley 1999; Grosz 1994, 1996; Lindgren 2004). By the time of the Enlightenment, as Evelyn Fox Keller's work (1985) has shown, to be a woman was also to be an object of science, not a maker of it. In these ways, the category of woman has been closely aligned with the category of disability as a term that has marked deficiency and disqualification.

In contrast, we recognize the positive signification of disability and believe that feminism's engagement with disability can refigure the face, body, and voice of rhetoric(a). We reframe disability, not only by turning around this word's usual function as the ultimate specter of derogation, but also by making use of its gathered meanings in order to shape and focus a new critical lens built on the generative potential of an alliance between disability studies and feminisms. A feminist, disability studies perspective impacts methods—not only in our scholarly projects, but also in teaching and service, which also are frequently areas where composition and rhetoric research is undertaken and applied. We believe that five key concepts from disability studies provide methods for the work of critique, recovery, and invention of new rhetorical futures. These concepts grow out of, and deepen, feminist critiques of the rhetorical tradition. Rolling through each of these concepts is a key rhetorical strategy in disability studies—the move to investigate the history of bodily norms in order to unmask the powers and processes of "norming" and the construction of "normality."

DEMYSTIFYING NORMAL

Normal always highlights particular power relations that affect everyone, but especially people with visible disabilities. "When we think of bodies, in a society where the concept of the norm is operative," Lennard Davis writes, "then people with disabilities will be thought of as deviants" (1995, 29). As Davis and other disability studies scholars have pointed out, the categories of normal and abnormal, able and disabled are invented and enforced in service of particular ideologies, for instance a valorization of the bourgeois subject or of the middle class (1995, 26–29).[1] These categories are useful fictions that mark unwanted elements while reinforcing the hegemony of the dominant group.

The term normate has been developed in the field of disability studies to connote the ways normalcy is used to control bodies—normalcy, as a social construct, acts upon people with disabilities.[2] Normate designates the unexamined and privileged subject position of the supposedly (or temporarily) able-bodied individual. As with the concepts of male privilege, of whiteness, or of heteronormativity, the individual assuming the normate position occupies a supposedly preordained, unproblematic, transparent, and unexamined centrality. A normate culture, then, continuously reinscribes the centrality, naturality, neutrality, and unquestionability of this normate position. Such cultures demand normalcy and enforce norms, both marking and marginalizing those bodies and minds that do not conform.

Disability studies scholars critique normalcy by studying the history of norms, challenging their centering mechanisms and the politics that construct disability as deviance. The field of disability studies therefore also challenges those rhetorical moves that attribute deviance to a society's others—those discourses that suggest that inequities based on disability, race, class, gender, national, and other divisions are attributable to biology. Importantly, in challenging the idea that social imbalance can be explained by biology, disability studies challenges both the attribution and the construction of deviance—not just reversing attributions of deviancy, but also deconstructing the mechanisms by which an individual or group might be stigmatized.

Challenging attitudes about normalcy is difficult work, however, because normate thinking is deeply entrenched within the academy and deviations from the norm make people uncomfortable and become justifications for exclusion. As director of composition at a Midwestern University, Cynthia Lewiecki-Wilson mentored and supported instructors teaching first-year composition. Working with the disability resources office, Cindy placed a blind student into the class of a seasoned instructor, thinking that this instructor's experience and easygoing style would be a good fit for a student needing accommodations. However, this placement turned out to be a disaster because the instructor felt strongly that the usual way that she did things was being disrupted. Despite several conferences with Cindy, the instructor kept saying, "He doesn't seem 'normal.' He makes me nervous." Even given the institutional pressures to accommodate his different learning needs, the instructor felt emboldened to be frank, saying—finally—"I want him out of my class."

It does not take a great leap to imagine how strong (and potentially destructive) the unspoken structuring force of the norm is as it is exerted upon other students with differences, whether of race, class, or sexual orientation, when accommodating their learning needs is not even institutionally mandated. We all can call up anecdotal evidence of this sort. Yet, from the perspective of a feminist disability studies methodology, we recognize that one must not wait for or rely on anecdotal evidence, but actively interrogate the assumption that the white, male, and able-bodied position is central and natural—one must acknowledge that commonplace attitudes and institutional practices represent a normate perspective. This instructor, like many in the academy, views the "norm" as the universal, not as a set of particular hegemonic values, instituted and maintained by a ruling class that excludes many. Our point is that teachers would be more aware that certain actions and attitudes are discriminatory if they had knowledge of disability studies' critique of the norm. All classroom researchers should be critically aware of the ways that the norm reifies some students and practices, placing them inside, and others outside, the usual parameters or expectations. The teacher in Cindy's story was finally discriminatory—the attitudes she expressed before this final step, however, are widespread, and are in fact too often the "normal" way of thinking.

The article "Constructing a Third Space: Disability Studies, The Teaching of English, and Institutional Transformations" (Wilson and Lewiecki-Wilson 2002) extends this discussion of how we might work toward new ways of thinking about classroom equity, arguing that we can change entrenched practices and encounters with difference by developing reflective and reflexive pedagogy and research, modeled on postmodern feminist epistemology allied with disability studies. In their roles as administrators, Jay Dolmage and Cindy Lewiecki-Wilson have also both worked extensively to promote pedagogical practices of universal design (Dolmage 2005b). Universal design, a concept borrowed from architecture, holds that one should design spaces *and* learning environments for the broadest possible access—with ramps in the front door, figuratively and literally, and with varied and flexible pedagogical doorways wide enough to invite in all learning styles. In *Disability and the Teaching of Writing: A Critical Sourcebook* (Lewiecki-Wilson, Brueggemann, and Dolmage 2008), in their teacher training of new graduate student teachers, and in faculty development workshops, Jay and Cindy argue for the importance of universal design principles and practices for every class and demonstrate UD features so that hopefully fewer and fewer teachers will proceed from exclusionary normative assumptions.

[margin note: norming = rhetorical move]

Following from the thesis that norming is an essential rhetorical move, we can read rhetorical history as itself a normative text. Just as feminist researchers have challenged the idea that women were not fit rhetors, a study of the rhetorical tradition, through a disability studies lens, reveals the ways that rhetoric became disembodied and rhetorical fitness came to be ascribed to just a narrow range of (white, male, able) bodies. A disembodied rhetorical history also informs a certain epistemology, which denigrates the rhetorical value of the body and, more specifically, of bodily difference.

Central to disability studies is a reengagement with embodiment, although disability studies theory is not monolithic and uniform in the ways that the body is conceptualized.[3] What all disability studies theorists have in common is interrogating the social and historical constructions of able and disabled bodies. Just as feminist historians have defused the charge that only men can be persuasive, disability studies methodologies challenge the idea that bodily differences, often viewed as deficiencies, perversions, or deformities, can have only negative rhetorical value, and can only disqualify the subjects upon whom such stigma is culturally located.

This normative matrix comprises a narrow range of rhetorical ability, which is impossible to maintain; it also overlooks the ways that rhetors make use of disability as rhetorical power. For example, while popular stories suggest that the Greek rhetorician Demosthenes overcame his stutter and his perceived effeminacy to speak perfectly (Hawhee 2005, Fredal 2006), other versions of this history suggest that the great orator used his "abnormal" body and voice for generative rhetorical effect (Rose 2003). The historiography by Jay Dolmage (2006), for example, reclaims the rhetorical value of *metis*, symbolized both by the Greek goddess of the same name, eaten by her husband Zeus because her crafty and feminine knowledge is more powerful than his brute force, and by Hephaestus, a Greek god with a physical disability.

Jay's work with Hephaestus argues that there can be positive models of disability rhetoric, that disability did not, and does not, disqualify one from rhetorical opportunity and efficacy. Hephaestus's feet are represented (in art and myth) as being turned outward, away from one an-

[margin note: + models]

other. Yet in the mythical world, this "disability" symbolizes rhetorical cunning or *metis*—the ability to move from side-to-side more quickly, and to "think on one's feet," so to speak. Although such stories may seem foreign to the modern reader because of the powerful hold of embodied norms, Jay's work shows that much bias has been exported into the past and suggests the need for further exploration of the rhetorical history of stigmatized bodies.

Jay's work on the Greek goddess Metis (Dolmage 2009) also argues that our neglect and oversight of this history of divergently embodied rhetoric is connected to the denigration of the female body. Metis was eaten by her husband Zeus because he saw her *metis,* or cunning intelligence, as a threat to his power. This story of ingestion serves as an analog for the consumption and erasure of *all* embodied rhetoric, of the female body, figuratively, and of the rhetorical potential of bodily difference, by the rhetorical tradition. Jay maps this trend from Metis to Helene Cixous's reclamation of the Medusa myths and Gloria Anzaldúa's *mestiza* consciousness, concepts that share more than just an etymological connection. Jay's work provides a model for refiguring rhetorical history by rereading past norms of bodily diminishment or propriety that serve to devour and expel all that does not conform to a very narrow bodily norm.

While feminist researchers have the tools to reanimate the rhetorical tradition and re-invest the body with rhetorical meaning, they should recognize that disability reaches into all bodies, not only those that appear "abnormal." It isn't enough to simply reclaim the body—we must examine the ways that this body shapes possibilities for expression by disciplining bodily difference or enforcing bodily norms.

Understanding the embodied foundation of disability studies, feminist research methodologies should include a critique of the construction of disability as a marker of rhetorical defect and should seek ways of understanding bodily differences as rhetorically generative. For example, another response to having a blind student in class would be to develop rhetorical practices that are enabled by other senses and not dependent upon sight. The poet and teacher Stephen Kuusisto, who is blind, recommends teaching all students the generative powers of listening, memorizing, and reciting, skills that blind students master (2008). In this way, the presence of bodily difference could lead to recovery of neglected aspects of the rhetorical canon—memory and delivery—which, we believe, are largely overlooked in composition and rhetoric classes at all levels of the curriculum.

CRITIQUING THE MEDICAL MODEL

While the rhetorical tradition solidified the rhetoricity of the word and figured bodily difference as disqualification, the rise of medicine and science further schematized and multiplied categories of bodily deviance and deformity. The disabled, now categorized and labeled in ever more refined dissections of deviance, came under this new regime of science or—to use Foucault's term—bio-power. Science, medicine, and later therapeutic discourses and practices cast disability as a personal deficit or deviance to be cured. The modern medical paradigm has done more than categorize and control people with disabilities; it has enforced sterilization, institutionalization, and eradication—a history of oppression that disability studies scholars are now recovering and studying (see Mitchell and Snyder 2006; Stiker 1999; Trent 1994).

The rise of science brought with it cultural logics (e.g., the belief in value-free observations, context-independent methods, an objective truth) that sustained historic exclusions and founded new ones on scientific grounds, through the arrangement and discipline of abjected others around the rational subject-observer. To be a complete, bounded, rational subject, disability had to be expelled—disowned or eradicated.[4] Whether women, slaves and foreign others, or the disabled, science used its instruments of measurement, its gaze, and its taxonomies to array these others as passive and lesser objects to be studied by the unexamined examiner, the "modest witness" described by Donna Haraway (1997, 23–24), whose invisible subjectivity shores up his objective authority.[5] Disability extended beyond actual impaired bodies to become an operative and essential element driving subject/object dualism—any body subjected to the medical gaze becomes disabled to some extent, through its positioning as passive object, and through the over-signification of bodily deviation.[6]

In opposition to the prevailing model of science as hierarchical domination over the passive object of study, feminists Evelyn Fox Keller and Christine R. Grontowski (1999, 39) propose an interactionist, dialectical process not only between the scientist and what s/he studies but also in the complex interaction of biological forms and their contexts. Interaction can be conceptualized both at the cellular and, as N. Katherine Hayles argues in her work (1999), at the environmental level. In a similar move, disability studies holds that disability is a complex political and cultural effect of one's interaction with an environment, not simply a medical condition to be eliminated. Indeed, the more we understand the complexities of the human genome, the more it appears that simply erasing or snipping out defects may jeopardize other important genetic safeguards (Wilson 2002). On the other hand, the rhetoric supporting gene research frequently claims that in the future disability will be eradicated.

The scholarship of disability studies has shown how this medical dream to eliminate disability has had dehumanizing results. Programs based on scientific assumptions and attributions of disability have been used to violently reinforce racial and national exclusions—from the pseudoscience of eighteenth- and nineteenth-century racial theories that justified collecting and displaying human specimens like the "Hottentot Venus," to twentieth-century eugenics, its apogee in the Holocaust, and its dissolution and reconcentration in myriad other contemporary forms. Jay's most recent research, for example, focuses on the creation of categories such as the "feeble-minded," the "moron," and the "idiot" as products of American anti-immigration rhetoric in the early twentieth century (Dolmage 2007). Jay shows how these terms were used to justify new race-based categorizations, hierarchies, and exclusions. Disability was the accent applied to a new corporeal lexicon and served to mark out what was not American. This new stratification was also reinforced by the first standardized IQ and literacy tests, and thus Jay shows how an investment in the *creation* of categories of race/disability serves as the impetus for these normative practices as well.

In such ways, disability history and feminist and disability critiques of science provide important methodological lenses, which help the researcher challenge epistemologies that do not self-reflexively examine their own dispositions toward and assumptions about the subject of study. In our work, whether editing collections or engaging in archival research, we strive to treat science in its complexity, being critical and careful to recognize its history of objectification of bodies (especially female bodies) and abjection of some (especially disabled bodies), but also its positive power to improve the lives of people. As an editor of two disability studies collections (Wilson and Lewiecki-Wilson 2001; Lewiecki-Wilson, Brueggemann, and Dolmage 2008), Cindy has offered revision suggestions that try to move writers away from arguments that oversimplify disability's relation to science by, for example, pitting the "true" meaning of disability in binary opposition to science. While science objectifies the disabled and understands disability through the categories of abnormality, deviancy, and deficits to be cured, the informed researcher also realizes that the various ways that science has defined and constructed disability are important constituents of what disability signifies at a particular cultural moment. Consciously seeking to avoid such binaries can, in fact, be a method for thinking in new directions. Drawing upon both feminist and disability studies analyses of the body and of science offers a powerful and generative way to avoid binaries and critically explore how women and the disabled have been objectified by the medical gaze.

GAZING UPON THE FREAK

Just as the doctor's gaze creates an objectified, passive body, focusing on defect, the patient is likewise interpellated to reproduce this gaze. The "scientific" gaze comes to permeate culture. How we see others and ourselves is shaped by the medical-scientific paradigm, which is in turn shaped by disability and normativity. Rosemarie Garland-Thomson extends this line of investigation in her scholarship on the freak show, arguing that there are cultural processes that make physical abnormality or particularity "a hypervisible text against which the viewer's indistinguishable body fades into a seemingly neutral, tractable and invulnerable instrument of the autonomous will" (1996b, 10). It is only against an othered body that the normal body is allowed to perpetuate its deceit (of transparency, of being standard, of being whole).

Freak shows of the late nineteenth and early twentieth century not only arrayed and framed physical abnormality, but also referentially constructed exotic others, asking the viewer to cross-diagnose alien ethnicities with defective bodies. For example, African American William Johnson, known as "Zip the Pinhead," was billed as "the missing link" and exhibited in a cage to enhance the illusion that he had been captured in Africa. British- and American-born Hiram and Barney Davis toured as Waino and Plutano, the Wild Men of Borneo.[7] The (supposed) physical and mental abnormalities of these men, respectively, received reinforcement from an invented ethnic marking. In return, alien ethnicities were made more freakish, arrayed around the blankness of the norm so that it might take ideal shape. And the incarceration, pathologizing, or deportation of the strange body/mind is the ground upon which the liberty, health, and citizenship of the supposedly able-bodied and rational subject, and the healthy nation, is based. The studies of bell hooks (1992) and Londa Schiebinger (1993), for instance, show how such freakification has functioned in the construction of African and African American women as disabled. As Jay's research into American immigration practices shows (2007), to preserve its wholeness, and to define its fitness through contrast, a nation must (opportunistically) mark out and exclude a range of others.

Many objective research methodologies reify the representative sample, the universal, and generalizable. They manufacture the reproducible and isolate and invalidate the outlier. Feminist researchers informed by disability studies might instead look to the margins to understand the function of the outlier as the ground against which particular forms of knowledge come into view. They should be aware of the processes of the specular—the dominance of looking as a sense for meaning-making, which carries with it the logic of the visual. As the work of Fox Keller and Grontowski (1999, 189) points out, such distancing from and objectification of the other has been tied to the intellect and male domination at least since Plato. Researchers also might do well to imagine how other senses (hearing, touch, smell) might provide different metaphors and ways for making knowledge.[8]

UNDERSTANDING INTERSECTIONALITY

Just as the term *woman* has been critiqued as an all-encompassing label that may actually mystify which identity groups enjoy privilege and power, *disability* names an identity group riven with differences. There is no doubt that people with disabilities have experienced real oppression; however, people with disabilities—like women—also experience oppression because of their race or ethnicities, their gender, their class, or national identifications. There is a disability hierarchy, as well: People with different disabilities face different kinds of stigmas and social barriers, some more than others. It might almost seem as though disability is a useless term, in that in contains more differences than similarities. Disability studies scholars, activists, and allies, though, find the identity label useful more because it draws attention to the social processes of stigmatization and marginalization than because it names a unified group.

Disability has functioned historically to justify inequality for disabled people themselves, but it has also done so for women and minority groups. As Douglas Baynton has written, "the *concept* of disability has been used to justify discrimination against other groups by attributing disability to them" (1997, 33). Disability as stigma is a sociocultural attribution in service of normativity in all forms. Doing the work of deconstructing these norms would be a way to invalidate the idea of biological purity and to question the hegemony of masculinity, whiteness, and heteronormativity, the supposed biological differences between first and third world, and so on. Each movement towards hierarchization relies upon the attribution of physical and cognitive difference or disability, the ensuing fear of "contamination," and the ongoing insistence on the marginality and marking of other bodies and minds—premised upon the invisible presence of a pure and unmarked center. Yet deploying an intersectional understanding of the operation of disability is a tricky rhetoric, because not all groups that are marginalized share an inherent disability. What is unfortunate is that many stigmatized groups, in challenging the ways that they have been constructed as disabled, reference disability itself as though it were a natural and stable category— disability becomes, in the words of Rosemarie Garland Thomson, the "ultimate not me" figure (1996a, 41).

A common methodological problem that we have encountered as book editors and teachers is this incomplete challenging of discrimination. A scholar or graduate student in a seminar, for example, might recover a previously ignored woman rhetor who in her time was considered disabled (having a "naturally" weak bodily nature not suited to public life) and so was disqualified as a public speaker because of her gender. The scholar or student constructs her argument by claiming

[margin note: need to interrogate basis of category]

that women of the period were unjustly limited by the prejudices of their time (that is, they were not "really" disabled), but stops there, recuperating the construction of gender, but not of disability as well.[9] This response only serves to make disability seem grounded and static, and to reinforce the stigma of disability, while it "obscures the multiplicity of identities and overlapping layers of experience which become overly simplified as discrete and inseparable" (May and Ferri 2005, 121).

However, if we suggest that disability is the ultimate category of abjection, or argue that we are actually all disabled, the risk is that disability is played as a trump card, neutralized, or seen as transcendent, abstract, or metaphorical (and somehow not materially real). Such statements often form in response to the idea that disability is just an add-on to the regular suspects of identity politics—race, class, gender, sexuality—and is retrofit onto the PC bandwagon. The danger of universalizing disability, or any other category of oppression, is that such claims erase the complexity and real material effects of multiple oppressions. For instance, as Robert McRuer and Abby Wilkerson write (2003), gender and ability are indivisible; one cannot have an intelligible gender without also having an intelligible—i.e., nondisabled—body. Robert McRuer (2003, 79) argues that disability studies must also be a feminist project, and a queer project, and an antiracist project. It should be noted that disability studies needs feminism, and critical race theory, and queer theory, and so on, just as much as these study areas need a disability perspective. This allows for an understanding of differing and overlapping processes of oppression and hierarchies of otherness. Unpacking the specific and multiple processes of oppression experienced by one subject can be extremely generative, opening up new avenues for research and producing much greater insight.

Researchers should understand the ways in which disability is used to stigmatize almost all minority groups, how identity groups often distance themselves from disability in a bid to overcome stigmatizing without challenging the category of disability itself, how forms of oppression are played off one another, and thus how these processes actually result in reifying and keeping alive the mechanisms of derogation. One place for rhetoricians to begin combating the interlocking processes of oppression is through an attention to language use.

As rhetoricians we know that language shapes action and attitudes, not only reports them. Disability studies scholars study the ways that language has been used to label and stigmatize the disabled, and to justify and contribute to oppressive social arrangements and practices. Rhetoricians should strive to avoid language habits that perpetuate negative attitudes toward the disabled and contribute to oppressive practices and to imagine instead new forms of expression.

James Trent writes about the history of labels like "feebleminded," noting that the invention of these terms in the late nineteenth and early twentieth centuries was tied to the invention of IQ tests and the segregation of people with disabilities from the rest of society (1994, 155). Once people with disabilities were labeled and sorted and arrayed on scales according to their deviation from standardized norms, it became easier to justify their institutionalization and erasure and this contributed to the "medicalizing" of disability through an array of "scientific" terms. Labeling may not have been a sufficient cause, but it nonetheless played a central role in the eugenics movement, providing a language and grammar that found its ultimate expression in institutional warehousing and in sterilization programs in the United States, and in the Holocaust in Germany.

Disability writers, such as Simi Linton, don't ask people to sugarcoat the words with which we name disability, but to be aware of the history and entailments, the common tropes and plots, that language carries with it. Euphemisms such as *handicapable* simultaneously convey the fear of disability (so terrible that we can't name it directly and honestly) and a sentimental attitude (are all people with disabilities capable of everything?). Most importantly, such terms foreclose the very important role that social arrangements play in disablement. As Linton's work (1998) points out, saying someone is *mobility challenged* lays the problem of nonmobility on the individual rather than on the environment, which can be made more or less accessible for those using wheelchairs, crutches, or braces. Other terms express the point of view of the nondisabled, not the disabled, Linton contends. The term *wheelchair bound*, for example, does not reflect the fact that wheelchairs actually enable movement for people with disabilities rather than binding them in place. Linton points out the power of reclaiming previously derogatory labels; just as African Americans reclaimed black as *beautiful*, disability activists reclaim *crip* as a powerful, twisted, and sexy term to unite the disability community. Others have developed crip to denote a method of critical turning, a double imagination for understanding both the processes that shape identities and the possibilities for reimagining them (see McRuer 2003; McRuer 2006; Sandahl 2003).

Jay's work (2005a) investigating the entailments of the word *retarded*, for instance, provides an example of the importance of, in his words, "asking questions about the construction of the meanings of disability. Why have definitions of disability been based upon discourse (largely scientific) that represents itself as objective and 'natural'? Why do metaphors of disability often function to hide an individual's humanity and highlight a deficit? Why have metaphors of disability come to entail all manner of negativity?" Jay's thesis was that "new, more accessible and more diverse representations of experience are desirable and possible through the critique of existing metaphors and the creation of new ones" (Dolmage 2005a, 112).

As teachers, and particularly as teachers of teachers, Cindy and Jay are both careful to discuss language practices, not to determine a set of rules for political correctness, but to interrogate the roots, the cultural meanings, and the transactional power of particular words. Our goal as teachers and as teachers-of-teachers is to help others to become reflexive students and practitioners—to help others recognize the ways bodies are constructed through language and through common cultural stories, discourses, and narratives.

G. Thomas Couser describes the "preferred plots and rhetorical schemes" that appeal to audiences because they reaffirm commonly held ideas. "What characterizes these preferred rhetorics," he writes, "is that they rarely challenge stigma and marginalization directly or effectively" (2001, 79). Couser names these the rhetoric of triumph, the medical paradigm, horror or Gothic rhetoric, the rhetoric of spiritual compensation, and the rhetoric of nostalgia. Whether conveyed through compressed tropes or longer narratives, these rhetorical schemes tell familiar stories about disability from an ableist perspective: that disability is about an individual overcoming obstacles, that it is about a cure, that it is so horrible that it evokes revulsion or pity, that its purpose is to make one a more spiritual or better person, or that it arouses a deep aching for the lost, pre-disabled life. Couser contrasts these with rhetorics of emancipation and political rhetoric in which disability becomes a story of movement toward social and political goals for people with disabilities.

Another area of study, closely related to Jay's research into the construction of particular terms for disability, is embedded in sensory metaphors. How is disability figured in our everyday language when and where we least expect it? Thinking critically about sensory metaphors— e.g., "turn a blind eye"—can often lead to the deepest questions about epistemology—to a reconsideration of "how we know" and how we think and write about knowing in ways that answer to multiple senses.

We encourage rhetoricians to attend to pronouns, to avoid writing about "them" as the object of study, whether the outsider is defined through race, class, gender, disability, or nationality. One need not directly invoke the terms *normal* and *abnormal* in order to convey normative thinking. As Simi Linton writes, "there is an assumed agreement between speaker and audience of what is normal that sets up an aura of empathy and 'us-ness.'" (1998, 23). This aura of unity also enforces abnormality and the exclusiveness of the out group. While we hope to avoid employing labels that carry stigma, we also strive to provide opportunities for naming. This is a delicate balancing act. For example, in assessing a new digital component of the writing program at Miami University, Cindy collaborated on a student survey, in which one question asks for self-disclosed demographic information, such as gender, sexual orientation, age, and major. The first version of this survey omitted disability as a category. This useful name/label could help us learn whether the new digital classrooms and pedagogy were accessible, accommodating, and attractive to students with disabilities.[10]

As scholars, writers, and editors we also aim to be aware of the negative implications of a label, word, or metaphor we use, but sometimes we fail. Disability-tinged metaphors, if used consciously, can be powerfully unpacked, but unconscious use seeps in and can—visibly or invisibly—reinforce negative stereotypes. So Cindy has used examples of such mistakes from her own writing and research in teaching students to be more aware of the implications of their language choices, and she has encouraged students and scholars to reflect on their own shifting pronouns (am I representing myself as I, we, us, them) as markers of the fluidity and intersections of one's identity. In "Writing from Normal," Margaret Price (2008) posits that this can be a powerful way of analyzing subject positions and identities. In our own work—as scholars, teachers, and administrators—we constantly try to remain vigilant to the ways we use language and structure arguments, to avoid us/them binaries, and to be more fully aware of the implications of the terms and labels we choose. This is ongoing and difficult work, but also potentially very generative both for writing and the teaching of writing.

Disability studies disrupts the idea that individuals with disabilities can be defined solely through their disabilities and heightens our rhetorical awareness of the ways that language practices perpetuate or can be deployed to reimagine common representations of disability. Disability studies keeps us rhetorically alert to the centering or exclusion of some senses, the mechanisms of derogation, and the importance of careful intersectional analysis. This field of study also provides an essential critical perspective on the ways knowledge is created, categories are enforced, and bodies are valued across time periods and geographies.

To the degree that normativity facilitates certain forms of understanding, disability studies reminds us that it is worthwhile to investigate all of the entailments of this cultural logic—from assumptions about who and what constitute rhetorical fitness to uncritical use of research that objectifies its subjects or is based on unacknowledged constructions of normalcy and deviancy.[11] An understanding of the function of normativity, disablement, and enfreakment is essential to feminist research and an important subject for further study. Informed by disability studies, the feminist researcher understands that disability affects us all, not just because we are all only temporarily able-bodied, but because the categories of able/disabled prefigure all of our relationships, discourses, and dispositions. The rhetorician should read with and against the practices that produce normalizing categories of all kinds as she remains open to locating new possibilities.

Queering Feminist
Rhetorical Canonization

K. J. Rawson

In *The Western Canon*, Harold Bloom (1994, 35) describes the canon as "exist[ing] precisely in order to impose limits, to set a standard of measurement that is anything but political or moral." As Bloom describes it, canonization is an inherently normativizing process—canons exist by virtue of exclusion, selectivity, and standards. Feminists have long opposed canonization since those who have the power to "impose limits" act from a privileged position that is anything but politically neutral. Bloom's desire, and that of others, to establish a "standard of measurement" that is politically or morally neutral fails to account for the complexities of canon formation. Disciplines tend to create canons over time, cumulatively, through scholarly publications, anthologies, and courses. Through these channels, canons develop when some texts emerge as seminal, as do the methodologies that scholars use to engage these texts.

Feminist rhetoric has now reached a point where we have a discernable canon—a group of texts, including feminist rhetors and feminist scholarship, that we engage with regularly. My goal here is not to argue for the texts and methodologies that constitute the feminist rhetorical canon; rather, it is to investigate methodological patterns in the feminist rhetorical canon that shape our field. While the existence of the feminist rhetorical canon signals feminist rhetoric's secure presence in rhetoric and composition, it also functions to establish methodological norms that determine what constitutes feminist rhetoric, and perhaps more importantly, what does not.

The feminist rhetorical canon has been guided by two primary methodologies. One is feminist rhetorical recovery of previously ignored or unknown women rhetors. The other is theorizing of women's rhetorics, or what some have called "gendered analysis," which involves developing a rhetorical concept or approach that accounts for rhetors who are excluded from traditional rhetoric. In "Sappho's Memory," Susan C. Jarratt (2002, 11) similarly identifies two methodological approaches to feminist rhetoric, though her argument is specific to feminist rhetorical historiography. She calls these two approaches "recovery of female rhetors and gendered analysis of both traditional and newly rediscovered sources."

I understand these two methodologies in terms of movement. For feminist rhetorical recovery scholarship, the movement is often from individual figures or particular groups to theorizing about the contribution of those figures or groups (see, for example, Logan 1999). This work often begins with a single individual (e.g., Anna Julia Cooper) or a specific category of individuals (e.g., nineteenth-century black women rhetors) to then create broader theories about how women use rhetoric. Feminist rhetorical theory, on the other hand, moves from broader rhetorical theorizing to focus on individuals by engaging a single, though complex, topic or conceptual category (e.g., delivery) and applying it to specific examples of rhetorical practices (see, for example, Buchanan 2005.).

While these two approaches—recovery and gendered analysis—have been extraordinarily productive and have essentially created and established a field of rhetorical study where there wasn't one before, both have relied upon normative notions of gender to identify and categorize what counts as feminist rhetoric. Feminist rhetorical recovery work has thus far used fixed identity categories, typically "woman" or "female," and has mostly recovered a gender-normative body of texts—those produced by biologically born, self-identified, or historically identified women. What Jarratt (2002) calls "gendered analysis" has similarly normativized the feminist rhetorical canon; while it has engaged with oppressive gender roles and stereotypes (i.e., male and female), it has not yet challenged gender binaries and logics (i.e., masculinity and femininity).

How is "woman" defined in feminist rhetorics? Is our definition hinged on a simple biological, anatomical, or chromosomal basis? If so, we might do well to keep in mind the disabilities studies concept of *normate*, which in this context, might shed critical light on the privileging of people whose birth-assigned, anatomical, biological, social, and psychological genders are all neatly and unquestioningly aligned. Since I have never encountered a definition or extrapolation of "woman" in feminist rhetoric, does that imply that feminist rhetoric reifies the idea that there's no need to define "woman," that women simply *are*? If that is the case, I would suggest that we might benefit from engaging with historical and political projects that define and locate "woman" as a complex identity *production* and performance.[1] With such careful contextualization and critical location, our work might avoid exclusionary pitfalls, which threaten any well-intentioned feminist project.

My initial attempt to *queer* the feminist rhetorical canon engages with the methodological norms that define feminist recovery and gendered analysis in rhetorical studies. Though queer, as a concept, framework, and methodology, hasn't yet been taken up much in feminist rhetorics, it has the potential to offer productive insights about the complexities of identifying "woman" as a key concept upon which feminist rhetoric is founded. Queer theory can be a useful analytic for feminist rhetoric because it provides a lens to scrutinize normativities, including gender normativity and heteronormativity in the field. While I think it is important to engage with the heteronormativity that has been an unspoken presence in feminist rhetoric, in this chapter I focus on gender normativity by employing an emergent strand of analysis that I call transgender critique.

The discourse defining queer and transgender is multifaceted and complex, but a short summary will suffice here. In his introduction to *Fear of a Queer Planet*, Michael Warner (1993) provides a useful overview of queer. He writes, "For both academics and activists, 'queer' gets its critical edge by defining itself against the normal rather than the heterosexual, and normal includes normal business in the academy." As Warner argues, queer does not mean non- or even anti-heterosexual. Instead, queer, as it is used in queer theory, provides a critique of the normal, wherever and however normalcy exists. As I am using it here, queer is not an identity but an analytic. Queer theory is often primarily interested in normalcy that functions to desexualize or erase the non-heteronormative, but it is not exclusively concerned with sexuality as an identity, particularly not to the exclusion of other identities. I deploy queer theory in order to investigate the normativities that dominate the two primary methodologies that constitute the feminist rhetorical canon, or the "normal" business of feminist rhetorics.

Transgender critique, which I see as a specific application of queer theory, examines the complex nexus of assigned biological sex, socially perceived sex/gender, and chosen gender. In the introduction to *Transgender Rights* (Currah, Juang, and Price Minter 2006, xiv), the editors describe transgender as a term "generally used to refer to individuals whose gender identity or expression does not conform to the social expectations for their assigned sex at birth. At the same time, related terms used to describe particular identities within that broader category have continued to evolve and multiply." In other words, transgender can be understood as the umbrella term that refers to people who do not conform to social expectations of their assigned sex/gender. While transgender includes specific identities, such as transsexual, transvestite, and butch, it also refers to those who self-identify as transgender and to those who act in gender nonnormative ways. I deploy transgender critique as a way to challenge the gender normativity that has been the invisible but central focus of the field of feminist rhetorics. Transgender critique queers feminist rhetorical studies by pushing for an engagement with broader, more expansive definitions of gender that more closely mirror the complexities of lived gender.

IDENTIFYING A FEMINIST RHETORICAL CANON

Feminist rhetorical normativity is systemic, not merely individual. Canonization is an inherently normativizing process because it requires limits and standards of judgment that are oppressive to those who don't fit its norms. The feminist rhetorical canon has emerged in a grassroots fashion, thanks to individual scholars' efforts to challenge the dominant rhetorical tradition and to growing interest in these challenges, but it is still, on the whole, susceptible to normative standards.

My introduction to feminist rhetoric began in a course during the fall of 2005 in my first semester as a PhD student at Syracuse University. We used a hefty course packet of readings to supplement works by Ritchie and Ronald (2001), Glenn (1997), Logan (1999)—there was no shortage, it seemed, of scholarship in feminist rhetorics. With this introduction to the field, feminist rhetoric never struck me as a secondary or minor subfield of rhetoric; instead, I met feminist rhetoric as an established discipline with a historical lineage that predated my entrance into the field by two decades. I was introduced to an impressive body of scholarship that functioned like a canon, full of important figures, notable scholars, rhetorical theorists, and a vast array of scholarship including noteworthy anthologies and edited collections. Though I read anti-canon arguments within feminist rhetorical scholarship, such as Joy Ritchie and Kate Ronald's argument that their anthology *Available Means* was not meant to establish a canon of women's rhetorics (2001, xvi), I could not escape the sense that feminist rhetoric had grown into canonization in spite of itself.

Though conversations about canonization did not emerge in feminist rhetorical studies until the late 1990s, the canonization debate thrived in literary studies from the 1980s through the mid-1990s. Feminist literary scholars began responding to the Western literary canon, though not explicitly in terms of canonization, as early as 1977 with Elaine Showalter's publication of *A Literature of Their Own*. In her introduction to the expanded edition, Showalter recollects, "I had imagined *A Literature of Their Own* as a book that would challenge the traditional canon, going far beyond the handful of acceptable women writers to look at all the minor and forgotten figures whose careers and books had shaped a tradition" (1999, xxi). While Showalter's work was attacked from many fronts, fellow feminist Toril Moi wrote one of the most scathing critiques in her book *Sexual/Textual Politics: Feminist Literary Theory*. Moi strongly opposed Showalter's challenge of the traditional canon through recovery because "Showalter's aim, in effect, is to create a separate canon of women's writing, not to abolish all canons. But a new canon would not be intrinsically less oppressive than the old" (2002, 77). In sum, the point of contention between Showalter and Moi was over whether or not to revise the traditional canon or abolish canonization altogether.

This debate over a feminist literary canon parallels the debate in feminist rhetorical studies over attempts to uncover and recover a canon of women's texts. In a well-known exchange, feminist communication scholars Barbara Biesecker and Karlyn Kohrs Campbell rehearse the same ideological differences that separated Showalter and Moi. In Biesecker's commentary on Campbell's two-volume history of women's suffrage public address/essays *Man Cannot Speak for Her* (1989), Biesecker describes Campbell's work as "an affirmative action approach to the history of Rhetoric"; she notes that such an approach does not "challenge the underlying logic of canon formation and the uses to which it has been put that have written the rhetorical contributions of collective women into oblivion" (1992, 144). Like Moi, Biesecker resists the feminist recovery method of folding women into the rhetorical tradition—the add and stir approach—while leaving the tradition unquestioned and unchallenged. Though she does not articulate it as such, Biesecker calls attention to the normativity of canonization inherent in the tradition, which structurally (re)produces oppression. Importantly, neither Biesecker nor Moi critique the gendered normativity of Campbell or Showalter's work, but rather, they take issue with a willingness to work within the traditional canon and thus uphold and perpetuate the canon as a system of normativity.

One way to avoid the problem of gender normativity in canonization is to attempt to avoid canonization altogether. Some feminist rhetoric scholars, such as Joy Ritchie and Kate Ronald, oppose canonization outright in their recovery efforts. Near the beginning of the introduction to *Available Means* (2001, xvi), Ritchie and Ronald write, "we begin first by offering seventy women rhetoricians in a room of their own, not out of our desire to name or fix a women's canon of rhetoric . . . ," yet they acknowledge that collecting a body of texts implies a potential move toward canonization: "Although we realize that this anthology runs the risk of 'canonizing' the writers we have chosen to include, we also hope that in conversation and context the study of women's rhetorical practice . . . will unsettle homogenizing tendencies that recreate traditional, exclusive rhetorical frameworks" (xix–xx). Ritchie and Ronald share Biesecker's concern that canonization means stabilization, homogenization, and normalization of a body of texts, but they are willing to take the risk of creating the anthology because, like Campbell, they see the potentially radical destabilizing effect of the project.

Available Means epitomizes the frustrating paradox of much work in feminist rhetoric—scholars often produce feminist rhetorical scholarship in order to actively revise the androcentric rhetorical tradition but in turn create new traditions, new canons of feminist rhetorics that become exclusive of people who are not biologically born or identified women. From a transgender perspective, the feminist rhetorical canon perpetuates gender normativity (presuming and upholding traditional definitions of "woman") even as it resists the gender normativity (i.e., male-privileging) of the rhetorical tradition.

QUEERING FEMINIST RHETORICAL CANONIZATION

Feminist rhetorical recovery work, the dominant body of work in feminist rhetoric, is often presented in anthologies of recovered women rhetors, including those edited by Donawerth (2002), Logan (1995), and Mattingly (2001). It is not uncommon in these texts to read justifications and explanations of why these women deserve consideration as rhetorical figures and to see a critical questioning of what counts as rhetoric. Alongside anthologies of recovered women rhetors, numerous books have been published as companion volumes or edited collections.[2] In these texts, scholars engage with women rhetors by analyzing their rhetorical practices, which often include nontraditional sites of rhetorical invention and deployment.

While figures in these anthologies may have identified as feminist or not, woman or not, or by some queerer gender construction, we often recover them as single (or dual) identity figures whose identities are seemingly fixed and consistent over the course of their lifetime.[3] For some scholars, such as Ritchie and Ronald, one way to avoid anachronistic labeling is to carefully use "woman" while omitting any use of "feminist" or "feminism" (though the work itself might be rightly labeled feminist rhetoric). This editorial decision to omit "feminism" has the potential to spark valid debate, certainly. But even in this approach, what is seemingly uncontestable in Ritchie and Ronald and across the scholarship that has thus far been produced in feminist rhetorical recovery is the naturalized category of woman. By beginning a research project with specific individuals (e.g., Aspasia) or groups of individuals (e.g., ancient Greek women), the category of "woman" emerges as the concretized staple of a given rhetorical project. Doing so allows us to focus on one part of a historical figure's identity, in this case "woman," while leaving out other identities such as race, age, ability, religion, and sexuality, which are integral to a person's rhetorical experiences. Isolating "woman" as a singular category for feminist analysis is only possible when we recover otherwise privileged women, including white, heterosexual, gender-normative, able-bodied people. While scholars such as Shirley Wilson Logan and Jacqueline Jones Royster have pushed feminist rhetorical scholarship to take up race in meaningful ways, sexual and gender normativity in the field of feminist rhetorical studies remain largely invisible because of heterosexual and gender normative privilege. Though it is certainly the case that no one research project can account for all identities, it is possible to become increasingly aware of the identities we privilege to the exclusion of others.

My argument about gender normative privilege in feminist rhetorics is similar to the debates that take place in queer studies over race. In *Queer Race: Cultural Interventions in the Racial Politics of Queer Theory*, Ian Barnard provides an important challenge to queer studies that resonates with my challenge to feminist rhetoric's reliance on the category of gender: "As queer is currently used by queer theorists, it almost without fail refers to sexuality; this very privileging of sex, sexuality, and sexual identity as axis of analysis means also that its model subjects are assumed to be white, since, as I have suggested, in a society structured around race and racism at every level it is only white queers (and white people in general) who can have the luxury of not naming race, not naming their own race" (Barnard 2004, 15–16).

Barnard provides a queer critique of queer normativity—a consequence of privileging sexuality to the exclusion (or failure to recognize) of other identities. Queer is not an identity but a strategy, a politic, an outlook on the world. Once it becomes merely a sexual identity, it loses its utility as an analytic. Taking inspiration from Barnard, we might begin to address the problem of gender normativity in feminist rhetorical scholarship by also using gender as an analytic rather than an identity category. As Barnard critiques white people's privilege of not naming their race, we might also recognize the privilege of cisgender people not having to name their gender normativity.[4]

If we work from an understanding of gender that insists on the cultural constructions and productions of gender, that recognizes transgender and gender nonnormative subjectivities, and that pushes against the naturalized categories of man and woman, what happens to feminist rhetorical recovery? One way to answer this question would be to imagine feminist rhetoric as work that publicly supports a spectrum of gender rights and a variety of gender expressions. Recovery efforts could focus on figures who have engaged in gender advocacy or on work that supports free expression and embodiment for an infinite range of genders, supporting true freedom of gender expression. This work could also recontextualize already recovered women rhetors alongside a newly formulated lineage of gender expression advocates that is not limited to women or to a particular historical context.

In this vein, recovered figures might include Patrick Califia, Mark Anthony Neal, and John (Radclyffe) Hall—diverse figures that could teach us a great deal about feminist rhetoric through their gender expression advocacy work.[5] These figures raise a number of important questions that we, as feminist rhetoricians, need to consider: How does one rhetorically advocate for gender expression from differing historical, racial, social, class, and sexuality contexts? In what ways does gender advocacy work redefine or reposition our field's work on feminisms and rhetorics? Where do we find the rhetorical work of gender advocacy and how do these contexts matter? These questions will help us as feminist rhetoricians reimagine rhetorical recovery across a variety of discourses that include sex and gender but that are not bound to a single and presumably stable gender or sexual identity.

To take Patrick Califia's work as a brief example: if we look to the preface of the second edition of his book *Sex Changes: The Politics of Transgenderism*, we can find evidences of his feminist rhetorics of gender advocacy. Reflecting on the project of the book, he writes, "Rather than assuming that variant gender expression was a pathological condition requiring treatment, an artifact of the patriarchy, or a maladaptive response to widespread hatred of homosexuals, *Sex Changes* took the radical position that diversity in gender identity, opposition to normative notions of social sex-roles, and even 'anomalies' in genetic sex are natural and universal phenomena, a rich and valuable part of human physicality and society" (2003, xi).

Originally published in 1997, Califia's celebration of (trans)gender diversity is a groundbreaking contribution to the growing field of transgender studies. *Sex Changes* has considerable implications for the feminist project of allowing for a free range of gender expression and embodiment while working against normative sex roles. Califia's gender advocacy work is done through an examination of transgender politics but is not limited to transgender people. Might his work share some commonalities with other, already recovered feminist rhetors such as Gloria Anzaldúa who writes, "But I, like other queer people, am two in one body, both male and female. I am the embodiment of the *hieros gamos*: the coming together of opposite qualities within" (1999, 41)? As feminist rhetorics begins to include people such as Califia, we may open up opportunities to reexamine our already existing figures, such as Anzaldúa, to find that their rhetoric offers expansive definitions and theories of gender that go far beyond what the editors of *The Rhetorical Tradition* refer to as Anzuldúa's "significance for women's language and rhetorics" (Bizzell and Herzberg 2001, 1583).

If gender identity is a category that we still want to maintain in our recovery efforts, we could further challenge the boundaries of our feminist recovery work by examining the rhetorical practices of transgender rhetors such as Leslie Feinberg, Kate Bornstein, Emi Koyama, and Virginia Prince.[6] To take Leslie Feinberg's work as a brief example, we needn't look any further than the introduction to *TransLiberation: Beyond the Pink and Blue* for evidence of Feinberg's rhetorical prowess. Ze[7] writes, "if you do not identify as transgender or transsexual or intersexual, your life is diminished by our oppression as well. . . . Your individual journey to express yourself is shunted into one of two deeply carved ruts, and the social baggage you are handed is already packed" (1998, 6). Though Feinberg writes from a clear location as a transgender person, ze tactfully reaches out to nontransgender people to form alliances and to provide education that transgender oppression is an injustice that affects everyone.

This type of feminist rhetoric, which works to educate transgender and nontransgender people alike about gender oppression, resonates with the scholarship that has already been done in feminist rhetorical recovery. A researcher studying these activists would take individuals as the starting point for developing rhetorical theory, but could conceive feminist rhetoric across a broader feminist spectrum by bringing together a range of people who embody multiple gender expressions. Admittedly, the sampling of figures I have provided is somewhat lim-

[handwritten marginalia: invitational— interesting]

ited because many are contemporary, self-identified transgender people. And even further, many of these figures identify as feminist, so the dilemma of anachronistic labeling—calling someone transgendered and/ or feminist who would not identify that way in a given historical time period—is a nonissue. Still, by considering such figures as feminist rhetors, feminist rhetoricians might begin to ask: what is feminism and how do we employ the concept in feminist rhetoric? Like women's studies departments that are renaming themselves gender studies departments, feminist rhetoric might also shift from studying women's rhetorics to studying the rhetorics of genders.

Gendered analysis, though not neatly severed from recovery and reclamation work, broadens the scope of feminist rhetoric by beginning to interrogate the category of gender. This work begins with a conceptual category of analysis, such as silence or listening, and then demonstrates examples of how that category functions as a feminist rhetoric. Often, these conceptual categories of analysis reconfigure rhetoric in ways that push against gender norms. Two prime examples of this are Glenn's *Unspoken: A Rhetoric of Silence* (2004) and Ratcliffe's *Rhetorical Listening: Identification, Gender, Whiteness* (2006), which both strive to reclaim practices that have not been considered rhetorical (silence and listening, respectively), to carve out space for new feminist rhetorics. Taken together, Ratcliffe's and Glenn's books demonstrate how feminist rhetorical theorizing can analyze the power dynamics of rhetorical situations, asking key questions such as: Who gets to speak? Who is made silent? In what contexts? How do we hear/understand these discourses? What are the fundamental parts of our discourses that we are not challenging? The result is not only a feminist expansion of rhetoric to include silence as a rhetorical use of language and listening as a rhetorical approach to discourse, but also a revision of where we find rhetoric and what it looks like.

Ratcliffe positions "gender" as a trope in order to destabilize it as a seamless or natural category. She writes, "*Gender* is a trope that signifies socially constructed 'common-sense' attitudes and actions associated with men and women. This definition is predicated on the existence of two sexes, men and women" (2006, 9; emphasis original). By calling into question the very terms of feminist discourses, Ratcliffe challenges rhetorical theory to take seriously the ways discourse can shape experiences and epistemology. She introduces gender (and race) as a trope, not out of reflex, but as an indispensable component of her project that forecasts her diverse applications that follow, including her considerations of identification, the Audre Lorde/Mary Daly debate, and listening in the classroom. Such a strategy shows that gender and race are categories that are debatable and open for rhetorical analysis while other feminist rhetorical concepts are simultaneously theorized.

While this work of scrutinizing gender connects Ratcliff's work to arguments made in queer theorizing and transgender critique, she stops short of unsettling the categories of man and woman. To take one example, she writes, "Gender functions as a cultural category that is embodied and performed differently by each person, depending on his/her culture's socializing messages about gender, upon his/her particular identifications with gender, and upon his/her reactions to these messages and identifications" (2006, 11). This description of gender is progressive in that it situates and contextualizes gender in ways that few feminist rhetoricians have done, which recalls Judith Butler's groundbreaking work on gender performativity. Yet Ratcliffe continues to rely on the "his/her" (man/woman) binary in her writing, which upholds biological sex as a naturalized category. This isn't to say that pronouns such as his and her are not still viable, but like gender, they require scrutiny and should be treated as constructions.

One way to begin destabilizing the his/her binary would be to further interrogate Ratcliffe's theorization of the role of gendered rhetorical identification. Preliminary questions could be: What options are available to those who do not identify with either side of the his/her binary? What other identifications are possible for transgendered people and how do those identifications *queer* gender more broadly? Furthermore, when transsexuals transition from an assigned gender at birth to a chosen gender later in life, do they not deconstruct the perceived naturalization of biological sex? While I am using *sex* to refer to the biological assignment of male/female to a particular body, and *gender* to refer to masculinity and femininity, as most feminist scholars also do, my proposition is that transsexuality renders sex as mutable and socially constructed as gender.[8] In other words, transgender critique allows us to see where sex is normativized in feminist rhetorical scholarship and can assist scholars in the deconstruction of gender normativity.

Like Ratcliffe's interrogation of gender, Glenn's *Unspoken* (2004, 153) similarly uses feminist rhetoric to challenge invisibility, in this case the dominance of the "verbal matrix" and the consequences of silence and silencing. She explains, "Silence is too often read as simple passivity in situations where it has actually taken on an expressive power. Employed as a tactical strategy or inhabited in deference to authority, silence resonates loudly along the corridors of purposeful language use" (xi). By flipping the verbal matrix and including silence as a tactical strategy and a type of language use, Glenn offers a feminist rhetorical theory that accounts for those who are both made silent, and those who refuse to speak.

Glenn's *Unspoken* is a good example of the power of feminist rhetorical theorizing and its potentially limiting gender politics. Glenn's overall project to pioneer the study of the rhetorics of silence pushes feminist scholarship toward new sites of analysis and rhetorical consideration. Glenn works against gender normativity by detaching imposed silence from femaleness and femininity. She writes, "In other words, whether people are male or female, masculine or feminine, is not so important to their purposeful use of silence or speech as their willingness to use silence or speech to fulfill their rhetorical purpose, whether it is to maintain their position of power or resist the domination of others" (2004, 23). This argument, which is sustained for much of the book, provides an important lens for analyzing silence and the relationship between systems of power and (male and female) bodies.

Yet, as she outlines in her "Word (or Two) on Terms and Categories" (2004, xix–xx), Glenn continues to use "masculine" and "feminine" as "terminology for gendered power differentials." In arguing that "silencing can be 'feminine,' while purposeful silence can be 'masculine'," Glenn upholds and furthers troubling assumptions about masculinity and femininity. As work in transgender theory, such as that of Leslie Feinberg, Kate Bornstein, and Riki Wilchins, has argued, femininity and masculinity are not stable cultural descriptors.[9] Rather, gender oppression happens at the axis of (perceived) sex and (perceived) gender, irrespective of (perceived) masculinity or (perceived) femininity. Such an interrogation of gender might prompt us to ask: What new or existing rhetorical strategies do transgender discourses utilize? What theoretical frameworks might we construct that encourage a genuinely cross-gendered (male, female, and transgender) scope of feminist rhetorics?

Our methodologies have enabled some types of work to flourish—scholarship on women's rhetorics—while other types remain unexplored, such as scholarship on transgender rhetors and rhetorics. While some scholars may still use the concept of woman in strategic and productive ways, such scholarship could be strengthened by a thorough consideration of who and what is made silent in taking that approach. In this transgendered critique of the dominant methodologies in feminist rhetoric—recovery and gendered analysis—I hope to have opened up the possibility for feminist rhetorical recovery work that does not uncritically rely on the category of woman, and gendered analysis that does not neglect careful interrogation of gender. Working toward such a goal would move us closer to a feminist rhetoric that would be more aligned with the developments in feminism and gender theory that are flourishing in queer studies and elsewhere, inside the academy and out. After all, it isn't just biologically born women who produce feminist rhetoric—gendered people of all varieties are invested and engaged in feminist rhetoric, we just need to develop ways of accounting for all of our voices.

Cosmopolitanism and the Geopolitics of Feminist Rhetoric

Wendy S. Hesford

> Hillary Clinton, head covered in a flowing chador of golden silk, stands barefoot outside the Citadel of Cairo. The chants of the Muslim call to prayer echo through the winding streets. Quietly declining the slippers set aside for privileged visitors, she walks barefoot into the ancient mosque like a common Egyptian woman, her head bowed, her face turned away from the reporters and photographers.
>
> Lucinda Franks, "The Intimate Hillary,"
> *Talk Magazine*, September 1999

In "Hillary Rodham Clinton's Orient" Caren Kaplan demonstrates the power of cosmopolitan travel and its imperialist entailments in global feminist discourse. In this romantic image of Clinton as a "citizen of the world," taking up the cause of third world women's oppression, we see the concurrence of colonial and cosmopolitan discourses (2001, 225). Lucinda Franks's coverage of Hillary Rodham Clinton's and Chelsea Clinton's 1999 trip to North Africa, at the onset of Clinton's run for a seat in the U.S. Senate, articulates the cosmopolitan ideal through a visual rhetoric of identification, namely Clinton's projected bond with "common Egyptian women," and representation of her as an "enlightened" Western traveler (Kaplan 2001, 230).

Representations of global feminism in rhetorical studies may similarly hazard Western-centric cosmopolitan narratives that romanticize certain forms of travel and engagement with non-Western subjects. As its deployment in postcolonial theory, feminist theory, and cultural anthropology suggests, the term *cosmopolitan* reveals contradictory uses and meanings (Wilson 1998, 352). On one hand, the term has been used negatively to signify liberal self-invention, tourism, and global travel, and to refer to carnivalesque cosmopolitanism (Buell 1994). On the other hand, it has been used affirmatively to categorize a new class of transnational cosmopolitans (Hannerz 1990), and to refer to migration, diasporic movements, and refugees (Clifford 1991).

The philosophical dimensions of cosmopolitanism can be traced to ancient Greek and Roman thought, namely Diogenes the Cynic (404– 323 B.C.), who coined the term *citizen of the world,* and the Stoic philosophers. Diogenes refused to be "defined by his local origins and group memberships, so central to the self-image of the conventional Greek male; instead, he defined himself in terms of more universal aspirations and concerns" (Nussbaum 1996, 6). The Stoics followed Diogenes' lead, arguing that we each dwell in both our local communities and the community of human aspiration (7). In *Cultivating Humanity,* Martha Nussbaum adopts a cosmopolitan stance in her call for the reform of liberal education based on our "imaginative capacity to enter into the lives of people of other nations" (1997, 51). But what Nussbaum's notion of cosmopolitan education does not address is how cultural predilections and entrenched conceptions of identity and difference limit our "imaginative capacity," including the Hegelian self-other dialectic—the warring struggle for recognition—itself symptomatic of the "pathology of oppression" (3). What, we might ask, are the ethical ramifications of the confinement of the subject of human rights internationalism within the parameters of a binary identity? For instance, despite the professed egalitarian imaginary of human rights internationalism, non-Western sociocultural practices have been its prime targets; the "messianic ethos" of human rights is pitched to "help those who cannot help themselves" (Mutua 2001, 231). I want to be clear, it is not that the human rights project is irredeemable, but rather that its cosmopolitanism mimics the history of morality emerging from the West and brought to the rest of the world (Mutua 2001, 209).

I use the term *cosmopolitan* to refer to individuals who have the freedom and capital to move about the world, and the term *feminist cosmopolitanism* specifically to refer to feminist formations of global citizenship, particularly as these formations inform human rights advocacy, and the privileging of Western feminist cosmopolitans' encounters with the women and children of third world countries, namely those construed as non-Western or marginalized U.S. subjects.

In order to respond to the risks of cosmopolitanism for feminist rhetorical studies, we need to rethink how we theorize the spatial and temporal as part of a transnational feminist rhetorical methodology, which brings together transnational feminist studies and rhetorical studies through critiques of cosmopolitanism and its particular focus on the consumptive practices of vision and spectacle. Such practices turn the subject represented into an image-commodity, and erase, or at the very least reduce, the complexity of mitigating material and political circumstances. I offer a critical engagement with earlier feminist perspectives on the politics of location and situated knowledge and rhetorical configurations of identification, agency, and the public sphere. My efforts are not, however, without risks, which include falling prey to the binary logics and methods that structure feminist cosmopolitanism. Indeed, the lure of feminist cosmopolitanism is strong, as my analysis of the cosmopolitan rhetoric of feminist playwright and activist Eve Ensler and transnational feminist videographer Ursula Biemann suggests. This lure may be strongest when attention is focused on human rights violations outside of the United States, which in far too many accounts reinforces aesthetic and geopolitical distance. Therefore, instead of viewing feminist cosmopolitanism and transnational feminism as oppositional rhetorical stances, we might view them as rhetorical actions on a volatile but no less methodological continuum.

Ensler might seem like a counterintuitive figure to turn to since she does not align herself with or offer a cohesive methodology for transnational feminism. But her work (2006) illustrates a prominent model of feminist cosmopolitanism and thereby serves to highlight the methodological risks that such models pose for developing a transnational feminist rhetorical analytic. In contrast, Ursula Biemann's experimental videos on women's experiences in the global sex industry (2001b; 2001c) provide a critical opportunity to think further about the identifications that transnational feminists imagine and how space and time may be read differently through *kairos* than through either cosmopolitan or locational rhetorics that rely on fixed identity categories. Kairos is a multidimensional term that refers to a situational understanding of space and/or time and the material circumstances—namely the cultural climate—of rhetorical situations (Crowley and Hawhee 2004, 37). To foreground kairos in both the creation and analysis of cultural texts is to represent a qualitative notion of time and space that is adaptable, opportune, and contingent on material circumstances. Kairos is an important concept to feminist rhetorical studies as scholars wrestle with articulating the temporal and spatial features of transnational identifications and transnational publics.

Ensler's *Insecure at Last: Losing It in our Security Obsessed World* (2006), offers an account of her excursions around the world to interview women whose lives have been dramatically shaped by the atrocities of war, sexual violence, and social injustice. Ensler describes herself as a "traveler, a woman who exists in motion, a nomadic being, a citizen of the world" (xix). Her itinerary reads like a map of turn-of-the-century global feminism, which has brought awareness of human rights violations against women, particularly sexual abuses, to the international stage. Among Ensler's expeditions are a two-month trip to Croatia in 1994 to interview Bosnian refugees and victims of rape warfare, and a 1999 journey to Pakistan and to Afghanistan to witness women's lives under the Taliban.[1] Despite the efforts and achievements of feminist activists to engage a wide range of concerns that affect the lives of women and children, including poverty and the lack of education and health care, spectacular representations of sexual violations against women and girls continue to attract the international media, in part because such stories ascribe to Western myths of deserving victims and to the shaming tactics of human rights organizations.

Like Clinton's imagined orient, Ensler creates an international mosaic of women's oppression and a global feminism framed by the discourses of feminist cosmopolitanism (with its promise of freedom to move about the world) and feminist orientalism (wherein "feminist travel enacts its own imperialism in the name of personal or gender liberation" [Kaplan 2001, 220]). Ensler's cosmopolitanism articulates the collective—her sought-after unification—through personal disclosures and inclusion of women's stories and their resilience to gender oppression. *Insecure at Last* vacillates between stories of violence against women across the globe and stories about the author's alcoholic father, whose anger permeated her world. "Our house, our family, was his empire. I was his subject. Or his tortured prisoner" (Ensler 2006, xvi). Ensler's use of the metaphor of imperialism to describe the father-daughter relationship sets up a parallelism between her childhood trauma and the trauma experienced by refugees, homeless women, and women in prison. A sense of shared vulnerability prompts the author to purge her past. "Until recently," she writes, "I was always waiting for something . . . most of the time it was like a reflex, a verb that was my verb: waiting"—an "existential yawn," a "repository wound," "a residue of memory of another world" (105, 107). Ensler traces this waiting to the moments of childhood terror while in her bed at night: "After the punching and whipping and screaming had stopped. . . . Waiting was better than cutting myself or making myself bleed. Waiting was better than murdering my father" (109).

Forty years later, she travels to the Rift Valley in Africa, where she meets Agnes Pareiyo, an activist working to stop the practice of female genital mutilation. Pareiyo's story of her own victimization and activism prompts Ensler to make a financial contribution through her V-Day foundation so that Pareiyo can buy a jeep to travel more easily to educate communities about the health risks of female cutting and to offer alternative rituals to celebrate girls' coming-of-age. The money also enables Pareiyo to build a safe house for girls (Ensler 2006, 112–13). Seeing the newly built rescue center two years later, Ensler realizes that she is no longer waiting. As she puts it, "We get rescued by giving what we need the most. What we are waiting for has always lived inside us" (114).

Ensler finds strength through her identification with the women she meets who save her from her fears, preoccupations, and "falsely constructed notions of security." "Drawn to that which [she] feared," Ensler's search to "understand brutality and violence began as a search for logic and security but became the journey that freed [her] of the false need for these protections" (2006, xviii). Vivid descriptions of bodily reactions—"cold, shivering impoverishment that crept deep into one's skin"—give readers access to Ensler's perceived corporeal connections to the women. The "dissolution of all kinds of borders"—geographical and psychological—authenticate her actions: "I have held the hand of a woman whose face was melted off by acid in Islamabad, Pakistan" and an Afghan woman thrown into a seizure by the memory of "torture and murder that took place in a stadium in Kabul" (xix). Like the father-as-emperor metaphor, this litany sets up a paratactic rhetorical structure—

an equivalence—between Ensler and the women that is based on memories and experiences of suffering. To allow another's pain to "enter us,"
Ensler argues, "forces us to examine our own values . . . insists that we
be responsible for others . . . compels us to act" (18). Although Ensler
imagines solidarity as a byproduct of identification with another's pain,
a common trope in Christian political theology and human rights discourse (Downey 2003), rhetorical identification and reflexivity function
in her narrative in ways that validate her presence. Imagining the suffering "other" is one of the central challenges of human rights advocacy,
but cosmopolitan identifications and structures of sentiment alone can
not set the standard of aspiration for global justice. Indeed, as Kaplan
reminds us, "If the cosmopolitan subject is a 'citizen of the world' by
virtue of independent means, high tech tastes, and globe-trotting mobility, then the cosmopolitan intellectual or writer is especially culpa-
ble, proclaiming liberation politics from that safety zone of privilege"
(1996, 126).

Yet Ensler also struggles over her privileged mobility, with her "desire to rescue the women," and with her need for control, definition, and
interpretation. Importantly, she recognizes, for instance, the bombard-
ment of women war victims, particularly in the former Yugoslavia, by
Western journalists in pursuit of the "most sensationalist aspects of
these women's lives—the gang rapes, the rape camps" (2006, 8). Likewise, transnational feminists are concerned with the hierarchical and
spectacular politics of interpretation. However, Ensler addresses these
concerns through the creation of a primarily psychological journey narrative—a cosmopolitan feminist bildungsroman, which privileges individual transformation over and above an analysis of structural injustices
and the contradictions of globalization.

Ensler's sense of global feminist citizenship is predicated on the
coupling of rhetorical identification and transnational sentimentality
(which presumes that the recognition of one's vulnerability will lead one
to act to eradicate the other's pain) that cosmopolitanism makes possible. Moreover, for those of us who do not have the means to travel, Ensler travels for us; her self-reflexivity presumes a level of intimacy with
readers that parallels her rhetorical identification with her subjects. In
contrast to the women's autobiographical stories, which appear in quotations so as to designate their authenticity, in her poem, "Under the

Burqa," Ensler aligns herself and her reader with the experiences of Afghan women living under the Taliban through the use of second-person narration, generous imaginings, and rhetorical projections: "Imagine a huge dark piece of cloth / hung over your entire body / like you are a shameful statue," the poem begins. The poem concludes:

Imagine muttering and screaming
inside a cage
and no one is hearing.
Imagine me inside the inside of the darkness in you.
I am caught there
I am lost there
inside the cloth
that is your head
inside the dark we share.
Imagine you can see me.
I was beautiful once.
Big dark eyes.
You would know me. (Ensler 2006, 37–40)

For Ensler, travel appears to be the primary way to move beyond a detached voyeurism and the xenophobic security of the nation-state. Ensler sees her travels as a counterexample to the post-9/11 U.S. nationalist obsession with homeland security, solidification of identity markers, and restriction of knowledge: "you can no longer feel what another person feels because that might shatter your heart, contradict your stereotype, destroy the whole structure" (2006, xv). But to what extent does feminist cosmopolitanism and the mobility of feeling reinforce the very national proclivities that Ensler seeks to disrupt? Ensler's cosmopolitanism is associated with a worldliness available to those not fighting for their lives, which allows them, as public intellectuals, to interact with other transnational subjects, including refugees and migrants, whose lives depend on the social welfare state. Ensler's authorial position and authenticity as a global feminist actor is dependent on the estrangement that travel brings. For Ensler, rhetorical identification with others enables personal liberation. Ensler presents several of the women she meets as complex human beings whose lives are in a state of flux. Nevertheless, the journey narrative that dominates *Insecure at Last* positions non-Western subjects, as well as marginalized U.S. subjects, in subsidiary rhetorical roles as the basis for the author's self-actualization. This hierarchical relationship is precisely the cost of the self-revelatory process, and thereby the risk of its extrapolation as a methodological principle.

As we move away from cosmopolitan identifications toward political engagement we need not deny that solidarity "may be aroused by suffering" (Arendt 1963, 88–89) or that compassion may be a means of directing political resources. Rather, as Elizabeth Spelman suggests in *Fruits of Sorrow: Framing Our Attention to Suffering,* we need to recognize that "[e]xisting inequalities between persons may be exacerbated rather than reduced through the expression of compassion" (1997, 89). We can begin to critically demystify feminist cosmopolitanism and its limitations by articulating the goals and methods of transnational feminism. At this historical juncture, transnational feminism might be best characterized as an interdisciplinary analytic, attentive to the constraints of neoliberalism and to the power differentials and inequalities that shape geopolitical alignments. A transnational feminist analytic enables, as Inderpal Grewal puts it, an examination of the "interarticulation of consumption and identity formation as caught up within the movements of people, goods, and ideas across national boundaries," including the movement of feminisms (2005, 28). Grewal's concept of interarticulation effectively brings together the rhetorical and material analysis of context and its intertextuality.[2]

Despite all the work on revisionary histories of rhetoric, feminist rhetorical studies continues to be defined, in large part, by a fairly exclusive focus on rhetorics within the borders of the United States or Western Europe (Schell 2006). Moreover, the recent turn of rhetorical studies toward the "global" tends to be more "internationalist than transnational" in its focus, emphasizing a nation-to-nation analysis or "unidirectional comparativism—West to East, North to South" (Hesford and Schell 2008; see also Hesford 2006). The cosmopolitan impulses are most discernable in the field's approach to multicultural rhetoric, which has celebrated the poly-vocality of border writers, such as Gloria Anzaldúa, and romanticized mobility over and above a geopolitical analysis of the material structures that define alternative rhetorical practices (Bahri 2004). Rhetorical studies has not sufficiently engaged the complex material and rhetorical dynamics of transnationality or addressed the need to revisit key rhetorical concepts, such as the public sphere, to account for transnational publics generated by the movement of people, goods, and ideas across and within national boundaries (Grewal 2005, 28).

The concept of the public sphere and its correlation with sovereign states and national citizenry is a normative feature of rhetorical studies and political theories of democracy and communication. To transnationalize the public sphere is to trouble nationalist conceptions of citizenry, language, and communication (Fraser 2005, 2) but not to deny their influence. The interarticulation of transnational and national discourses and the regulatory apparatus of neoliberalism transcend and secure nationalist agendas. For instance, the privatization of the military and of the prison industry complex may disaggregate the national locus, but these institutions remain vital components of state domination. Moreover, to suggest that the nation has exceeded itself—a "postnational constellation" (Fraser 2005, 1)—is to deflect attention from the nations that benefit from transnationality—a term I use to disrupt top-down views of globalization (Ong 1999). Transnational publics can be viewed as "arena[s] of struggle in which certain groups emerge and are legitimized (by governments, institutions, and other groups)" (Keck and Sikkink 1998, 33–34). To view transnational publics as arenas of material and discursive struggle calls for disciplinary and methodological renovations supplied by feminist transnational theories that account for rhetoric, specifically.[3]

Rhetorical methods are particularly conducive to identifying how nation-states instantiate and empower certain elements of transnationality and its imagined publics. Transnational publics may be protean, but they are no less governed by rhetorical principles, hermeneutic methods, cultural norms and identifications, and national formations and imperatives. In contrast to common characterizations of transnational publics as "discursive arenas that overflow the bounds of both nations and states" (Fraser 2005, 1), we need to explore how transnational public spheres are bound to and intersect with national publics and their discourses.

Methodological challenges accompany the call for a shift from a nationalist to a transnationalist emphasis in feminist rhetorical studies and from a consumptive feminist cosmopolitanism to a critical transnational feminism. Two videos by Ursula Biemann, which focus on the geopolitics of global sex work and the mail order bride industry, provide an opportunity to reconcile the feminist methodological focus on the local with an awareness of overlapping localities and interarticulations of the local and global. If rhetoric is action and not reduced to the study of artifacts, its potential to illuminate transnational movements becomes clear. The notion that rhetoric needs to move beyond the study of individual texts or individual authors is fairly standard now. Scholars are moving away from the anthropocentrism of earlier criticism, seeing texts as fragments of larger discourses, and focusing on ideologies and ideographs rather than on authors as agents. With few exceptions,[4] however, rhetorical scholars have not anticipated or sufficiently articulated the methodological challenges posed by the transnational movement of rhetors-texts-audiences.

Within a transnational feminist analytic, to read rhetorically is to read intertextually for explicit connections and resonances; it requires that we think in relational terms and reexamine the spatial and temporal dimensions of our methods. Indeed, intertextuality is a key element of a transnational analytic that reads across contexts and focuses particular attention on how arguments travel across cultural and national borders and how symbols and symbolic practices are appropriated, translated, and historicized. To analyze discursive intersections—the rhetorical webs of thought—that constitute action at a particular historical moment and context is to newly imagine the classical concept of kairos.

Kairos was illustrated in classical rhetoric by the figure known as Opportunity, a man (originally nude) depicted balancing on a stick while balancing a set of scales on a shaving knife (Miller 2002, xii). Balance is achieved and sustained to the extent that kairos can anticipate the needs and values of imagined or intended audiences. In contrast to interpretations of kairos as a transformation of contentious discourse into a harmonious situation, however, I want to foreground a view of kairos as an analytical method that breaks the cycle of oppositions in order to enable new knowledge (Petruzzi 2001). To view kairos through a transnational lens is to recognize transnational publics not as static but as always in the process of becoming, and audiences as waxing and waning as publics form and disperse. To employ kairos as part of a transnational feminist methodology, therefore, is also to engage kairos with the problem of identification as it operates across a range of discourses and to examine the experiences and narratives with which particular acts of identification are entangled or associated.

To recognize how identifications are both imposed and claimed is to foreground identity as embodied rhetorical action, or, as Patricia Williams suggests in another context (1991, 10–11), to understand identity categories as rhetorical gestures. Such recognition "complicates the supposed purity of gender, race, voice, boundary [and] allows us to acknowledge the utility of such categorization for certain purposes and the necessity of their breakdown on other occasions." Thus, I call for us to shift our focus from the identity categories of victim and agent to consider identification practices within action-defined contexts. Such a shift opens up important new ground for thinking through the complexities and particularities of women's agency and processes of identification that define the terms of transnational feminist scholarship and advocacy.

CYBERSEXUALITIES, COSMOPOLITICS, AND TRANSNATIONAL IDENTIFICATIONS

Ursula Biemann's experimental videos *Remote Sensing* (2001b) and *Writing Desire* (2001c) trace the routes and displacements of female bodies in the global sex industry. Biemann is a Western, white, experimental videographer, whose interests lie in revealing the constructedness of different positions articulated by trafficking NGOs rather than in reducing issues to messages that can be used to bring about legislative change. *Remote Sensing* points to how global capital and technologies sexualize and facilitate women's movement into the sex industry and at the same time police geographical boundaries and hinder women's migration for work other than sex work, namely because states hold onto structures that forbid women to migrate for work in other professions.[5] *Remote Sensing* reports, "500,000 women migrate into the European sex industry every year. Two-thirds come from post-socialist countries." As the narrator notes, migration laws reveal "the place of sex in . . . national space. These laws protect the flourishing sexual life of male citizens as privileged, and a source of power." The video also challenges the victim/agent binary through its portrayal of the identity of sex workers at the former DDR/Czech border: "Here, everything is transitory, no sentimentality, no clinging to the past. The prostitutes are from distant places, many smuggled in, captured, and illegal. They all know that where they are, and what they are is only temporary. The consumers, the German tourists just passing through, they too are aware that their time here is only temporary. Everything resonates with impending change."

Neither of Biemann's videos resolves these contradictions or solidifies identity categories, but they do expose the oppositional logics, cultural values, and public policies that create and sustain such categories. Both *Remote Sensing* and *Writing Desire,* as they struggle against the logic of oppositions, reveal just how profound the obstacles are to systematic change and processes of resignification even within transnational feminist advocacy. Despite Biemann's claim that she is not primarily interested in the evidentiary function of representation, or in reinforcing the victim/agent binary, both films include narratives of women lured and tricked into sex work. For instance, *Remote Sensing* focuses on a case involving a group of Filipinas who were recruited by a German man and his Filipina wife in Metro Manila. One woman, part of a group of eight who had the same experience, recounts, "One morning the recruiter approached me personally and promised me $350 a month if I agreed to work in a restaurant in Germany. We didn't have to pay any placement fees . . . all the fees would be gradually deducted from our salary. At the moment of departure, we noticed that on the ticket it said Nigeria instead of Germany as we believed."

This "lured and tricked" narrative is complicated by several factors, including the narrative of Naomi, who was recruited from Manila, then sold in Nigeria, then sold in Togo, and finally fled to Cyprus, where prostitution is legal. She used the money she earned through prostitution there to return home. Naomi further complicates the victim/agent binary in her conversation with Biemann about relationships. When Biemann asks Naomi if she has ever had a boyfriend, Naomi responds that she has never had sex without getting paid for it. "No boyfriend . . . someone you loved," Biemann repeats. Naomi clarifies, "I never say to a customer . . . I love you." But she is perplexed by the question itself: "No boyfriend. But customer, yes. But free, no. Why?" Naomi conveys a radically different set of values than those inherent in Biemann's question. The cosmopolitics of this exchange resides in the videographer's insertion of the cultural and rhetorical commonplace of the romance narrative. Naomi's reaction, and the fact that this exchange did not end up on the cutting-room floor, draws the viewer's attention to the risks of comparativist methods and the need to see exchanges such as that between Biemann and Naomi as interarticulations—as rhetorical (dis) identifications shaped by their contact with each other.

The sonic level of representational construction in *Remote Sensing* provides yet another framing device for the women's experiences. In the case of Filipinas in Nigeria, Biemann includes a strong mediating device—an English voice-over—that she seldom uses. Biemann has expressed that she typically aims to let her subjects, who include former sex workers and NGO women, speak and analyze the international situation, rather than theorizing their experiences in a voice-over. One could read this voice-over as an ethical breach by the Western white videographer in representing sex workers in the global south (an exchange that reproduces the social hierarchy of the global north), yet we might also view this editorial decision as indicative of the challenges of transnational feminist methods and as evidence of how Biemann's video vacillates between transnational feminist rhetorical analytics and cosmopolitan feminist rhetorical analytics.

Biemann generates a critical ambivalence through her critique of the victim/agent binary and her simultaneous inclusion of testimonies of women victimized by the sex industry. This ambivalence illuminates the representational challenges posed by the rhetorical conventions of human rights discourse for transnational feminist scholars and advocates, especially the challenge of how to document victimization. For instance, *Remote Sensing* exposes the risks of documentary techniques in revealing multiple layers of surveillance: "Locked up in tiny rooms, confined in semi-darkness, guarded closely, she lives in the ghettos and the bars of the underworld, the semi-world, living a half-life. Guarded step by step, number by number, trick by trick." The camera travels down long dark corridors of brothels at night, dimly lit by streetlights and the lights from clubs. The corridors echo the "semi-darkness" and the "underworld" quality of the narrator's description of sex workers' lives. They are dirty and crowded, choked with prostitutes and potential customers. Given the danger of filming in this milieu and the fact that the women didn't want to be filmed, the camera does not focus on any individuals. The camera instead lingers on women's eroticized body parts—

breasts, lips—fragmenting the bodies it seeks to represent. Here the video plays on the cultural expectations that women will be objectified. But are such rhetorical identifications necessary as forms of persuasion in transnational feminist advocacy? And in what ways does the video reproduce or rearticulate the spectacle of women's objectification? This choice, according to Biemann, is a result of difficult recording circumstances, but it also indicates the internationalization and limitations of certain representational strategies and journalistic conventions. These images of captivity progressively dissolve, as later parts of the film speak to more self-motivated decisions to enter the sex trade. As a visual metaphor, the presence and dissolution of the spectacle suggests yet again how Biemann navigates the continuum of cosmopolitan and transnational rhetorical analytics.

Writing Desire suggests that critical agency resides in the strategic mobilization of rhetorical and cultural commonplaces and the juxtaposition of dominant discourses and counter-discourses. The video opens with an exotic beach scene, palm trees, and upbeat music. Over this tourist image, the following text appears in succession: "Geography is imbued with the notion of passivity. Feminized national spaces awaiting rescue. With the penetration of foreign capital." The opening sequence foregrounds the increasing disembodiment of sexuality, the links between sexual desire and electronic communication technologies, and the production of subjectivities through the compressed space of virtual exchanges. This sequence also constructs the viewers as consumers: we hear Internet dial-up sounds, then categories and links appear on screen, representing a search by the categories of country, age, height, weight, education, and ID code. The cursor scrolls down a list of third world countries. The link for the Philippines is then opened, and digital representations (photographs and online videos) of young women appear. Women are ranked and described according to their country of origin; in this way the video highlights locational identifications and cultural stereotypes and myths. Women from the Philippines are described as the "most friendly." Women from Brazil are listed as the "best lovers." Women from Thailand are listed as the "most beautiful" and women from Costa Rica as the "most eager to please."

Writing Desire focuses on commercialized gender relations on the Internet, namely the mail-order bride market and virgin market in the former Soviet Union and the Philippines (one of the poorest countries in Southeast Asia). The video argues that women's bodies, as symptoms of global culture, are racialized as objects of desire either waiting to be conquered or rescued. The video implies that new media and technology create mobile subjectivities and sever context, and, in so doing, enable alliances that otherwise might never occur. The video portrays the fantasies of individuals bridging the distance through technology without confronting the consequences of those fantasies—"a stream of desire troubled by nothing." As a woman lying across a bed says, "What's interesting about it [e-mail desire] is that you create these love stories in which you are the protagonist. . . . What is important is the act of writing, while the real bodies are absent, it's all in the writing. That's why the sexual discourse becomes important. It would be wrong to infer that it replaces the body." Instead, the body is "present in the writing." This sequence highlights the challenge of technology in configuring a locational feminism, where identity is embodied as technology. Here the body and identity become first and foremost rhetoric, highlighting Biemann's feminist agenda of representation, which, as she puts it, is "To bring the representation of women in poverty in connection with high technology and other concepts [such as mobility] that have a progressive high status in our eyes." In the case of *Remote Sensing*, "women become agents of transport and transformation for countries who struggle to make themselves a place on the global chart." The video proposes a link between the proliferation of global sex work and sex tourism and the technology of the Internet, which "capitalizes on this vulnerable set of motivations" (Biemann 2001a, 3). *Writing Desire* fractures presumptions about the stability of identity and geographical contexts, and yet also reminds us of how these new technologies are embedded in—and foster—inequitable material relations and oppressive conditions for much of the world's population.

At one point in the film, the rhetorical competence and strategies that women in the global sex industry employ becomes strikingly clear: on the screen overlaying Qtime videos advertising brides from post-Soviet areas, the following text appears: "she is beautiful and feminine / she is loving and traditional / she is humble and devoted / she likes to listen to mellow music / the smile is her rhetorical gesture / she believes in a lasting marriage / and a happy home / she is a copy of the First World's past." The phrase her "smile is her rhetorical gesture" acknowledges the rhetorical dimensions of identification and agency in the context of transnationality. As Biemann notes in her commentary on the film, "To present herself as humble and unambitious, she denies the desirability of the financial and social rewards of marrying a Western man. Morality remains an economic issue, but if women want to be seen as moral at all, they better mask their awareness of their relationship to property, mobility, and privilege" (2001a, 3).

In this sense, *Writing Desire* exposes the foundational Western idea, as Caren Kaplan notes in another context, that "travel produces the self, makes the subject through spectatorship and comparison with otherness" (1996, 36). Just as in *Remote Sensing,* a critical ambivalence characterizes this video. In *Writing Desire,* however, the critical ambivalence does not emerge so much from the deployment and critique of victimization narratives as from the portrayal of cosmopolitan conceptions of identity. These conceptions are acquired through travel, virtual or otherwise, and depicted in the figure of Maris Bustamante. Bustamante is an artist based in Mexico City who finds an American husband through an Internet dating service. She is middle-aged, a self-identified feminist, a widow, a mother, a university professor and, as she puts it, "radical of my own will." After an "examination of [the] Mexican environment . . . the 'Cradle of Machismo,'" and after working through "intellectual guilt," she posts her profile on an Internet dating service. She corresponds for six months with a man named John, a lieutenant with the U.S. Marine Corps, who she later marries and with whom she establishes a new family. Bustamante indicates that the Internet enabled her to suspend judgment and to reformulate her expectations; she would not ordinarily have been attracted to a military man. Bustamante's narrative is emblematic of the historical trajectory of future promise (construed in familial, heterosexual terms), a narrative that recasts the white middle-class feminist subject at the center and as normative. She and the lieutenant are pictured in a classic familial portrait. The centerpiece of the black-and-white photograph is the father, seated front and center, surrounded by his wife and three teenage children. His wife's hands are folded on his shoulder. The whole family is smiling.

Bustamante is figured as kind of virtual cosmopolitan, whose worldliness is acquired, in large part, via technology. Bustamante might be said to have seized the technological day, to have enacted kairos as a form of cultural cosmopolitanism, which encompasses cultural and virtual tourism, self-invention, and discursive mobility (Kaplan 2001, 220). The position of Bustamante's story, defined by a conventional narrative arc, affords her character a certain status in *Writing Desire*. We might read this narrative as an example of the idiomatic particularity of contemporary geopolitical feminisms or as exemplary of the temporal rhetoric of awakening and rebirth common to second-wave feminism. Either way, Bustamante's narrative highlights the venerable power of rhetorical stasis to usurp the transnational feminist project by reclaiming rhetorical commonplaces and hegemonic notions of freedom, movement, and liberation, and securing normative identifications through structures of opportunity (technology, privilege). Finally, the rhetorical weight of Bustamante's narrative in *Writing Desire* offers a cautionary tale to transnational feminist scholars and advocates about the risks of transference (rhetorical, methodological, cultural, national), including the force of "traveling feminisms" (Thayer 2000, 207), and the lure and risks of cultural cosmopolitanism.[6]

While the configuration of identity as a field of action allows us to trouble the victim/agent binary and to consider the strategic deployment of such contrasts, such a conceptualization also has risks. If it loses all traces of the materiality of rhetoric, it becomes the methodological equivalent of cultural cosmopolitanism. Just as we need to look beyond the academic transmission of new conceptions to consider how "social movements appropriate and transform global meanings, and materialize them in local practices" (Thayer 2000, 207–8), so too do we need to understand how identities and identification practices are enabled and constrained by kairos—that is, by material and rhetorical circumstances. Placed against the geopolitical backdrop of the early twenty-first century, the classical figure of Kairos therefore emerges not so much as an accommodative figure of balance but as a critical subject negotiating the contradictions of transnationality.

An understanding of identification through kairos is one that recognizes the colonial and imperial histories that shape the terms of identification associated with global sex work and feminist advocacy, and the identificatory practices that transform women into subjected others in increasingly transnational and cosmopolitan public spheres. In other words, the dynamics of transnationality compel us to read the geopolitical (spatial) elements of identity and positionality rhetorically, in terms of the timeliness of certain identifications and their deployment, and to develop an analytic attuned to the continuum of feminist cosmopolitanism and transnational feminist rhetoric in our own work. What is needed is not a routine methodology or prescribed style but greater critical acuity about the material conditions, compositional challenges, and disciplinary expectations that pull us to one side or another on the continuum. A transnational feminist rhetorical analytic highlights the discourses of mobility in unique ways; it enables us to see the differential conditions of mobility (who/what moves or travels across borders and who/what doesn't, and why). These considerations are crucial for studying the contradictory effects of globalization and the geopolitics of feminist rhetoric. A transnational rhetorical analytic calls for an ethical vision grounded not in recognition of our likeness to others, not in seeing "ourselves in their eyes," but in a utilitarian conception of identity and difference as rhetorical-material fields of action. A relational understanding of subjectivity can shift the ground of global feminist rhetoric from uncritical cosmopolitan practices to interpretive practices that acknowledge the different axes of domination and shifting relations among women in diverse locations (Kaplan 1996, 184). Finally, transnational feminist provocations are no less imperfect than the hegemonic internationalisms to which they respond.

Growing Routes

Rhetoric as the Study and Practice of Movement

Ilene Whitney Crawford

In 2002, I began collecting literacy narratives from postwar generation Vietnamese women in order to understand the ways in which acquiring English is sponsored and compelled by capitalism's expansion in the third world (see Crawford 2007). At that time, I categorized the project as feminist literacy studies. But I had a rhetorical problem: the tendency I shared with my U.S. audience to freeze Vietnam in time, circa 1975, impaired my ability to work on the terms the physical space of Vietnam offered, and impaired my ability (and that of my readership) to see the future Vietnam my subjects were imagining, a modern nation respected for its intellectual and technological contributions to the world. To learn the lesson of Vietnam—a lesson about the twenty-first century, not the twentieth—I needed to be moved rather than persuaded. I needed to develop a different methodology, one better suited to a project I now think is feminist rhetoric as well as feminist literacy studies, a methodology I call "growing routes."

To be moved, I first had to reconstruct Vietnam as *topos*. When I began collecting literacy narratives from women living in Ho Chi Minh City (HCM City), the set of images that signified Vietnam to me were more real at times than Vietnam itself; it took some time for my vision to adjust. I had to learn to see—and then learn to remember—a dynamic place with a present and a future that will be shaped more by the rapidly evolving forces of late capitalism than it will be shaped by the legacy of the Vietnam War. Mapping "my" route through Vietnam, a route that turns out to be a well-worn one, demonstrates how the materials that fashion topos are collectively assembled. This seems obvious. It seemed obvious to me too, and I went to Vietnam fully prepared to critically interrogate my perspective; but let me assure you that physically experiencing the power of Vietnam as topos, discovering that you can't think your way out of walking the streets in a preprogrammed way, really drives the point home.

In his discussion of topos, Roland Barthes notes the significance of the "metaphoric approach to place," citing Aristotle's claim that "to remember, it suffices to recognize the place." "Place," Barthes glosses, "is therefore the element of an association of ideas, of a conditioning, of a training, of a mnemonics; places then are not arguments themselves but the compartments in which they are arranged" (1988, 65). I want to put some pressure on Barthes's assertion, however. As Frank D'Angelo shows, "*topoi* became displaced as inventional strategies and embedded in discourse as methods of organizing ideas" between antiquity and modernity, becoming "structural patterns" that bear a "heuristic burden" (1984, 67). Places, topoi, are indeed compartments for arguments. But compartments need to be built, and because they are built they also function as arguments in and of themselves. Vietnam certainly continues to function as a container that shapes arguments about the lessons the late twentieth century has for U.S. status and identity. But what is our cue to make those arguments? How do we recognize Vietnam as the topos that invokes these arguments? Many of us in the United States recognize Vietnam via a select set of codified images and terms.

On my first trip to Vietnam in 2002, I traveled with my friend and colleague Thuan Vu. Thuan was returning to Vietnam for the first time after fleeing Saigon in 1975 by boat with his family as a two-year-old. I was not returning to Vietnam; I did not have family who served in Vietnam. But I found that I also "remembered" Vietnam; while not a homeplace for me like it was for Thuan, it was a place I had composed out of a series of very predictable memories, which I later described in this journal entry excerpt:

> Born in the United States in 1970, my memories of Vietnam take the shape of a frozen-in-time feedback loop of photographs, news footage, and movie scenes that document or reference the Vietnam War: wounded

soldiers, napalmed children running down a dirt road, burning villages, and people frantically clinging to the last helicopter leaving the American Embassy, all set to the sound of thumping helicopter blades and "Flight of the Valkyries" à la *Apocalypse Now*.

If you also know Vietnam primarily through 1970s and 1980s U.S. media, you are likely to recognize my memories as your memories. For example, picking up Anthony Bourdain's 2001 collection of travel essays *A Cook's Tour* after writing the journal entry above, I was at first dismayed to read this:

> In Saigon, walking the streets, it's hard to separate the real from the fantasy, the nightmare from the wish, a collection of film and video images that have long ago been burned into so many of our cortices. The ceiling fan in *Apocalypse Now*, the choppers coming in slow with a *Whuppwhuppwhuppwhupp* . . . the running girl, flesh hanging off her arms from a napalm strike . . . burning bonzes toppling over . . . the point-blank bullet to the head. . . . Feeling nauseated and guilty, I read for a while, afraid to go back to sleep. I'm rereading Graham Greene's *The Quiet American* for about the fifth time. It's his Vietnam novel, set in the early days of the French adventure here. He wrote much of it—it is said—at the Continental Hotel, just down the street. (Bourdain 2001, 54–57)

I was dismayed to find not only that the Vietnam Bourdain remembered and the Vietnam I remembered were remarkably similar places, composed from the same collection of memories, but also that our memories guided our vision and our physical movements in the same ways, creating nearly identical routes through the material space of Vietnam. In fact, just previous to this passage, Bourdain describes his experience of encountering American soldiers' war-era artifacts, an experience also nearly identical to mine, which I write about elsewhere (Crawford 2005).

The Vietnam War is the kind of event Ron Eyerman would call a cultural trauma, which, as opposed to physical or psychological trauma, "refers to a dramatic loss of identity and meaning, a tear in the social fabric, affecting a group of people that had achieved some degree of cohesion" (2001, 2). The Vietnam War clearly both echoed and amplified dramatic challenges to American identity made by Civil Rights activists, feminists, and gay rights activists. Once a traumatic event tears a group's social fabric, Eyerman argues, the event must be "understood, explained, and made coherent through public reflection and discourse" and "mediated through various forms of representation and linked to the reformation of collective identity and the reworking of collective memory" (2). The kind of traveling Bourdain and I did participated in this reformation and reworking: the similar routes we made through the physical space of Vietnam participated in the imagination and creation of a coherent narrative about the meaning the U.S. presence in Vietnam had for the United States.

It is difficult not to participate in such collective meaning-making projects. Lynn Worsham reminds us that trauma is an ahistorical, arhetorical event: to be traumatized is to be "possessed by an event that cannot be narrated into a frame of intelligibility" (2002). Subjects need coherent narratives in order to recognize themselves not only as individuals but as individuals connected to other individuals. Until a coherent narrative is fashioned, they become stuck in time. When Bourdain and I looked at and then represented Vietnam in ways that echoed our cultural training, we were responding to this cultural trauma, participating in the reworking of a collective memory. The aim of such a reworking is to reinstall and preserve the identity of the United States as moral, just, well-intentioned, and physically powerful—but we craft this identity at Vietnam's expense, freezing it in time, making Vietnam a place, a topos, that continues to serve our own ideological needs.

Watching Philip Noyce's film *The Quiet American* (2002) shortly after I returned from my first trip to Vietnam also helped me to understand "Vietnam's" effects as topos. *The Quiet American*, an adaptation of Graham Greene's novel of the same title, is set in 1950s HCM City (then Saigon); a good deal of it is filmed in front of the Continental Hotel and the Municipal Theatre at the intersection of Le Loi and Dhong Khoi, a few blocks from the hotel where I stayed during my first visit. While people walked down the street in mid-twentieth century clothes, pedaled mid-century bicycles and cyclos, and drove the occasional mid-century car, the twenty-first century also jumped out at me: the blue awning of the Versace store on Dhong Khoi peeped past Michael Caine's shoulder. Noyce also shuttered the actual Continental Hotel, on the northeast corner of the intersection, and recreated it on the southwest corner, where the Caravelle Hotel is, which gave me the sensation of being backward the entire film.

Watching the film kept forcing Noyce's imagined mid-century Saigon and a real turn-of-the century HCM City into the same irreconcilable field of vision, illustrating for me critical anthropologists Akhil Gupta and James Ferguson's distinction between "space" and "place" (1997, 40). Spaces are physical, material locations. Places are remembered and/or imagined locations. When people collectively remember and imagine a space, making it meaningful to them, it becomes a place. For example, Gupta and Ferguson note how displaced peoples create diasporas in the image of "remembered or imagined homelands" (39). Thus "India and Pakistan seem to reappear in postcolonial simulation in London, [and] prerevolution Tehran rises from the ashes in Los Angeles" (38). Similarly, a section of Orange County, California, has become "Little Saigon," which the *New York Times* has described in terms of a collectively reimagined ending to the Vietnam War—"what Saigon would have been if South Vietnam had won the Vietnam War" (Mydans 2002).

By the time I saw *The Quiet American*, I knew I needed to heed Gupta and Ferguson's encouragement to politicize this meaning-making practice that constructs "places" out of "spaces" and, in the context of my work in Vietnam, to explore the questions that they ask: "How are spatial meanings established? Who has the power to make places of spaces? Who contests this? What is at stake?" (1997, 40). To paraphrase D'Angelo (1987, 51), how do *topoi* come to bear their heuristic burden?

My initial experiences traveling in Vietnam and suffering disorientation while watching *The Quiet American* also taught me a great deal about the role that memory and imagination play in shaping perspective. Perspective became more than a spatial reasoning problem for me, more than a matter of figuring out where I was physically in relation to what I was looking at, or how my physical and emotional location affected what I could see and comprehend intellectually. Perspective became a diachronic problem as well, a matter of figuring out when I was looking from, how the particular moment from which I was looking affected what I could see, and what future I was able to look into.

I treated my disorientation, the irreconcilability of the whens I was looking at Vietnam from, as both a signal and an opportunity to rethink my feminist literacy studies project, to invest time in accounting for and recomposing my own perspective as part of my work in Vietnam, and to reconceptualize my work as also a project in feminist rhetoric. From the beginning, I wanted my project to be transnationalist. I was seeking opportunities to broaden my study of U.S. histories of race, class, and gender formation to include their global histories and I was seeking ways to travel again. Like Inderpal Grewal and Caren Kaplan, I recognized that acts of travel could be analyzed, that "forms of movement and displacement in the modern world such as immigration, forced removals, diasporas, refugee asylum, as well as travel for educational or corporate needs [can be] analyzed [for] how inequalities of class, gender, nationality, sexuality, and ethnicity are created through movements over time and space in particular ways" (2000, 2). I was already persuaded that we need to study "how women become 'women' (or other kinds of gendered subjects) around the world," rather than study what different women are like, and I knew for myself that I needed to more directly experience "the impact of global forces such as colonialism, modernization, and development on specific and historicized gendering practices that create inequalities and asymmetries" in order to learn about them (9). I thought that moving for work would challenge me to test this theory.

I was already persuaded that Vietnam could teach me a lesson about the twenty-first century, but I found that my path followed a twentieth-century script that reconstructed a twentieth-century Vietnam. To script a current path in Vietnam, I needed a theory of movement. I began theorizing rhetoric as the study and practice of movement, rather than the study and practice of how language achieves its effects, i.e., persuasion. What moves us through time and space—physically, emotionally, and intellectually? How are these three registers of movement connected and interdependent? "Growing routes" describes a mode of feminist rhetorical practice that constructs and accounts for our roots in the world and our routes through the world over time. "Root" and "route" are homonyms where I grew up; "growing routes" invokes both, treating both roots and routes as complex compositions of physical, emotional, and intellectual movement.

My current work attempts to recompose Vietnam as topos by interweaving my literacy narrative and my Vietnamese and Vietnamese American subjects' literacy narratives with the partial literacy narratives of subjects I know only through left-behind photographs, letters, and scrapbooks I have collected in Vietnam. As such, the text reflects the silences and gaps produced by war with and displacement of Vietnamese people in order to acknowledge the impact this history continues to have on the literate lives of young women in the postwar generations. Contemporary young women's literacy narratives are born out of an irresolvable clash of contradictory forces rooted in Vietnam's complex history of foreign occupation: there is a free(er) market economy emerging but there is also restricted freedom of expression; there is an economic imperative to participate in the transnational exchange of goods and services but there is also a fear of Chinese and American cultural imperialism; and there is a yearning to achieve the status of a modern nation, but there is also a calcified political infrastructure that sacrifices human intellectual potential to maintain itself. These forces move human beings physically, emotionally, and intellectually.

My work acts alongside a tradition of Asian American cultural production that Lisa Lowe describes as an "alternative site where the palimpsest of lost memories is reinvented, histories are fractured and retraced, and the unlike varieties of silence emerge into articulacy" (1996, 6). In order to recompose Vietnam as an alternative topos for arguments about globalization in the twenty-first century, I practice growing routes by accounting for how my point of view has been shaped by mass media "memories," how my movement in Vietnam has interrupted and changed that shaping, and how I am attempting to compose new perspectives with recovered texts and images.

Our interwoven narratives show how global forces unevenly compel first and third world women's literacy and travel. There are points of connection and disconnection in our literacy narratives. There are also stark differences in our access to literacy sponsors, the degree to which we are compelled to acquire particular foreign language literacies, the degree to which we are compelled to travel or prevented from traveling, and the relative material benefits of globalization we enjoy.

Joy Ritchie and Kate Ronald argue that feminist rhetorics explore women's "relationship not only to their own physical embodiment but also their integral connection to the wider bodies and spaces of the physical world in which women reside" (2001, xxvi). Chandra Mohanty also speaks of bodies when she argues that "feminist scholarship, like most other kinds of scholarship, is not the mere production of knowledge about a certain subject. It is a directly political and discursive practice that is purposeful and ideological . . . it is a political praxis that counters and resists the totalizing imperative of age-old 'legitimate' and 'scientific' bodies of knowledge" (2003, 18–19). I am attempting to enact body-conscious writing in both senses, seeking to "find the means to enact and 'compose' the fluid, fragmented subjectivity of women . . . by creat[ing] new styles and generic forms," as well as constructing "new *topoi*, new topics/places from which arguments can be made" (Ritchie and Ronald 2001, xix–xxiii).

In order to interrupt, comment on, and recompose my perspective on Vietnam, I juxtapose twenty-first-century images, including my own digital photographs, with collected twentieth-century images of Vietnamese women that foreground the ordinary in their lives—work, shopping, lunches, family dinners, outings with children, graduations, work. My work has both revealed to me and allowed me to show how my gaze was also shaped by an impulse to see and represent Vietnam in terms of its Otherness. I have found it important to call attention to and mock my own slightly exoticizing gaze by repeating images of conical hats, fruits, street vendors, and the like. Composing with images as well as text is allowing me to think and write about perspective very differently than working with text alone. Instead of remembering Vietnam in terms of a Hollywood war in a exotic faraway land, my substitution/use of ordinary images photographed by ordinary Vietnamese people is helping me to remember Vietnam in terms of the local ways of living in and documenting space (routes) and local ways of building relationships and lives (roots).

Once I had traveled from the United States to Vietnam, aside from taking taxis to cultural and historical sites and dodging imaginary helicopters, I realized a great deal of my initial work in HCM City was stationary—I sat to conduct interviews, to write, to study Vietnamese. I wasn't moving, and I didn't theorize this degree of stasis initially. It came as a surprise to discover that ordinary physical movement was one of the strongest catalysts for my emotional and intellectual movement. When subjects-turned-friends Trang, Chi, Chung, Mai, Tuan[1] and others insisted on taking me via motorbike to run errands, to visit friends, to see the sights in different neighborhoods, I discovered that I needed this very local mode of physical movement, this experience of having to manage and organize a sensory overload of shoutsexhausthornstoucheslights, in order to understand how their movement, the ways they inhabit and move in HCM City, their routes, compose HCM City and make it a twenty-first-century place. At the same time, their movements construct their desire for and attachment to HCM City as a place, growing their roots.

Another local movement that I adopted was using Vietnamese. But while I am claiming it as one of my movements now, I resisted truly studying Vietnamese for some time. I justified this by saying that the point of the research was to find subjects who spoke English. Truth be told, I didn't know how far the project would go, if it would be worth the investment—physical, emotional, or intellectual. And Vietnamese is difficult for me. Although it is written with a Romanized alphabet, it has six distinct tones, and the sounds signified by consonants like d-, t-, tr-, ch-, c-, and ng- and vowels like ă-, u'-, and o'- are very different from anything in English. So I relied for a long time on Thuan's and a host of other people's abilities and willingness to speak English to facilitate my movement.

Literacy can be a means of connecting; it can also be a means of disconnecting, of making one's self distinct from the hoi polloi: look what I can do that you can't. In my life, literacy has been my primary route to power. My college infatuation with Greek and Latin, for example, was really about my own status vis-à-vis others. I am not naturally good at speaking languages. I am good at reading and writing. So I chose to major in Latin and Ancient Greek because they were the hardest majors I could imagine succeeding at and they only required reading and writing, not speaking or listening. With Vietnamese I was confronted with the speaking piece and the listening piece—the slowness of it, so counter to the frenetic pace of globalization, and the unevenness of it, in that I am able to read and write it much better than I can speak or understand it. There are the old impulses to read and write to show off, to show other people I can do something that they can't, to hold power in this way. But there is something else, a feeling that grows whenever its grammars and tones and rhythms temporarily take hold before flitting away again. "You have to study a language because you love it," Kim said as we were wrapping up our study session one night this summer, chatting about her work teaching Vietnamese to the kids at the temple in Bridgeport. And it struck me, pedaling home afterwards, friction-powered headlight *whrr whrring* like the wheels in my head, that I hadn't ever really chosen to study a language because I loved it. Trang and Tuan and Kim love Vietnamese, and that love is infectious when they teach. I have been infatuated with languages, yes. Writing systems romance me; I wonder to what degree my alphabet fetish propelled my study of Ancient Greek and Japanese. But have I loved a language other than English? Literacy is performance; I think I have loved my performance, loved the feelings my performance reflects more than the language. I am trying to perform differently, to drop the need to feel like an expert, know it all, better than, best in show, and to love for a different reason—to love the feelings that come with performing as student, partial knower, mistake maker, never-going-to-be-fluent learner, but as someone trying to connect versus trying to distinguish herself from, to separate herself from others.

This means I have to acknowledge the feelings of discomfort produced when I show I am a beginner—speaking with an accent, making mistakes. After teaching basic writing every year since 1994, I have an entirely new understanding of what it means to be a basic writer, to have to invent a writing process without feeling the deep structures of a language, to have to invent the feelings that will allow me to grow some roots in this language. Sometimes my accent is unintelligible, especially to Vietnamese speakers with little experience listening to foreigners speak Vietnamese—like the parents of the two Vietnamese children I tutor, to whom I can write more clearly and in more detail than I can speak with them. My tongue feels like a new, unfamiliar object in my mouth. I get tongue-tied; unable to make my mouth, lips, tongue, and palate move in the coordinated way I need them to in order to produce the sentences that are in my head. "Oh, that was a good *thích*," Kim tells me last week during our Thursday night class. I repeat: *Tôi thích tập nói tiếng Việt.* "Hmm, now you lost it again," she says. (Why does "I like" have to be the verb that gives me trouble? Why couldn't it be a less important verb?) In Vietnam, Tuan made me practice t- and th- over and over with a piece of paper in front of my mouth—t- does not move the paper; th- does. I giggled when I visited my third-grade tutee's ESL reading class in the spring, sitting in the tiny chairs alongside the eight- and nine-year-olds doing the same kinds of pronunciation drills Tuan and Kim have done with me.

Movement again. Fingers similarly learn to make different routes across my keyboard to compose in Unicode with Vietnamese tone and accent marks. I am letting myself love something I am not naturally good at, something I cannot master. It is another way I can commit to practicing movement, along with moving back and forth from physical space to cyberspace, from page to screen, from familiar academic genres to invented new genres, from the United States to Vietnam—whether that means driving across town or getting on a plane for HCM City. From Hollywood image to old photograph to digital photograph. From taxi to motorbike. Each register of movement that I practice—intellectual, physical, emotional—informs and deepens the others. I need to keep asking: how else can I move?

I have made other moves. In Vietnam I moved my online work from my hotel room to its public spaces and neighborhood coffee shops. I moved interviews out of hotels and into cafes and restaurants and apartments where they could became conversations over coffee, lunch, and dinner; individual conversations became conversations in groups of two, three, four, five, six. One-time group conversations became repeat conversations, and conversations with established friends became conversations with new friends. I began deliberately introducing hometown strangers to each other, helping new friendship route/root systems to form.

These route/root systems have also become digital—in-person conversations became e-mail exchanges and instant message sessions and photo sharing and webcam chats when we were half a world apart and could no longer meet in person. The ways in which access to the Internet, private computers, and DSL have broadened since 2002 and the ways in which instant messaging and computer-to-computer Internet calling and photo sharing programs have become available have transformed the kind of routes/roots I can make with my subjects as individuals and as a group. We construct and reflect on our lives as women—how and why we are making our choices about children, education, work, sexuality; which cultural ideas about gender, nationality we accept and resist. We negotiate similar questions about whether and when to have kids, how to balance work and family, how to make time for relationships, and how much education to get and when in relation to all the rest. We also share the more mundane—what happened at work this week, at

English Club, at dinner, what's the news and gossip about so-and-so. Woven into the e-mails and IMs and webcam chatting is the study and practice of English and Vietnamese, consistent encouragement about our relative progress, acceptance of where each of us is. We use hardware and software to grow routes in a digital diaspora, constructing this virtual place and constructing our connections to each other.

Moving on local terms will continue to require physical travel, not just virtual travel, on my part—being in the space of Vietnam in real time, trying local modes and routes in addition to tourist ones, recognizing the differences and using them. It requires not forgetting the relative privileges of movement and access I enjoy. It requires actively constructing myself as a participant in a conversation, actively constructing the conversations, but not using my credentials to dictate pace or purpose or product. Moving on local terms also forces me to acknowledge how my specific material circumstances shape the kind of physical movements I can make in Vietnam. I am a five-foot-three, thirty-eight-year-old white woman, perceived as approachable and friendly, more peer than researcher, by the Vietnamese women in their twenties and thirties who choose to work with me. I have a partner to take care of household issues when I travel. I do not have kids, so I can travel for weeks or months at a time. And unlike most of my subjects, I can easily get a passport and visa to travel back and forth between Vietnam. I can earn research grants to cover my travel expenses, move freely in expatriate and foreigners' spaces in Vietnam, and gain access to some people and places because of my status as professor of English and women's studies at a U.S. university. I treat these "signals" of difference, as Grewal and Kaplan call them (2000, 3), as opportunities to gain perspective, access, and insights that I can return to the collective as we continue to cosponsor our linguistic and cultural literacies.

I now use Deborah Brandt's concept (2001) of literacy sponsors to describe our relationships with each other and our relationship to the technologies we employ: "any agents, local or distant, concrete or abstract, who enable, support, teach, and model, as well as recruit, regulate, suppress, or withhold literacy—and gain advantage by it in some way." Our movement is organized around our present needs: cosponsoring each others' linguistic and cultural literacies on the terms local economies make possible. Our shared economic moment compels us (unevenly, yes) to move transnationally, to acquire the linguistic and cultural literacies we need to negotiate, create, and gain access to emerging opportunities that materially transform our lives, that create new hybrid economic and cultural spaces at this time. In the case of my subjects, English literacy (as well as Chinese, Japanese, and French) can secure a job with a foreign company that pays significantly more than a domestic company and enables the exchange of ideas and perspectives. In my case, Vietnamese literacy creates skills, partnerships, and perspectives, all of which increase my capacity to think, teach, write, and travel globally. These are liberal objectives in many ways—working within existing (albeit emerging) economies, believing in the transformative power of literacy and education and dialogue. But these objectives have emerged as the common ground my subjects and I share with each other, a meeting in the middle of a socialist to capitalist continuum, the point from which we work together to move ourselves intellectually, physically, and emotionally.

Vietnamese women are living through a remarkable moment of change. Those changes—the growth of a market economy, the opening of Vietnam to foreign investment, Vietnam joining the World Trade Organization—are moving many women within Vietnam and making it possible for me to travel back and forth to Vietnam. Our relationship is further shaped by this new economy—by the need for Vietnamese women to acquire English literacies, by the material difference it can make in their lives, by the tensions it is creating for women and their families, by my ability to serve as a sponsor, by the ways we can create in-person and virtual meeting spaces and forums to exchange literacy sponsorship, to fashion English for Vietnamese trade routes. We are (re)writing Vietnam as a new place and (re)writing ourselves in it.

I am writing Vietnam rather than writing about Vietnam. This distinction marks intellectual movement I have made since 2002. It is a signal that I am able to narrate Vietnam into a frame of intelligibility, that I am no longer unstuck in time, no longer Billy Pilgrim in *Slaughterhouse Five*; that I am making the frame, the place, the topos Vietnam bear an alternative heuristic burden—showing the effects of globalization's push-pull by telling a story about women creating the language needed to route/root ourselves in each others' lives. But I could not make this intellectual movement of inventing the form my work is taking, of clarifying its purpose in relation to its audience, of conceptualizing my role as rhetor—in short, negotiating my rhetorical situation—until I practiced physical movement on local terms often enough to rewrite my own emotional landscape, until I grew different routes and roots, until I loved being a part of writing a twenty-first-century Vietnam more on its own terms.

This work makes me acutely aware of what James Clifford calls the "the paradoxical nature of ethnographic knowledge": believing in "human connectedness" while "questioning any stable or essential grounds of human similarity" (1988, 145). I am attempting to practice what Clifford calls surrealist ethnography: as I narrativize Vietnam, I do not "begin with the different and render it—through naming, classifying, describing, interpreting—comprehensible," but rather use collage, "an assemblage containing voices other than the ethnographer's, as well as examples of 'found' evidence, data not fully integrated within the work's governing interpretation," where "the cuts and sutures of the research process are left visible" in order to "leave manifest the constructivist procedures of ethnographic knowledge" and—possibly—"avoid the portrayal of cultures as organic wholes or as unified, realistic worlds subject to a continuous explanatory discourse" (146–47). Feminist rhetorics can and must participate in this work of simultaneously narrating connection and instability, not with hope of resolving the tension between them, but as Audre Lorde reminds us, to "take our differences and make them strengths" (1984, 112). Here is where feminist rhetorics complement the work of critical anthropology and ethnography and transnational feminism most clearly for me. With Vietnam in particular, the U.S. cultural impulse is to try to resolve, to finish, to end the story—we see the ruinous effect of this effort every day in the current routes through Iraq and the concurrent narrativizing of those routes that fill the headlines and the cable news networks. The U.S. impulse to write the end of the story on its own terms is deadly for a whole new place. The task of feminist rhetorics is not only to rediscover, reframe, and rewrite open stories; it is also to grow the routes necessary to find the languages, the pieces, and the forms we need to do so.

[7:48:35 a.m.] *Le Thi Thu Chung says:* what are u doing?

[7:48:57 a.m.] *Ilene Crawford says:* I am writing now. I was finishing some emails to colleagues and students.

[7:49:23 a.m.] *Ilene Crawford says:* The revision of my article is due Sept 15

[7:49:33 a.m.] *Ilene Crawford says:* so I am making changes to it.

[7:49:38 a.m.] *Le Thi Thu Chung says:* i c

[7:49:46 a.m.] *Ilene Crawford says:* The editors like it, but it is too long (you knew that!)

[7:50:01 a.m.] *Ilene Crawford says:* so I need to cut it down, so it is no longer than 21 pages.

[7:50:09 a.m.] *Ilene Crawford says:* I need to cut it in half.

[7:50:14 a.m.] *Le Thi Thu Chung says:* :D

[7:50:21 a.m.] *Ilene Crawford says:* I know.

[7:50:29 a.m.] *Ilene Crawford says:* Big job!

[7:50:35 a.m.] *Le Thi Thu Chung says:* pls do not omit what u write about us

[7:50:37 a.m.] *Le Thi Thu Chung says:* :)

Two

Reflective Applications

Making Pathways

Inventing Textual Research Methods in Feminist Rhetorical Studies

Kathleen J. Ryan

> ... rhetorical invention has migrated, entered, settled, and shaped many
> other areas of theory and practice in rhetoric and composition.
>
> Janice Lauer, "Rhetorical Invention: The Diaspora"

As a scholar first trying to establish a research agenda as a tenure-track
faculty member, I found that early efforts to articulate my research
agenda to a general scholarly audience in faculty evaluation reports and
grant applications were uncertain at best. I lacked a language to satis-
factorily name my research methods and agenda in feminist rhetorics
to make arguments for my scholarly potential. Because I was not practicing a more familiar research methodology like historiography or ethnography, I did not have a way to describe my work effectively in these
important evaluative contexts, let alone for the sake of my professional
development. I struggled over questions like these: Is feminist rhetorical studies a discipline or a subdiscipline of rhetorical studies?[1] What
are the characteristic questions, issues, and research methods of this
disciplinary landscape? What shape can my contribution take? More
concretely, how can I create a research agenda to identify my scholarly
work to myself, to others? My experience illustrates challenges other
junior faculty and graduate students in feminist rhetorical studies also
encounter. Since disciplines are marked by methods of study (among

other things), these are questions of disciplinarity and ones to guide individual scholarship. They should be seen as full of inventive possibility rather than sources of anxiety, extending what feminist rhetorical studies is and might become.

My writing helped me to answer these questions. As I researched and drafted an article (see Ryan 2006), I became comfortable defining feminist rhetorical studies as a field of study that both overlaps with and distinguishes itself from rhetorical studies. More recently, I've come to understand feminist pragmatic rhetoric as the perspective that guided that project and continues to shape my scholarship. Feminist pragmatic rhetoric basically brings together feminist pragmatism and rhetoric. Richard Rorty writes that feminist pragmatists work to create "a better set of social constructs than the ones presently available" (1990, 35). My articulation of feminist pragmatism, which draws on the work of (among others) John Dewey, Paolo Freire, Lorraine Code, and Charlene Haddock Siegfried, emphasizes the importance of subjectivity, experiential knowledge, and ongoing reflection on experience and action in order to better act in the future. Janet Atwill's research on rhetoric as *techne* (1998) complements feminist pragmatism's emphasis on contextual, practical knowledge directed toward "beautiful results in the midst of power and oppression and ignorance" (Cherryholmes 1999, 5). My use of Atwill expands feminist pragmatism to include productive knowledge as a flexible, context-dependent way for people to intervene in and invent the world. Atwillian rhetoric likewise reinforces feminist pragmatism's reformist agenda. The aim of rhetoric as *techne* is "neither to formalize a rigorous method nor to secure and define an object of study but rather to reach an end by way of a path that can be retraced, modified, adapted, and 'shared.' The purpose of such a path . . . is not to find a thing. [It is] to produce an alternative destination" (Atwill 1998, 69). Like feminist pragmatism, this art is an alternative to the analytic model of knowledge, which assumes knowledge is a neutral, certain, objective search for truth. Instead, a more appropriate model for feminists in the humanities is one that stresses situated knowledge making and acting in the world to better the world—a feminist pragmatic rhetoric. My aim in turning to feminist pragmatic rhetoric is to offer recovery and gender criticism, especially theorizing, as a feminist means to practice textual research as disciplinary invention, and thus to create a new pathway for articulating and conducting textual research in feminist rhetorical studies to continue to thoughtfully explore, invent, and transform this "dynamic territory" (Royster 1995, 389).[2] In other words, this critical reflection— itself an enactment of feminist pragmatic rhetoric—offers a pathway for practicing feminist textual research as a means of individual scholarly invention and, more broadly, disciplinary invention.

STRATEGIES FOR PRACTICING RECOVERY AND GENDER CRITIQUE

My previous work offers composition and communication scholars an opportunity to consider the relationship between feminisms and rhetorics in the context of edited collections.[3] In "Recasting Recovery and Gender Critique as Inventive Arts: Constructing Edited Collections in Feminist Rhetorical Studies" (2006, hereafter "Recasting"), I found that an early either/or relationship between the arts of recovery and gender critique gives way to a both/and approach that opens multiple possibilities for rich lines of inquiry in and reflection on feminist rhetorical studies for editors, and, by extension, other researchers. Recovery, often figured as "merely" adding to a canon, and gender critique, which I defined as both the analytical work of rereading and rewriting the rhetorical traditional from a gendered viewpoint and the theoretical work of, in Cheryl Glenn's words, "regendering" the rhetorical tradition, emerge as transformative research methods. They are not, ultimately, so easily distinguished from or opposed to one another as one might first suppose, particularly given the polemical debate between Karlyn Kohrs Campbell (1989, 1993) and Barbara Biesecker (1992) about recovery and theory that played out in the pages of *Philosophy and Rhetoric* in the early 1990s and became a tool editors used to position their collections. Rather, recovery can be as transformative as analysis, criticism, and theorizing.

I learned to see recovery and gender critique as textual research methods by approaching the project through the lens of invention studies—in particular, Janet Atwill and Janice Lauer's framing of their collection *Perspectives on Rhetorical Invention* (2002). Lauer's observation that rhetorical invention has "migrated" into different contexts got me thinking about invention of/in feminist rhetorical studies (2002, 2) while

Atwill's call for scholars to return to early Greek depictions of invention furthered my effort to consider research practices in feminist rhetorical studies because she invites new perspectives. She writes: "Early Greek conceptions of invention depicted the art as a process and act of 'making a path.' To make a path is to enable new perspectives, new points of contact—even new destinations" (2002, xx). My interest in invention thus became my means—my path—to research, compose, and (now) articulate a feminist pragmatic rhetoric that uses textual research methods as one valuable research methodology.

I began my research with the intent to identify all the invention strategies in texts operating in the interstices of feminisms and rhetorics. Though I quickly learned this desire far exceeded the scope of a single article, this agenda highlighted invention as one of my primary research methods—my approach to defining and analyzing recovery, gender critique, and theorizing—and became an activity that, in turn, developed my definition of invention. I've come to define invention as *rhetorical strategies*—heuristic, imaginative, interpretive, epistemic—for gathering and shaping material to compose the content of effective discourse. My research has convinced me that invention is, as LeFevre (1987) says, a social act; it is also a work of imagination, shaping, and interpretation in the tradition of Vico (1990); and, in the hands of feminists like Cheryl Glenn (1997), Gerda Lerner (1997), and Jacqueline Jones Royster (2000), a productive, dialogic re-vision of texts and activities that stresses knowledge construction. I thus specifically understand and practice rhetorical invention as a dialogic, creative, revisionist, and epistemic act—a feminist pragmatic rhetorical perspective.

To invent "Recasting," I reread papers, bibliographies, articles, and exam responses I had saved in various electronic and print forms to revisit what I already knew and gather this material together to take a new look.[4] This activity of gathering and rediscovering texts I had forgotten or neglected—this recovery—reminded me that I did know something about feminist rhetorics and gave me direction for seeking out new material to deepen my reading as I researched databases anew and followed bibliographies and references to other historical and contemporary texts. I took copious notes on articles, chapters, and books that I read and reread, creating a textual memory map of key words, favorite quotations, and emergent responses. My note-taking practices were often guided by Rich's notion of re-vision as reseeing (1986), Fetterley's resisting reader (1981), and Fahnestock and Secor's definition of rhetorical analysis (2002, 183–84), in which the rhetorician "pays attention to the who, when, where and probable why of an argument, identifies language choices that serve the rhetor's ostensible purpose or perhaps, depending on the interpreter, his or her unconscious or subverted purposes," and "seeks to uncover the argument of a text."

As a feminist pragmatic rhetorician, I define *argument* more broadly than Fahnestock and Secor—often mentally locating *purpose* or *end* in its place and remembering feminist challenges to traditional notions of argumentation. I thus did not rely fully on their strategy to use "an identifiable vocabulary drawn from the rhetorical tradition and/or from a particular school or theorist" to be open to new vocabularies (2002, 183). I ultimately created an annotated bibliography as a quick reference of what I had read and needed to read, and what characterized my reaction to each text. At one count, I had generated over fifty pages of bibliographic entries and notes. Compiling texts, reading and rereading, researching new texts, and note taking became significant strategies for entering this conversation as an observer and listener. This recovery process, in all its inventive dimensions, helped me find my footing as a feminist rhetorician.

The canon of arrangement served as a second, interrelated canon to guide my research. Like Winifred Horner (1988, ix–x), I see all the rhetorical canons in a synergistic relationship; in particular, I have learned—especially from women's historian Gerda Lerner (1997)—to understand the canons of invention and arrangement as overlapping at the site of *shaping* material: imaginative, interpretive, and conceptual work to make and represent knowledge in a particular genre. By arrangement I mean rhetorical strategies—heuristic, epistemic, generic—for managing material, for organizing and ordering discourse effectively. Here, rhetorical arrangement exceeds the narrow sense of partitioning a text to include shaping material epistemologically and literally—a process of strategically selecting and placing textual claims and evidence to communicate to a particular audience in a particular genre. Through reflection, I understand I used these canons simultaneously as tools to address my research questions, which ultimately narrowed to the following: What rhetorical contributions do editors of feminist rhetorical collections make? What can a study of these texts teach us? My article offers a partial answer to these questions.

As I shifted between invention and arrangement activities, I moved slowly from the role of reader, observer, and interpreter to meaning-maker, writer, and theorist. The concrete practice of studying and organizing notes informed my meta-thinking and my project slowly took a firmer shape in my mind and on the page. I worked extensively with my notes, marking them for patterns, divergences, and key words, borrowing interpretive and organizational research strategies I had learned to do with Ann Berthoff's double-entry notes (1982). I cut out quotations from my notes on recurrent topics (including metaphor, recovery, discipline, and collaboration) and moved them around in different piles on my office floor to help me observe different patterns, construct my argument, and choose a way to represent my understanding of these framing texts to others. While these activities may not seem unique to feminist research, they emerged from feminist and revisionist readings of classical canons, feminist reading practices, and my subjectivity as a feminist rhetorician and new, woman faculty member. Conducting this kind of research helped me create tools for reading and interpreting feminist texts, catching the drift of conversations, and becoming an agent in my discipline.

Two important rhetorical decisions significantly shaped my move from data collection to interpretation to representation on the page. These choices, which helped articulate my point and organize my argument, further illustrate how shaping—a recursive blending of invention and arrangement—is a significant part of feminist textual research. First, I decided to focus on the framing material of edited collections to attend to my interest in the relationship between genre and disciplinarity, and, second, I chose to use the Campbell–Biesecker exchange in *Philosophy and Rhetoric* as a framing device of my own. Reading Gail Hawisher and Cynthia Selfe's "The Edited Collection: A Scholarly Contribution and More" (1997) and Laura Micciche's "The Role of Edited Collections in Composition Studies" (2001) persuaded me to focus on edited collections because this genre aligned with my disciplinary questions about feminist rhetorical studies, since, as Hawisher and Selfe indicate, this genre "seems especially critical to those fields we would label as relatively newly-constituted areas of inquiry." They further explain, "By bringing to scholarly conversations voices that might not otherwise be heard, the edited collection defines and broadens fields of inquiry, while at the same time identifying issues that demand attention" (103-4). Likewise, Micciche's description of the rhetoric of the framing texts in edited collections resonated with my desire to make sense of the intersections between feminism and rhetoric. Micciche writes, "in the framing texts editors may define key terms, offer readings of the rhetorical and historical contexts to which their text contributes, and foreground particular theoretical approaches. More broadly, editors establish an intellectual and often political context, describing the sort of intervention the edited collection seeks to make" (103-4). Anis Bawarshi's discussion of genres as "socially constructed, ongoing cognitive and rhetorical sites—symbiotically maintained rhetorical ecosystems, if you will" further augments the disciplinary rhetoricity of edited collections for scholars in feminist rhetorical studies (2003, 39). These perspectives on genre and edited collections thus coincided well with my interest in contributing to conversations about feminist rhetorical studies' disciplinary status in the spirit of such articles as Patricia Bizzell's "Opportunities for Feminist Research in the History of Rhetoric" (1992), Karlyn Kohrs Campbell's "Consciousness Raising: Linking Theory, Criticism, and Practice" (2002), and Krista Ratcliffe's close study of Woolf, Daly, and Rich as feminist rhetorical theorists (1996). These texts, and Royster's metaphor of disciplinary landscaping (2003, 148), expose gaps in the landscape of feminist rhetorical studies that I wanted to address, too.

Using the Campbell–Biesecker exchange as a shaping method was a means for me to assert my shift from bystander to agent since my notes repeatedly showed editors positioning themselves in terms of this "debate," often quite explicitly. Turning the terms of this debate into a lens to interpret and shape my response to the texts I was studying became a significant way for me to shape my text and better understand rhetorical, dialogic moves in this emergent discipline. My research taught me that such polemic—as the "debate" first seemed—might rather be characterized as a traditional (patriarchal) means of responding to an academic work and creating dialogue in an academic community. This polemic actually gave way (over time) to more entangled discussions in the framing texts, where recovery blended into theory. By the time *Avail-*

able Means: An Anthology of Women's Rhetoric(s) was published (2001), Joy Ritchie and Kate Ronald had identified women's writing as theory, altogether disrupting criticism and theorizing as a more privileged research method than recovery.

As I crafted my article in terms of evolving responses to this "debate," I decided for clarity's sake to separate my definition of gender critique into critical writing and theorizing, because gender critique covers such a wide range of activities, from rhetorical analysis and rhetorical criticism to theory application and creation. "Recasting" defines critical writing as rhetorical analysis and critique of new and familiar texts and theorizing as "efforts to apply theoretical perspectives to the topic of gender and rhetoric and create new rhetorical theories drawn from women's writing and speaking" (2006, 25). The article goes on to offer heuristics to enact both interrelated practices; those on critical writing focus on the results of resistant rereadings of familiar/new texts, while theorizing emphasizes creating new ideas and conceptualizations about rhetorical practices and (feminist) rhetorical studies as a discipline. I see better now how a decision I characterized as one related to lucid organization is also, in fact, a personal/professional act of making sense of research methods in feminist rhetorical studies, particularly distinguishing (for myself and then others) theorizing from rhetorical analysis/criticism.

THEORIZING AS A TEXTUAL RESEARCH METHOD

To me, theory is a method of conceptualizing and systematizing experience through observational, interpretive, imaginative, organizational, and reflective practices. A theorist tries to better understand some phenomenon in a generalized way with the intent to participate effectively as a citizen in the world in general, and, for the purposes of this project, to contribute to feminist rhetorical studies. Theorizing, then, is an ongoing experiential, contingent, reform-minded activity of creating new understanding and actions. In this framework, theory becomes an empowering means to understand and construct our lives and our discipline. This accessible definition offers new scholars in feminist rhetorical studies means to (re)see their efforts to enter the discipline using the textual research methods I advocate. It's critical not to underestimate the power of this view of theorizing as it both authorizes the scholar as theorist and explains the need for theory. It is this definition of theory that enabled me to embark on and compose "Recasting." It guided my exigency for writing; my ongoing, recursive conceptualization of the project; and my composition of it for *Rhetoric Review* readers. My hope is that this definition also confers greater agency onto other feminist researchers as creators and path-makers in feminist rhetorical studies— an agency that a typical definition of theory does not proffer to most new scholars.

Because I am a feminist pragmatic rhetorician, my definition of theory, not surprisingly, diverges from high theory and its character-istic pretense toward universality and timelessness, opaque language, and remove from the lives of ordinary women and men, including femi-nist scholars trying to make their way in graduate school or as junior faculty members. My definition draws on (among others) interrelated perspectives on theory by Sidney Dobrin (1997), Shirley Rose and Irwin Weiser (2002), and Karen A. Foss, Sonya K. Foss, and Cindy L. Griffin (1999)—scholars who self-identify or can be characterized as pragma-tists and/or feminists as well as rhetoricians. In the foreword to Sidney Dobrin's *Constructing Knowledges*, Patricia Bizzell sets up the critical distinction between Theory and theory that frames Dobrin's book: "Whereas 'Theory' tends to be thought of as something static, like a table of laws, 'theory' is better thought of as a process or an activity— 'theorizing' or 'theory talk'" (Bizzell 1997, 2). Dobrin further clarifies dimensions of theory as an activity, writing: "Theory provides a frame-work within which one can operate, ask questions, even alter or refine principles of that theory based on new experience, new observation" (1997, 9). Dobrin's identification of theory as dynamic—changeable or evolving—is one I welcome for its inventive potential, while his empha-sis on theory as a way to make sense of phenomena based on studying experience is consistent with feminist pragmatism's privileging of expe-riential knowledge.

This sense of theory as an activity for changing, framing, and un-derstanding is reinforced and complemented by Foss, Foss, and Grif-fin's feminist definition of theory as "a way of framing an experience or event—an effort to understand and account for something and the way it functions in the world." Their emphasis on theorizing as something individuals do daily in composing their lives makes the prospect of theorizing accessible to new scholars: "Individuals theorize when they try to figure out answers for, develop explanations about, and organize what is happening in their worlds" (1999, 8). The sense of agency their definition conveys is particularly compelling and empowering for those of us who are used to thinking of theory as reserved for esteemed, often male scholars. Understanding theory as a way to conceptualize and order one's world deflates the mystical quality typically attributed to academic Theory and the reverence accorded to Theorists. If we theorize regularly in our lives, we can learn to better extend this practice to theorize, to invent, research methods like these feminist textual ones. According to Rose and Weiser, "We turn to theorizing when . . . we are faced with a new situation and we need to understand that situation in order to decide how or whether to act, and when we need to explain or rationalize a practice" (2002, 191-92). In trying to position myself as a feminist rhetorician and junior faculty member, I faced exactly this need for theory—an exigency I know my students and other scholars share when situating themselves in relationship to a new discipline or project. I now recognize that in the specific activity of seeking to make sense of edited collections in feminist rhetorics I was theorizing to understand, enter, and contribute to a disciplinary conversation. Theory was a crucial means of inventing my research agenda, means, and myself as a feminist researcher. Had I known then to define this impulse to self-position and understand these textual research methods as kinds of theorizing, I would have had an inviting definition of theory and some specific practices to authorize my impulse to understand and guide my invention. I would have had a pathway to follow, even if I chose—as invention encourages us to do—to strike out and make my own path.

In addition to offering us ways to frame and authorize our work, Dobrin and Foss, Foss, and Griffin teach us to recognize *questioning* as a heuristic for theorizing, a strategy I used in numerous ways while drafting "Recasting." I began my project with a series of questions that expressed my exigency for writing. The heuristics I offer in making my argument for reseeing recovery and gender critique as inventive arts also takes the form of questions. For example, I offered the following heuristics to define theorizing as an inventive act to readers: "How can critique of texts and traditions lead to new theories and conceptualizations of rhetoric and the history of rhetoric as an area of study? What new rhetorical theories are women creating through their writing and speaking? How can feminist rhetoricians extract new theory from women's writing and speaking practices? What theoretical perspectives can be productively applied to studies of women's rhetorical practices?" (2006, 26). These questions helped me explicate and distinguish among key terms so that readers would understand my analytical framework for studying my chosen framing texts, but I also intended for researchers to employ these questions, just as I did during the course of my project. Moreover, I hoped these heuristics might prompt further scholarly research responses and projects. I wanted to contribute to this disciplinary conversation by offering a new way for feminists to consider textual research methods and make their own offerings in response.

Dobrin and Foss, Foss, and Griffin also offer explaining and organizing as theorizing activities. The note-taking process I have described is a mixture of evaluative, interpretive, and contextual work; the way I organized my notes—often looking for patterns—helped me ponder, observe, and reflect on the meaning I was making from ordering and reordering the material I gathered. This work I referred to as shaping is a kind of theorizing that blurs invention and arrangement. Attunement, which Louise Wetherbee Phelps describes as "a kind of background state of attention by which one continually sifts information and ideas for what might be useful in some context that is not presently focal" (1988, 222), is a kind of organization since it is a way of sieving multiple pieces of information through processes of selection and discarding. For me, that process included decisions like selecting edited collections, choosing particular edited collections, focusing on framing materials, and organizing my understanding of these texts and representing them to readers via Campbell and Biesecker's exchange. All this framing/shaping is theorizing because ordering experience, in this case textual experiences, is a conceptual act.

Because acts of definition figure significantly in my research, I emphasize this specific kind of explaining as another strategy for theorizing. Certainly, the holistic impulse to recast recovery and gender critique is a significant act of redefinition. More specifically, heuristics I offer enumerate my definitions of recovery and gender critique as inventive arts, drawn as they were from my interpretations of the framing texts in the context of my reading in feminist rhetorics, invention, and genre. Moreover, in redefining the classical canons of invention and arrangement, I was again theorizing—this time as a way to reflect on my process of composing the article, thereby offering a specific approach to feminist textual research. I have increasingly found definition, or rather, redefinition, as well as feminist encouragement to resee and revise to be powerful means of theorizing to create change as a feminist pragmatic rhetorician. I don't mean to create new definitions to be reified, but to embrace the ways definitions change and evolve as a result of feminist perspectives. Defining is also a valuable means of enacting agency and promoting reform to, in this case, rethink concepts in a feminist context.

It is largely through reflection and my own interest in reform that I've embraced definition as a critical theoretical act, additional theoretical strategies Weiser and Rose also privilege. They define a theorist as "a reflective agent seeking explanations of phenomena and situations in order to understand them better and to act on that understanding in a particular context for a particular purpose" (2002, 183). Dewey's understanding of reflection, whereby "'[t]houghtful persons . . . weigh, ponder, deliberate'" (qtd. in Phelps 1988, 209), situates consideration, explanation, evaluation, and questioning as additional strategies for practicing reflection on the world to theorize about it in order to act on that theorizing. Bizzell explains Dobrin's work on theorizing as "thinking about what one is doing—reflecting on practice—but thinking about it in a systematic way, trying to take as much as possible into account, and using the ideas of other thinkers wherever they may be helpful" (1997, 3). This effectively describes how an individual might theorize her scholarly and personal worlds in much the same way, with an additional emphasis on using dialogic thinking, or responding to others' ideas.

While the texts I read served a shaping function, so did friends, journal editors, and readers who commented on or verbally reacted to my article. Repeated drafting and talking about my writing helped me reflect on—and better express—my theory about research methods that editors and others do/might use to contribute to the dynamic discipline of feminist rhetorical studies. Answering these readers' questions helped me reflect on my emerging project and understand how I could use questions to explain my definitions of recovery, critical writing, and theorizing to give evidence of my claims about these research methods as inventive arts that editors use and also to offer strategies for practicing these methods that other feminist textual researchers/editors (can) use in their projects. Karen Burke LeFevre writes, "To enhance the possibility that invention will occur, people must be able to work, to think, to be part of a past tradition and continuing community, and to have their works received by others so the inventive act is completed" (1987, 75). This dialogue that began with me reading and talking back to texts developed into a relationship with my own readers, and will hopefully extend as other readers take up their own projects and continue the kind of dialogic exchange that is such a hallmark of the feminist rhetorics community.[5] In my own redefinition and contribution, I wanted new and established scholars to see what reseeing this opposition of recovery and theory might mean for how we conceive of research methods—recovery, gender critique, and theorizing—in feminist rhetorical studies, and how we might go on to do so in new ways—how we might, as agents, contribute to the development of this emergent discipline. I was significantly concerned with creating alternative visions and paths in feminist rhetorical studies, for myself and other researchers to embark on together and along different routes. Jacqueline Jones Royster speaks effectively to this motive: "While, with each run through a territory, we must inevitably choose a path, we need more than one crossing to see what is really going on. . . . The more pathways we create . . . the greater the chance we have of accounting more adequately and more sensitively to complex worlds" (1995, 389).

As a means of knowledge construction, theorizing is a critical part of disciplinary development and reform, though it takes on different shapes in different disciplines. I find that theory in feminist rhetorical studies reflects the dynamism of disciplinary landscaping because scholars like Royster welcome the inventive potential of new research methods and directions in the field.

According to Maureen Goggin (1995, 28), a traditional definition of discipline identifies a specific territory, a physical space and an intellectual space, where like-minded scholars practice common research methods, attend specific scholarly conferences, publish monographs, build graduate programs, belong to specific professional organizations—generally talk to one another in shared, accepted ways in specific sites to contribute to and enact the rules of their discipline. This definition suggests that disciplines are closed systems, but while I value these disciplinary elements, I privilege, as a feminist pragmatic rhetorician, a sense of disciplines as dynamic and always, necessarily evolving—with theory construction as a critical means—alongside recovery and rewriting—of scholarly agency and (disciplinary) change. It is, in part, with this knowledge of disciplinary fluidity—and the potential it implies—that I can conduct research in feminist rhetorical studies.

I'm not done theorizing about research methods or other questions I have about feminist rhetorical studies, but I have a better understanding of the kind of research methods I practice and why. I have learned that I am increasingly confident using the term *feminist rhetorical studies* to describe this discipline I embrace. I realize also that I had inadequately articulated my understanding of theory, and that I am more comfortable claiming the role of theorist. I understand that my current research agenda is guided by these textual research methods in the context of my stance as a feminist pragmatic rhetorician. I look forward to continuing my scholarship with a more informed sense that recovery and gender critique—critical writing and theory—are significant research methods intertwined with the rhetorical canons of invention and arrangement. I am also more aware of the significant relationships among disciplinarity, theory, and agency. Royster's notions of disciplinarity as landscaping and (new) research methods as new pathways offer compelling visions of feminist rhetorical studies' disciplinary present and future because of the potential for change they offer: they recognize where we stand as well as how we are called to shape this terrain as we encounter new texts, new experiences, and new exigencies. When Royster writes, "We landscape" (1995, 148), I interpret her to mean we invent, we theorize, we research. We make and follow pathways across the disciplinary terrain. It's in the spirit of this communal effort to share in the making of our diverse discipline that I offer feminist textual research as a useful means for faculty and students to conduct research.

Feminist textual research, then, includes particular approaches to recovery, rhetorical analysis and rhetorical criticism, and theorizing. I have focused primarily on theorizing to clarify that activity since I didn't define the concept fully in "Recasting." While the ways of theorizing I propose—framing, understanding, defining and redefining, questioning, explaining, organizing, conceptualizing, ordering experience, collaborating, reflecting, and reforming—makes evident that the canons of invention and arrangement characterize theorizing, so too does another concept that belongs in the list: shaping, the ways we manipulate material through selection, organization, and ordering. Identifying shaping and these other activities as ways of theorizing usefully enumerates and validates this meaning-making work for scholars and students. It's empowering to recognize these efforts to make sense of texts and worlds as theorizing since theory work is often unnecessarily figured as more esoteric than recovery and critique. Theory is simply another valuable way of making meaning in our discipline, as in our lives. As such, I place the textual research methods of recovery and gender critique, especially theory, alongside historiography and ethnography as available means for research in feminist rhetorical studies that offer further exploration of different pathways in our disciplinary landscape.

Rhetorics of Possibility

Challenging the Textual Bias of Rhetoric through the Theory of the Flesh

Bernadette M. Calafell

In the summer of 2002, I found myself in Mexico City looking for Malintzin Tenepal, known to some as La Malinche or Doña Marina Malintzin. This woman, who was Hernan Cortés's lover and translator, as
well as the symbolic mother of Mexican and Chicana/o peoples, had
been a part of my existence all my life, though at times I did not even
know who she was. I was in the midst of a crisis. Only two years earlier I
had moved to North Carolina from Arizona and found myself in a space
where literally no one knew what Chicana/o meant. I lost my grandfa-
ther, my only father, in February of the next year, and got married just
a few days before I left for Mexico City. I was caught in a trajectory of
uncertainty, fueled by a larger sense of loss and a desire to recover a narrative that might not only shed light on historical injustices and representations, but might also help me find my voice. I hoped that through
finding the story, voice, or even image of Malintzin, looking at the ways
Chicana and Mexicana voices had been lost or diminished in the postcolonial world, I would be able to recover my voice as well.

   This intimate connection between my experience and my academic
pursuits did not seem unnatural to me. My theoretical lineages are based
in women of color feminisms, primarily those articulated by Gloria
Anzaldúa (2002), Cherrie Moraga (1983), Lisa Flores (1996), bell hooks
(1994, 1999), and Patricia Hill Collins (2000). Each of these scholars has

necessarily informed the methodological approach that I have worked through, a methodology that is committed to the value of personal experiences, or what Moraga and Anzaldúa term theories of the flesh. In the groundbreaking book *This Bridge Called My Back: Writings by Radical Women of Color* (1981, 23), they describe the theory of the flesh as a place "where the physical realities of our lives—our skin color, the land or concrete we grew up on, our sexual longings—all fuse to create a politic born out of necessity. Here, we attempt to bridge the contradictions of our experience." Interpreting the theory of the flesh, Sandoval argues that it is not only a theory that allows for survival, but "that allows practitioners to live with faith, hope, and moral vision in spite of all else" (2000, 7). Others such as Alcoff and Mohanty have argued that identities can operate as theories and can thus "reveal and explain aspects of our shared world and experiences" (2006, 6). Theories of the flesh have been central to the survival of women of color and have been one of the primary ways in which we have been able to theorize about our experiences when we have been denied access to traditional forms of knowledge production. I am well aware of the critiques leveled against "so-called identity politics"; however, I am committed to a belief that, in the words of Alcoff and Mohanty, "Identities are markers for history, social location, and positionalities. They are *always* subject to an individual's interpretation of their meaningfulness and salience in her or his own life, and thus, their political implications are not transparent or fixed" (6). This commitment to experience and identity, along with my intersectional understanding of my identities that I have foregrounded (see Calafell 2001, 2005, 2007a, 2007b), has led to my work being constructed in a fringe position within the larger field of communication and rhetorical studies.

There is a need for many of women of color scholars in rhetoric to find and create our own homeplaces. I offer my homeplace and the experiential journey as a site to begin this conversation. Each of the choices I offer is inherently political and committed to a Chicana feminist project that values the theory of the flesh. Specifically, this feminist perspective, driven by a commitment to theories of the flesh, helps me to navigate the theoretical and methodological connections I make to rhetoric and performance studies. I locate some of the challenges faced by scholars of color in Rhetoric and Communication Studies by drawing on my experience as a way to perform the theory of the flesh and demonstrate the intimate connections between our work and our identities. The impulses and questions that guided my move from rhetoric to performance lead me, finally, to argue for a homeplace that brings together the theory of the flesh with a critical rhetorical perspective immersed in the politics of the performative. Within this homeplace, personal experience is valued as are other forms of knowledge production and representation. This space creates a space of possibility for me, as a cultural outsider in the academy. Following in the footsteps of other women of color, I create space in which to do my methodological pastiche.

In sharing this narrative, I am aware that when women of color give testimony to their experiences of racism, sexism, and homophobia in academia, they are often forced into the position of victims by others who may have little to no experiences with these kinds of daily traumas, or are constructed as part of a "culture of complaint," which "suggests that anyone who can claim victim status happily does so and proceeds to whine with an attitude of self-righteous martyrdom" (Alcoff 2003, 4). I offer my journey to give testimonies to the challenges faced by women of color in the academy and to demonstrate a trek for empowerment and agency within a hostile space.

LOOKING FOR A HOME OF ONE'S OWN

Rhetoric was the place where I began in the discipline of communication studies. Methodologically, I employ rhetorical criticism, critical ethnography, and autobiographical performance to understand or locate vernacular texts and knowledges: texts that may not be so public and that may take Other rhetorical forms. I mark this space of being on the fringe because in many ways it has been marked for me because of my methodological approach and my research presentation. But I am not the first minority scholar to question this fringe position. I ask myself the same questions that my mentor and friend Fernando Delgado has asked, "What if I cannot write on matters that I deem important? What if educated readers do not understand? Most frightening, what if they are simply not interested?" Delgado also asks, "How can Angelina Grimke or Harry Truman's discourse be any more (or less) salient in the 1990s than Rigoberta Menchú's or Louis Farrakhan's? And yet, somehow they are. [. . .] The above examples demonstrate the problem with minority voices, they often say things that others do not find important or valuable" (1997, 49–50). *Will anyone find my voice valuable? Can I make any contribution?* These are questions I often asked myself early in my academic endeavors. Anthony Slagle, commenting on the notion that his work on queer rhetoric makes him too specialized, sarcastically offers, "I have not done an adequate enough job of assimilating into the mainstream of the discipline" (2006, 320). Though these scholars have certainly opened the door in terms of getting us to consider the various ways to conceptualize the rhetorical critic, texts, and the act of criticism, much space still needs to be mapped. As Delgado writes, "The first challenge in engaging Other voices is uncovering their marginalized or subaltern expressions. The second is overcoming the institutional and academic barriers to documenting such voices" (1998, 420).

In addition to the barriers identified by Delgado and Slagle, Blair, Brown, and Baxter have addressed what they term as the "the imposition of the male paradigm" (1994, 383). They complicate discussions about voice even further in their description of the norms of academic writing: "Notably missing, or at least reduced to virtual silence, is the passion that obviously drives our choices to write about particular topics in particular ways. Our writings suppress our convictions, our enthusiasm, our anger, in the interest of achieving an impersonal, 'expert' distance and tone" (383). One aspect of this male paradigm is characterized by impersonal abstraction, which is "predicated on the separation of the person from contextual particulars" (389). Another notable aspect of this paradigm is disciplinary territoriality, which disciplines those operating from an interdisciplinary perspective (often women) (391).

While Blair, Brown, and Baxter pointed to alarming practices in the field, almost a decade later Shugart furthered their critiques by arguing about disciplinary practices in critical rhetorical scholarship, which is predicated on illuminating issues of power: "in order for one's work to be legitimized, recognized as scholarship, one must confirm to the scholarly tradition" (2003, 281). Ironically, Shugart argues that the aesthetic features of scholarship "subtly but profoundly undermine the critical project and reproduce oppressive paradigms" (284). The practices identified by each of these critics has certainly informed my disciplinary identity, my awareness of possibilities and impossibilities, and my understanding of myself existing on the margins of rhetoric; it creates the context for this discussion of my work.

A BEGINNING SPACE OF POSSIBILITY

From 1993 through 1995 I studied at the local community college in Phoenix, Arizona. This was not my first choice of schools, but given my financial options it seemed to be the best choice. The only other option with some financial benefits was a state university a few hours away. But being that far away from home and living on my own simply seemed unthinkable for both me and my family. After completing two years at community college, we decided that I would continue to live at home with my grandparents and commute every day from South Phoenix to Tempe by bus. When I finally arrived on the campus of the local university and in my first class, an introduction to methods course, I was terrified. It wasn't because I was unprepared for the work; rather, I felt culturally out of place. Years later I would read Cherríe Moraga describe her own college experience and the ways race and class informed it: "For years, I berated myself for not being as 'free' as my classmates. I completely bought that they simply had more guts than I did—to rebel against their parents and run around the country hitchhiking, reading books and studying 'art.' They had enough privilege to be atheists, for chrissake" (1983, 55). Like Moraga, I was initially uncritical about my place in the space, completely blaming myself for what I was feeling. All I knew was that I felt extremely out of place and awkward. Later I would come to understand that I was overwhelmed by the whiteness of the place. The whiteness was not just marked by bodies and personas that seemed vastly different and in many ways "free" as described by Moraga, but also by the feeling and affect of the place. My narrative of coming to the university seemed to be dramatically different from the others I talked to in the course who were living on campus or in their own apartments. Since I was a commuter, it seemed like my identity as student ended as soon as I stepped off the campus. I was in no way the "traditional" student, though I was the same age as my peers. To say I felt out of place would be an understatement. I rarely talked and, quite frankly, I was scared of my white peers. They seemed to belong; I felt naïve, clumsy, and unsophisticated. Ironically, these feelings in many ways are often still echoed in my feelings as a cultural outsider in the academy (Calafell 2007b).

My feelings of relative invisibility and unimportance quickly changed one day in class as we were required to read Lisa Flores's essay "Creating Discursive Space Through a Rhetoric of Difference: Chicana Feminists Craft a Homeland" (1996). It was the first time in my college experience that I encountered a text for a class that quite literally spoke to my experience. As Flores described the rhetorical strategies used by Chicana feminists to create a discursive home, I found my own struggle for space and voice echoed in her opening narrative of the story of Esperanza, the main character from Sandra Cisneros's *House on Mango Street,* who keenly understands the differences in class and culture around her and how they lead to her displacement (Flores 1996, 142). I cried while reading the essay, pouring all my emotion into my response to the piece. I searched the piece for any hint of Flores beyond her name as author. I wanted to know her story, how this piece could so deeply resonate with me, and how she felt when she wrote it. As luck would have it, Flores was a faculty member in that department and I was blessed to be able to work with her on a rhetorical criticism of *Latina Magazine.*[1]

My first encounter with rhetoric through Flores's essay set the tone for me in underscoring the importance of my identity in relationship to my role as a rhetorical critic and my negotiation of it, as well as my relationship to the various texts I would come to study. How could my voice not matter when the texts I was the most drawn to were so closely tied to my cultural experiences as a Chicana? Did my position as a cultural "insider" help illuminate meanings or, as others would argue, bias me? The answer seemed obvious to me, but as I entered graduate school I would come to understand that despite the ideological turn in rhetorical criticism, the norm within the field was for the critic's voice or illusion to selfhood to be relatively absent and criticism disembodied (Blair, Brown, and Baxter 1994). In many ways this lack of allusion to self was simply a way to reify the norm of the space as white, male, and heterosexual, essentially universalizing this experience and perspective. These perspectives governed what was deemed as important in rhetorical criticism and the lenses through which we should view issues of voice and texts. Other scholars, such as Olga Davis (1998),[2] have questioned the ways in which rhetorical scholarship lacks attention to the theoretical significance of the ordinariness of everyday life (i.e., experience) or everyday intellectualizing by black women, or as Ono and Sloop (1995) have argued, the attention is often placed on the rhetoric of the oppressor or the "exemplary" minority speaker. Davis further problematizes this by arguing that these "exemplary" speakers are most often male and are then essentialized as being representative of the race. My relationship with rhetoric was becoming increasingly more tenuous. Thus, I began to explore a relationship with performance.

The question of voice reemerged much more explicitly as I continued my graduate studies. Sitting in my introduction to rhetorical methods course in my second semester of graduate school I listened intently as the professor, a leading scholar in critical rhetoric, asked us to consider just how present a rhetorical critic should be in their readings of a text. Does the rhetorical critic acknowledge her or his subjectivity and relationship to the text? These questions would continue to emerge, though at this time I did not yet know how to theoretically articulate my response. Of course we all knew that the critic's voice was always present, but the question of subjectivity or positionality remained. Do we as critics explicitly disclose our identities and how they may inform our readings of texts? What perceived risks or social costs do we accrue in doing so? This was the question we debated in class, yet it was a question that was almost ridiculous to ask in my performance studies classes, where we were certainly expected to be accountable to our positionalities. I was suffering from academic schizophrenia and wondering how I would be able to reconcile all that I had learned about the dimensions of the field with what I was feeling.

THEORIES OF THE FLESH AND HONORING EXPERIENCE

Prior to going to Mexico City, I had extensively critically analyzed literature about Malintzin, both by Chicana feminist writers as well as others[3] to look for her story and try to understand the various frames through which she had been constructed. Drawing on my background in Chicana feminism and rhetoric, I was attempting to examine the dominant themes that framed the way Malintzin was understood culturally. This framing, in many ways, served as the context for what was to come and also grounded the project rhetorically. As I got deeper and deeper into each of the narratives of Malintzin, which essentially sought to determine whether she was a *vendida* (traitor) to her people, through her coupling with Cortés, or simply a woman with great foresight, intelligence, and spirituality, I began to reflect upon the ways that this narrative was symbolically and culturally written on my own body. As a mestiza connected to Malintzin through blood, I also bore the burden of the virgin/whore dichotomy into which she, along with the Virgin of Guadalupe, has been cast. This was a narrative that went beyond the written text, resonating with my experiences both in my literal present as well as through hauntings of my cultural past, and necessitated finding some sense of recovery or rehabilitation through a Chicana body, my own. In the published piece documenting this journey, I attempt to articulate the need for the connection between the self and the cultural:

> I am a woman without a voice who perhaps really never had a voice to call her own. The story of who I am is lost and now I need your help to find it. How can anyone understand the complexity of your life and your decisions? They can't it all comes out very one-dimensionally. You need to speak, your narrative needs to be heard. You need self-definition right now just as much as I do. I am hoping in my journey towards you, I will also find my voice and perhaps this pilgrimage, this performance in which I engage, can add to a Chicana feminist project of bringing your narrative to life because it is so embodied, because it is so performed. Thus, Marina, I ask you to let me work through my pain, my loss, my own experiences of nothingness and reclaim or find my narrative with you as I look for yours. Can this cultural pilgrimage not only give testimony to the cultural, but also to the personal in ways that show how Chicanas are deeply affected by the cultural narratives that dictate the proper roles of women and in a sense deprive us not only of your voice, but also ours? Can you help me find my way back? If I perform and honor your memory in a space that refuses to officially recognize it, can WE free ourselves? (Calafell 2005, 47)

This excerpt is drawn from my pre-pilgrimage writings in which I attempt to make sure of the connection between Malintzin and myself and the ways our narratives overlap through ideologies about proper womanhood. Malintzin's story and my own could not be told apart from each other. Between us were the intimate connections of our histories as well as the ways that issues of loss, desire, and home shadowed both of our narratives. In looking for Malintzin, I felt obligated to draw upon these intimate histories as a way to make sense of Malintzin's story and its resulting trauma as well as my own.

THE PERSONAL AGAINST THE MASTER NARRATIVE

Performance holds a world of possibility in that it encompasses the study of personal narrative, performative writing, performance ethnography, and generally the study of everyday life. In doing work in rhetoric, it always seemed as if I was always contributing to knowledge of others and never myself or people like me. I needed to make sense of my own place, as bell hooks (1999, 13) has described: "There are writers who write for fame. And there are writers because we need to make sense of the world we live in; writing is a way to clarify, to interpret, to reinvent." Frederick Corey (1998, 249) describes his love of theater as a child, and how, as he got older, he came to the realization that "Something was amiss. The drama never told *my* story." In the same way, aside from the essay by Flores, rhetoric never told my story and did not really seem to have any desire to do so. Performance offered a feeling of reciprocity that I was not getting in rhetoric by offering various ways to acknowledge, rather than suppress, my voice and commitment to experience and the everyday. One of them was personal narrative, which, as Corey argues, "is one way of disturbing the master narrative, and through the performative dimensions of the personal narrative, the individual is able to disrupt— and, dare I say *rewrite*—the master narrative" (250).

Given the possibilities that performance held in my academic trajectory, I began to immerse myself in it, all the while putting my rhetorical desires on the backburner. I turned all my attention to performance studies and specifically personal narrative, which allowed me to really consider how my identities informed the practices I was engaged in with my research. I came to understand the transformative power of personal narrative as I began to work in performance theory and practice, which, Langellier argues (1998), both provide a body to a voice that then resists colonizing powers of discourse. In these moments I understood that performance, and more specifically, performance ethnography, is "a cultural construction designed to counter the history of a body that is suspect, suspicious, suspended" (Corey 2006, 331).

These early ventures into performance soon moved from the stage to the page as I began to explore the possibilities of performative writing as evocative (Pollock 1998), persuasive, and in many ways pedagogical (Pelias 2005). Both Madison and Pelias describe the possibilities for social change inherent in performance. Pelias writes of performative writing's ability to create identification and empathy in the reader: "Performative writing features lived experience, telling, iconic moments that call forth the complexities of human life. With lived experience, there is no separation between mind and body, objective and subjective, cognitive and affective" (2005, 41). Madison writes of the performance of possibilities in personal narrative performance that implicates an audience into action and responsibility, and declares: "Performance helps me. It illuminates like good theory" (1998, 109). I found that the possibilities of the personal voice echoed the possibilities that were so seductive and political in Moraga and Anzaldúa's theories of the flesh, which also forefronted experience and the body. Anzaldúa elaborates on the theory of the flesh in her discussion of *conocimientos*: "Breaking out of your mental and emotional prison and deepening the range of perception enables you to link inner reflection and vision—the mental, emotional, instinctive, imaginal, spiritual, and subtle bodily awareness— with social, political action and lived experience to generate subversive knowledges. These conocimientios challenge official and conventional ways of looking at the world, ways set up by those benefiting from such constructions" (2002, 542). Anzaldúa's works seemed to echo Madison, who, writing of the relationship between performance and theory, argues: "Performance helps me live a truth while theory helps me name it—or maybe it is the other way around. My mind and body are locked together in a nice little divine kind of unity: the theory knows and feels, and the performance feels and unlearns. I know I am a un/learning body in the process of feeling" (1999, 109). The similarity in theoretical commitments to experience as theory building, and as a point of social change through the performance of experience, whether it be on the page or the stage, convinced me that performance seemed to go hand in hand with my commitment to Chicana feminist politics and theorizing. I was hooked on the possibilities of performance studies. Would I be able to bring these methodologies to an explicitly rhetorical space?

I was so enamored with the possibilities that performance held that I almost completely walked out on my relationship with rhetoric. It was sometime during my love affair with performance that I encountered Kent Ono's "A Letter/Essay I've Been Longing to Write in My Personal/ Academic Voice" (1997). This essay, written by a rhetorician who in many ways I aspired to be like, suddenly demonstrated more possibilities for me within rhetorical criticism, specifically critical rhetoric. Encouraged by Ono's discussion and performance of the politics of voice and vulnerability, I turned to his other work, namely his coauthored essay "The Critique of Vernacular Discourse" (Ono and Sloop 1995), which asks rhetorical critics to, in a sense, meet texts on their own terms, particularly those produced by historically marginalized communities. Ono's work not only allowed me to reconsider the question of voice within rhetoric, but it also allowed me to consider a way to see how the kinds of texts or artifacts I was interested in did not automatically have to be dismissed in debates about how criticism should be done and what counts as the object of study. Recognizing how history and power have factored into the ways historically marginalized communities have been studied or in many cases ignored, Ono and Sloop write of vernacular discourse, "At other times, it means reading pamphlets printed by community organizations, watching films by independent filmmakers, or talking about orations given on the street. Finally, the critique of vernacular discourse entails engaging in talk about everyday speech, conversations in home, restaurants, and 'on the corner'" (1995, 20). This intervention held promise in contextualizing the kinds of texts I would examine.[4] It also gave me a way to connect my burgeoning relationship with performance to my longstanding relationship with rhetoric because of its explicit relationship to the kinds of knowledges produced by historically marginalized communities in whatever forms they might take as well as whatever methodology might be used to better understand them.

Preeminent performance ethnographer Dwight Conquergood, like Ono and Sloop, has understood the need to challenge the ways we traditionally think about texts and knowledge production, noting: "The linguistic and textualist bias of speech communication has blinded many scholars to the preeminently rhetorical nature of cultural performance—ritual, ceremony, celebration, festival, parade, pageant, feast, and so forth" (1991, 188). Conquergood further argues, "For many people throughout the world, however, particularly subaltern groups, texts are often inaccessible, or threatening, charged with the regulatory powers of the state. More often than not, subordinate people experience texts and the bureaucracy of literacy as instruments of control and displacements" (2002, 147). bell hooks complicates this further by writing, "No one speaks about class and the politics of writing in this society. It is just assumed that everyone has equal opportunity when it comes to writing and publishing" (1999, 97). Augmenting the critique of power and textuality, Conquergood acknowledges the ways oppressed communities must often "veil their meanings" and how "we pay attention to messages that are coded and encrypted; to indirect, nonverbal, and extralinguistic modes of communication where subversive meanings and utopian yearnings can be sheltered and shielded from surveillance" (2002, 148). While Conquergood does not seek to displace a textual paradigm, he is committed to having a performance paradigm operate alongside it as a way to give authority and credence to the knowledges produced by historically oppressed communities (1991, 191). This paradigm shift away from the textual bias again compliments the work of feminists of color such as those I have already alluded to, but also Barbara Christian, who reminds us that people of color have long theorized in forms that may be different from the "Western form of abstract logic" (1990, 336), and Patricia Hill Collins (2000), who has written about black women's intellectualizing in the everyday.

In bringing together the work of performance scholars who give critical attention to questions of voice, reflexivity, and agency not only of those people we engage with in our work but also of researchers, rhetoric scholars concerned with Other types of texts and knowledge production, and feminists of color who have long been committed to the politics of the personal voice and Other forms of theorizing, I began to ask, would I finally have a way to articulate a methodological home?[5]

Before going to Mexico City, I was filled with desire for Malintzin. It was a desire that I could not quell through my rhetorical and archival work. I had come to know Malintzin through others' writings of her and through historical documentation, but the fleshed being, the real woman remained unknown to me. Armed with my understanding of the public discourses about Malintzin, I went to the city to look for her. I was trying to go home, in the way that Sandra Cisneros describes: "There. . . . You live there? The way she said it make me feel like nothing. There. I lived there. I nodded. I knew then I had to have a house. A real house. One I could point to" (1989, 5).

In looking for Malintzin, my journey consisted of placing my discussions, search for visual renderings of her, and lack of memorialization within the cultural context discovered within my analysis of discourse. However, my examination of images and my talks with people in the city existed alongside my embodied process of pilgrimage, which led me to walk through the streets she walked and go to the home she called her own. In these spaces, the affective charge and the force of history wore on me, coupled with my own sense of loss and desire to draw upon my theories of the flesh and my mestiza identity, which connected me right back to Malintzin. In understanding Malintzin, I brought together the larger cultural pieces through my analysis of narratives and documents about her, the performative and personal through my embodied pilgrimage and poetic writing of the experience, and the political and social through the insights of a Chicana feminist perspective that forced me to be reflexive about the ways my identity worked in the sense-making part of the journey. These pieces came together to form a methodological homeplace for me in this and later projects (Calafell 2007a; Holling and Calafell 2007).

I see this methodological homeplace as similar in many ways to hooks's description of homeplace, in that it has given me the opportunity as a woman of color to find a space of possibility within this academic world that brings to bear whatever academic tools are needed for the situation. The space of homeplace was necessary because, as hooks writes, "We could not learn to love or respect ourselves in the culture of white supremacy, on the outside" (1994, 449). Using this methodological homeplace, I have created spaces that allow me to work within the communities I engage on their own terms, often by not simply looking at a text and its rhetorical properties, but understanding the communities in which these texts are situated as a way to move beyond the false divide between text and context. The Malintzin project began with the archive, drawing on written or documented texts, but then moved beyond, ethnographically, to the site where she lived in Mexico City, drawing on the affect of the space, the narratives of those in the city who are affected by her legacy, and also my embodied pilgrimage. I called upon my theories of the flesh, my affective connection, to make sense of the contested narrative of Malintzin and how it informs the ways that I, many years later, am framed by her actions or the interpretation of her actions. In a sense, the story is not complete without my own. This methodological perspective, which is committed to feminist politics, has continued to guide me in other projects including a current examination of immigration after 9/11 that juxtaposes personal experience with an analysis of official discourses to reveal public and hidden transcripts. This is a methodological approach to which I am committed and that I believe is organic and ever-changing; at its core are reflexivity and vulnerability. These are key components of a homeplace for me.

Mining the Collective Unconscious

With Responses from Ruth Ray and Gwen Gorzelsky

Frances J. Ranney

Some two years ago, my colleague Ruth Ray, a composition scholar and feminist gerontologist (2000, 2008), told me about an archive of nearly one thousand case files stored in a closet at the Hannan Foundation, a senior services center in downtown Detroit, a short walk from our offices in the Wayne State University Department of English. Might I be interested, she asked, as director of women's studies, in these archives? Of course, I said—though I had no idea what I could do with them. We agreed that we would meet weekly that summer to go through the files, most of which concerned formerly wealthy elderly women who received aid from the foundation during the Depression years. At this point Gwen Gorzelsky, a scholar of literacy practices (2005), joined us. Certain that some themes of academic interest would emerge, the three of us proposed to present preliminary findings at the Biennial International Feminism(s) and Rhetoric(s) Conference at Michigan Tech that coming October (Ranney, Ray, and Gorzelsky 2005). As one who had been publishing on legal rhetoric and feminism for the past several years (Ranney 1999, 2000), I optimistically proposed to comment on first-wave feminist attitudes toward legal issues, what I thought of calling "first-wave feminist legalism."

Optimistic we were, indeed, including our plan to "go through the files" over the summer. We soon found that one file could occupy our interest for many hours—even days or weeks—and we were wading in data. Despite the massive source of material, I could find no apparent interest in feminism among the clients the foundation served; I was beginning to worry about the conference paper I had proposed.

And then we found "Fontia R."

Dramatic pause.

In the staff break room at the Hannan House, we were silently reading what we thought were separate files when Ruth suddenly spoke up. "You should look at this file," she said to me. "[quoting from the case notes] 'Woman has used the silk we bought to make herself a stylish suit.'" Ruth knew that I had, in the past, done a lot of sewing and was longing to find the time to do it again. "Um-hmm . . ." I mumbled, engrossed in the story of a woman approaching death who'd had to be separated from her scissors, with which she was cutting holes into her slippers, nightgowns, bed-clothing, and various upholstered items.

After exchanging a few quotations in a game of my-file-is-better-than-your-file, we realized that we were reading the first and final files of the same case, #133. Together with Gwen, we were soon immersed in and fascinated by the last years of Fontia R., born in 1858, whose sixteen years of aid from the Hannan Foundation had yielded three very thick files stuffed with over one hundred letters and postcards, some typed by her caseworker, some handwritten by Fontia R. herself. Containing seventy-four single-spaced pages of case notes; one or two photographs; medical records; expenditure logs; and transfer slips that documented her many moves from residence hotels, to boarding houses and, finally, hospitals, the files provided a detailed record of her daily life from June 1929, when she first applied for aid, until May 1945, when she died at the age of eighty-six.[1]

In the two years since our discovery, I've been steeped in the story of Fontia R. and in the Progressive Era scientific and economic discourses that dominated her middle adulthood and declining years. In my presentations and publications (forthcoming), I have focused on both the connections and the contradictions I began to see between Fontia R.'s need to be "fit" (in Progressive Era eugenic terms) and her desire to consume conspicuously (in the Era's economic terms) on an extremely limited budget. In part she managed these desires by wheedling her caseworker and the foundation into advances, and her residence hotels into terms of credit for her room and meal tickets; with funds still insufficient to fulfill her ambitions, she completed her performance of eugenic and economic fitness by buying clothes that would not fit her, so that she could return, re-buy, and re-consume variations of the same items continually.

Or at least that's what I think. My colleagues may think something entirely different. As the only one of the three to begin to write articles about Fontia R., I claim some interpretive priority that I of course don't deserve. In fact, I have become increasingly uneasy about writing about Fontia R. at all. Though the Hannan Foundation's lawyers cleared the legal issues before we began to publish our findings, they retained some reservations about the ethical issues. The foundation's board of trustees was more comfortable with the ethics of our research, reasoning that with the use of pseudonyms, the benefit to today's senior citizens was likely to outweigh any potential harm to their deceased former clients.

Lately I have begun to wonder, given my fascination with the file and my eager interest in writing about it, why that solution doesn't work for me. I have come to truly doubt whether it is ethical for me to presume to tell Fontia R.'s story. But I have come to wonder, as well, about the source of that doubt.

TRACES OF RESEARCH

The traces, questions, and answers I encountered in this project are like breadcrumbs strewn along the path I took as I attempted to justify my work to myself. I have attempted to determine whether my problem in writing about Fontia R. is truly an ethical problem and, if so, a problem susceptible to some resolution through feminist research ethics.

Though the chronology of my recollection is not always precise, my train of thought and investigation into the ethical work that I hoped would resolve my dilemma began with the foundation's utilitarian position, appealing to the greater good. I doubted whether my use of Fontia R.'s file and story could satisfy Kant's alternative to utilitarianism, the categorical imperative to treat Fontia R. not as a means to my own academic ends, but as a person—if, that is, she were a "person" according to Kant. I knew that both of those ethical systems had been interrogated by a great deal of work in feminist ethics. Could my work, perhaps, satisfy the standards of an ethic of care?

I decided to dive back into feminist ethics, which I had left behind some years earlier. The more I read, the more I began to wonder whether an ethic of care could apply to archival research. As I began to question my own ethics and personal involvement in the life of Fontia R., I also continued to question my construction of the problem. Did I owe any ethical obligation to a deceased woman whom I represented only through a pseudonym? Realizing that in large part "Fontia R." was a person of my own making rather than the woman who had actually lived the life I was examining, I began to investigate alternatives to care as a basis for a feminist ethic. Slowly, I came to suspect that my ethical doubts were the result of my lack of faith in my own moral authority. But I also realized that I was not alone in that predicament; in fact, it seemed to me that the feminist ethical project as a whole is handicapped by its grounding in the male philosophical tradition. To bypass that tradition, I attempted a rhetorical approach, one by definition outside it. Finally comfortable with my moral authority to respond to an ethical non-problem of my own invention, I posed the question—both to myself and to others—whether in a rhetorical world feminist ethics as we have struggled to create it may be unnecessary.

It was a long journey that took me back to square one, but the square itself had changed. In fact, it had started to look more like a circle, that shape loathed by formalist logic. But my journey into feminist ethics had, in taking on that form, reminded me of a statement I had run into more than thirty years before when I was working as a book-order clerk in the basement of a small-town library. I remember finding it in one of the books that I (secretly) read at my desk when I was supposed to be ordering. It was taken from a Native American tradition, and it said simply this: "There can be no power in a square." What it meant to me then, and what I am reminded that it means to me still, is that a square can't move because it can't get around its own corners. A circle, on the other hand, by its very shape and nature suggests movement, encourages it, and values both the movement forward and the return to beginnings that are never entirely the same as when we began. From wondering whether I had the right to write about Fontia R., I had returned to wondering—but now wondering why I wanted to deny myself that right.

I was surprised at how little I found when I searched for scholarship on feminist research ethics, or feminist archival research, given the vast numbers of works I found when I looked for feminist ethics or feminist research alone.[2] Two fairly recent collections of feminist texts culled from archives (Baxandall and Gordon 2000; Crow 2000) seemed promising but their "greater good" justification for the publication of archival work left me stranded once again with the utilitarian rationale. I also found that I could not share one foundational assumption grounding that rationale—that the texts involved could largely speak for themselves. Unlike the feminist activists whose works are published in those collections, Fontia R. was not making a public argument; she was just trying to persuade her caseworker to buy her a silk nightgown without a thread of rayon in it, or a black jacket instead of a pink cardigan, or shoes with stylish Cuban heels. I was rearranging and reassembling her texts so that she spoke about eugenics and laissez-faire economics. As to the ethics of doing so, I appeared to be on my own. My survey of feminist ethical thought led me not to a feminist justification but to a legalism—that it is not possible to slander or defame a dead person (Couser 2004). Highly unsatisfied, I was left with only the intuitive sense that my work was ethically justifiable on feminist grounds.

I sincerely hoped that the ethical problem I saw—what I believed was my complete fabrication of Fontia R. out of the real woman whose case I had found in the archives—would not occur to my readers.

Several months later, still dissatisfied with my conclusions regarding the ethics of my work and starting on another publication about the case of Fontia R. ("Down but not out in Detroit," forthcoming), I decided to take a second plunge into the work on feminist ethics. I found that, as Cole and Coultrap McQuin note (1992, 1), most of the feminist ethicists I was reading seemed to agree on two grounding assumptions: women have been subordinated to men throughout much of our history, and this subordination is ethically and morally wrong. One further agreement is implicit: most work in feminist ethics demonstrates that an ethic of care growing out of work by Carol Gilligan (1982), Nel Noddings (1984), and others has become so firmly established in the literature that whatever one's own approach, it must be addressed (see Tong 1993, Held 2004, Kirsch 1999, Maynard and Purvis 1994).

I had long been uncomfortable with the ethic of care, but had not attempted to analyze that discomfort; instead, I had simply ignored the ethic of care in my previous work. Now, struggling to use it, I was struck by Dianne Romain's critique (1992, 27) of the method Gilligan uses in *In a Different Voice*; why, Romain asks, would one consult women "raised in patriarchy" (Gilligan 1982, 27) to counter the patriarchal voice itself? Patricia Ward Scaltas further points out that the empirical evidence on caring is not only tainted by patriarchy but also does not describe all women (some of whom are not or do not want to be caregivers) and may play into patriarchal assumptions about women's inability to engage in rational moral thought (1992, 16–22).

These critiques speak to my own discomfort with Gilligan's work. Nevertheless, I believe there is more than coincidence manifest in the "different voice" of care, connection, and responsibility in the moral decision-making processes she observed. In personal terms, I recognize my own processes in those accounts—and am uncomfortably aware that those processes are thoroughly feminine in a patriarchal and misogynist culture.

I am also uncomfortable professionally, as a scholar of legal rhetoric, because the perceived conflict between "care" and "justice" that has persisted since Gilligan's identification of feminine and masculine themes seems grounded in a mistake that feminists ought not to perpetuate. Gilligan's work and a large body of scholarship that both endorses and opposes it—including work in feminist jurisprudence and legal theory— tend to assume that care and justice are at worst opposites and at best complements (Manning 1992, Held 2004, West 1992). But Gilligan is clearly not a legal scholar, and neither are the males from whom she derives her definitions of justice, Sigmund Freud and Jean Piaget. She passes on, then, conceptions of justice that are more concerned with the formulation of rules and their enforcement than with their own theoretical foundations. Freud and Piaget, as Gilligan cites them, suggest women have a stunted sense of "justice" because they refuse to accept "the great exigencies of life" (Freud qtd. in Gilligan 1982, 7), or because they want to adjust rules to preserve their "games" (Piaget qtd. in Gilligan 1982, 10). Those conclusions define justice inadequately and do not serve us well.

I won't belabor this point. Although the relationship between justice and care has been treated by the literature as intensely problematic

(Held 2004, West 1992), as I continued to dig around in the archives I realized that I had an even bigger problem with the ethic of care in the case of Fontia R. Naturally enough, an ethic of care (and other ethics termed relational, maternal, and so on) requires the presence of a "cared-for" (Noddings 1984) who at the very least receives our care and at the very best may reciprocate and work with us in analyzing our findings. According to Nel Noddings, it is the capacity for relation that creates the obligation to care in the first place (17). But neither the deceased woman whose story I had seized upon nor the woman I had invented as Fontia R. could function as a cared-for, because both lacked a capacity to respond to my care.

Now what? I wondered. And I also wondered: why am I so invested in this woman, these stories, and this problem? Why do I—care?

FR SQUARED

Fontia R. and I have far more in common than our first and last initials. In fact, as I've begun to construct her, I see that she is quite a bit like my late and very persnickety maternal grandmother, who was born in 1894, some thirty-six years later than Fontia R., but like her shows traces of the Progressive Era during which they both lived significant portions of their lives. As fastidious as Fontia R., my grandmother was not one to leave her house until every curl was carefully teased into place with a rat-tail comb into her trademark Mohawk-style upsweep. She was uneasy around lesser-groomed, differently-raced others; her clothes were of good fabrics and followed the billowing lines of her figure to a degree Fontia R. would have envied. The very model of early-twentieth-century taste, she made sure her furniture was of mahogany, her nightgowns of silk.

And, yes, though the interest in fashion and the willingness to spend on quality seem to have skipped a generation, I, too, love fine fabrics. My grandmother had abandoned certain Progressive Era traditions as soon as less labor-intensive or more "scientific" processes came along (unlike Fontia R. she had no problem with ready-to-wear clothing or manmade fabrics), but I loved to sew my own clothes far beyond the point where it was financially necessary. To be truthful, what I have previously described as digging through Fontia R.'s case files (hard work) was more

Cannot care for the dead? hm.

like running my hands along the edges of bolts of silk, rayon, wool, organdy, and lawn (sensory pleasure); it felt like taking the corner of a fabric between my thumb and forefinger to see how good the texture was, whether it stretched just enough on the bias, or whether it felt "cheap" and was thus to be dropped, hastily, like bad rayon. Reading her letters requesting suits, hats, shoes, gloves, undervests, and nightgowns of specific cuts and styles was like flipping through the pages of the pattern catalog in the vintage section. I couldn't wait to run from the case file to the local (expensive) fabric store.

Associating Fontia R. with the pleasure of finely coutured clothing in expensive fabrics, I came to love her. And associating Fontia R. with my late grandmother, I came to love *her*, or at least to find her memory less annoying. Weren't her hands with their carefully manicured nails lovely as they worked that rat-tail comb over the salt-and-pepper curls?

Perhaps my research methodology was neither objective, given my personal investment, nor caring, given the absence of my cared-for. In fact, my cared-for now appears to have been me. Could my care still be ethical?

SHE WON'T LET ME CARE ABOUT HER

I am not the first to notice that some things about which we may care—and even some persons, in extreme cases—are unable to serve as cared-for in Noddings's terms. This lack on the part of the potential cared-for has created theoretical frustration that has in turn generated alternatives to care as the foundation of a feminist ethic. Some alternatives revert to traditional ethics when care becomes impossible. Rita Manning, for example, suggests that when we are not able to directly interact with the objects of our care we "might want to appeal to rules" that "speak to us of what most would want as a caring response in a similar situation" (1992, 51). The utilitarian "greater good" comes to mind yet again. Alternatively, Cheshire Calhoun suggests that we need to include within our "paradigms for moral activity" the "emotional work" that many women carry out (1992, 118). Our traditional paradigms, she says, are too agent-centered—including, presumably, that of care. Calhoun recommends that we think of the moral act as including neither an agent nor a judge but an intermediary (116–18). This initially appealing recommendation, however, runs a risk that others have seen in such "feminine" ethics (Tong 1993)—that the moral self may disappear in the process of training herself to take on appropriate emotions based on internalized social values, as Calhoun herself acknowledges (1992, 118).

Ellen L. Fox and Winnie Tomm both deal with this risk, though Fox's recognition of it is more implicit than is Tomm's. She suggests as an alternative to care an ethics of "vision" that promotes an active practice (1992, 114) growing out of work by Simone Weil and Iris Murdoch. Though Fox maintains that both Weil and Murdoch overvalue selflessness, she argues that their passive version of vision has been made more active by scholars like Marilyn Frye and Maria Lugones, whose combined work makes possible an interdependence between two viewing subjects that does not harm either—indeed, that cherishes both (Fox 1992, 111–15).

But because Manning reverts to utilitarianism and Calhoun creates a potentially self-effacing ethic—and because Fox, once again, assumes two interacting persons—it was Tomm's contribution that began to intrigue me. Her provocative suggestion is that we adopt "desire" as an alternative to care—a desire for "inner space" that provides the resources required to motivate and fuel social action (Tomm 1992, 102). Tomm's inner space is not an isolated retreat from the world, but a space out of which we are able to act with purpose and effect. This idea seemed to provide a theoretical starting point from which I could work through my ethical dilemma. I saw it this way: By preserving my inner space, I thought, I might also preserve my self—care for my self—as I interacted with a set of apparently inert data to bring to life an idea that was not the data, not my self, but a new something that I could activate through my imagination. "Imagin-activation," I began to call it, and though it seemed a bit lame to me academically, I suspected I could make something ethical out of it.

DUPED BY PATRIARCHY?

Several weeks into my ethics reading project, it struck me that most of the scholarship in feminist ethics was being produced by philosophers. This fact is so obvious as to have been unnoticeable—after all, I knew very well that philosophy "owns" ethics. But as that pattern gradually became visible, it also became for me problematic. I knew that my own disciplinary bias was operating in that conclusion; rhetoricians and philosophers have been at odds at least since Plato. Understood by non-rhetorical scholarship, the public, and the news media (particularly when the talk turns to politics) as the deceptive use of presumably empty language, rhetoric as a discipline sees itself as far more. I have defined it for my own work as a conscious perspective on language that understands itself as such, and that uses that perspective purposefully to create a wide range of cultural "texts" (Ranney 2005, 17). Rhetoric, as I understand it, is social construction at work on itself.

According to the Platonic, academic, and popular traditions, rhetoric is also antithetical to ethics. That is not, as you might expect, my position. In fact, given that I had recently completed an entire book on the relationship between rhetoric and ethics, I was a bit disturbed by my failure to think of rhetoric—immediately—as a path to feminist ethics. Instead, I was following somewhat unconsciously along the trail blazed before me both by the patriarchs of ethics (Mill, Kant, et al.) and by those who have tried to widen the path. I am grateful to those who have done that hard work, but it is apparent to me that even feminist philosophers are disciplinarily tied to a definition of ethics itself that thwarts the project. Disciplined by philosophy, ethics seeks to provide a formula, however flexibly conceived, that we might somehow "apply" to ethical dilemmas. To sustain the metaphor of the pathway, no matter how hard we try widening it, diverting it, or even "telling it slant" (Glenn 1995, 292), it covers the same ground and conceives of itself as aiming at some kind of target that we know all too well we will never quite hit.

Part of the feminist ethical project has been to reassure us that "aiming" is ethically sufficient as long as the target is properly understood. I agree—with important caveats. I think that our aim has been misdirected. Certainly, the effort to rename the moral ground on which we might base our ethics has been and remains fruitful. But in our eagerness to incorporate what we have called "women's experience," we have created a path that is simultaneously too wide in its abstraction and too narrow in its ethnic focus (Maynard and Purvis 1994, 23). Further, as Nancy Naples notes in her study of the "survivor discourse" of sexual abuse victims, those experiences have taken place "within a social structure that made them possible"—the structure, I submit, of patriarchy, and of which we are all survivors. Feminism's determined focus on the role of "the other" (Kirsch 1999, ix) not only threatens to obscure the self and promote essentialism, as we have seen; it can also lead to the kind of ethical paralysis Kirsch notes (1999, 87), one that I have experienced with respect to Fontia R. My self has been frozen in its tracks as it faces the breathtaking responsibility of attending to the other, dead or alive.

Another caveat concerns the philosophical propensity toward formal design in the face of ethical quandaries. Maynard and Purvis, pointing out that feminist research has not created new methodologies, suggest that our innovation lies not in our methods but in "the framework or structure in which they are deployed" (1994, 46). They provide a convincing argument for the value of our research, but it seems to me that the form of our research processes cannot serve as the basis for our research ethics. In other words, the ethic behind our research processes cannot provide ready-to-hand answers when ethical questions arise. In fact, the very idea that a previously conceived form, formula, or structure may also structure ethical solutions seems antithetical to many feminist philosophical assumptions.

As a further caveat, it seems probable to me that we are attempting to over-define our target. The commonsense search for right answers, or at least good answers, to ethical problems cannot guide our aim— how can we aim at what we have yet to see? What we need, I have come to believe, is neither a structure, nor a formula, nor a target, but a process that, whatever outcomes it may produce, is in itself ethical.

Persuaded that my inner space might be a good place to start looking for such a process, I decided to clear my outer space by sorting through and giving away books. It was during that process that I found a book I had set aside, only partially read. *Jung on Active Imagination*, it was titled (Chodorow 1997). Oh, dear. Maybe "imagin-activation" wasn't as original as I had thought . . . originally.

ACTIVATING MY IMAGINATION

I am not one to wax poetic about imagination and have resisted the tendency I have seen to attribute automatic ethical value to imagination based on a presumably inherent ethic of narrative, to take one example

(Couser 2004) or on the assumption that the novel, to take another, is an inherently ethical genre (Nussbaum 1995). Furthermore, I am not a Jungian. I have turned to Jung and Jungians when I have been interested in dream interpretation for my personal development. But my coining of the term "imagin-activation" is an uncanny example of Jung's assumptions about the nature of our human (un)consciousness—and Jung's "active imagination" provides a way for me to assert the moral agency necessary to justify my archival work.

Jung is not the analyst of first resort for feminists. His tendency toward grand theory and reified archetypes (his construction of the category of "the feminine," for example) have drawn critical feminist attention (Rowland 2002, 73; Baumlin 2005, 180; Lauter and Rupprecht 1985, 223; Wehr 1987, 4–6). But feminist post-Jungian work asserts the value of Jung's understanding of the unconscious for feminist research and activism (Lauter and Rupprecht 1985, 224; see also Wehr 1987; Rowland 2002). Where Jung becomes helpful to postmodern feminists, according to Susan Rowland, is when "a system of ideas strays beyond scientific boundaries" (2002, 128). In my case, the invention of "imagin-activation" is an example of the recourse we all have to what Jung called the collective unconscious—a collection of what he described as "universal images and ideas common to the generality of men" (Chodorow 1997, 71) but which Rowland describes as a "radically disruptive and *unknowable*" set of images (2002, 129; emphasis in original). I did not, in other words, dredge "imagin-activation" up from nowhere, but in drawing on collective cultural memory I gave it a form that, as Jung claims, is "entirely subjective and individual" despite its origins in a collective substance (Chodorow 1997, 71).

For Jung, active imagination involved two steps: making oneself aware of images generated by the collective unconscious, and then engaging in dialogue with them. These "aesthetic" and "scientific" steps, respectively, became ethical when the results of the process were made concrete in daily life (Chodorow 1997, 10–11, 36, 43). To the extent that process may be turned around on itself, as my neologism imagin-activation suggests, it is a good candidate to replace the feminist philosophical emphasis on ethical structures. Certainly, it calls up all the elements of my archival research project and brings them together in a way that respects the integrity of each. The archive, a concrete example of the highly abstract Jungian collective unconscious, becomes a *materia informis*, an alchemical term Jung borrowed for the original chaos that contains the divine seed of life (Chodorow 1997, 165n3). As such, Jung claimed, it "is meant to be shaped," "to be treated like a person," like "something that does exist" (Chodorow 1997, 164). In the role of the "patient" using active imagination for self-development, I am charged with the responsibility of both witnessing the images that emanate from the collective (the archive) and engaging in dialogue with them. To the extent that I make what I learn concrete in my daily life and that of others, the process becomes ethical in Jung's terms.

Imagin-activation—what I feel constrained to call "my little invention"—differs from active imagination, however, in some fundamental assumptions. The images I see in the archives—those of eugenics and laissez-faire economics in the case of Fontia R.—are not "universal," as Jung would have assumed. They are, nevertheless, there. In Fontia R.'s shame at her crippled condition after she broke her leg at the age of seventy-four ("I have not the *courage* to go shopping in Hudson's . . . until I am able to look like a human being") I see the assumptions of eugenics; in her taste for high fashion ("Dear, dear Mrs. W., you cannot make me into a ready-to-wear model!") I see her class consciousness in Progressive Era terms. Finally, in her shopping cycle of purchases and returns I see the need both to "fit" and to engage in a very conspicuous form of consumption. Of a coat sent to her from Hudson's Department Store, Fontia R. wrote, "while it is all I thought, it does not fit—it will have to be returned." Note that it is the coat that does not fit—Fontia R., through her own making, does.

Imagin-activation as I see it is not intensely or even necessarily personal, as is active imagination; it is not directed toward the psychological development of one person (however much it might enhance that development), but is interested in the means by which the collective unconscious is shaped and made manifest as it silently and invisibly socially constructs us all. In active imagination, the purpose is to "find the images that are concealed in the emotions" (Chodorow 1997, 2); in imagin-activation, the purpose is to translate those powerful cultural images into yet more images—words, for example, or texts—in order to "actively see" (Fox 1992) the raw emotion on which they are all constructed.

Finally, I see imagin-activation as a rhetorical process rather than a philosophical one—concentrating not on the construction of a formula that, applied to ethical dilemmas, can lead us to "good" or "right" answers, but on a process whereby we may construct useful questions. Ultimately, as it "brings new energy and consciousness to the raw material" emerging from the archive (Chodorow 1997, 6), the rhetorical process of imagin-activation culminates in the production of a cultural text, one in which the images and emotions of the cultural unconscious take on the look of the unfamiliar rather than of the universally reified. Exposing the workings of social construction and "violating the reality structure" (Campbell 1973), the rhetorical process of imagin-activation acknowledges both the cultural archive and its basis in collective, accumulated human experience. Finally, it recognizes and provides the means with which to deal with the multiple points of entry into our cultural archive that can lead to differing experiential paths, differing points of exit, and even the aporia of dead ends.

FEMINIST ETHICS NEED NOT APPLY?

Though I believe we should rethink it a bit, I am not suggesting that we scrap the feminist ethical project. Indeed, I have found primary inspiration for my own process from the work on care, on feminine and feminist ethics, and especially on the concepts of vision and desire that I take from Fox and Tomm. I recommend that we consider the role of these and other key elements of the ethical process that have not been specifically recognized or sufficiently developed as such. Having found Tomm's inner space, for example, I believe we can usefully recognize this space or spaces, however private, as shared. Whether chaotic or carefully ordered, such spaces provide a fitting location for the operation of our intuition—not the women's intuition our culture both lauds and derides, but the "inner teaching" that even Aristotle recognized as a characteristic of the human psyche and as one of several pathways to wisdom (1926, 6:iii.1). Finally, I suggest we understand our selves as suitable objects of our own care and that we make a point of finding the inner space(s) required to do so.

What imagin-activation provides is a rhetorical process that is possible in ways that categorical imperatives, the greater good, and even caring are not. Seen as an ethic of the possible, imagin-activation also builds on the feminist ethical project—not in order to focus on the agent herself but on the idea that an "agent, *herself*" may exercise agency through her own moral authority and thus make her own ethical decisions. It was my lack of that sense of agency that led me to worry so about Fontia R. and my fabrication of her story—it is my imagin-activation that reassures me that the "living birth" (Chodorow 1997, 5) of an old story through new eyes is an ethical use of our collective unconscious.

RUTH RAY RESPONDS: SERENDIPITY AND ART

With tongue in cheek, Francie ultimately dodges the ethical questions she poses in regards to researching the archives. But it's an artful dodge and one that compels a response. Her claim—that the literature on feminist ethics of care doesn't adequately address the issue of "care" in regard to textual representations of the deceased—is actually a warm-up exercise for her main contribution, the introduction of "imagin-activation." This term is inspired by the feminist concepts of an ethics of vision and an ethics of desire. All of these seem to be aspects of the same thing—an ethics of self care that involves clearing out an inner space where one feels free to act creatively and with purpose and effect. With the intention of clarifying what imagin-activation might entail, I offer the following narrative example.

In 2001, I came across an article in the *Chronicle of Higher Education* about a feminist scholar who could no longer think or write. I found this story so compelling that I cut it out and put it in my "motivation file"—a manila folder in which I store ideas and images that inspire me to rethink my own scholarly life. Written by Janet Catherine Berlo, professor of gender and women's studies and of art history at the University of Rochester, "Quilting for My Life" is an excerpt from Berlo's memoir *Quilting Lessons: Notes from the Scrap Bag of a Writer and Quilter*, published in 2004. I now see, with Francie's help, that this is the story of Berlo's own imagin-activation.

A serious and productive scholar, Berlo found herself, in the summer of 1992, unable to finish her latest book on Native American artists, *Dreaming of Double Woman: Reflections on the Female Artist in the Native New World*. Suddenly, she was unable to read or write a single word. She had never before experienced writer's block, and she could not talk herself out of it. She couldn't even walk by her desk, never mind sit down at it. Even more terrifying, she couldn't talk about the subject of her book with her graduate research assistant, nor could she understand the young woman when she described an exciting discovery in the archives. Berlo says in retrospect that the right and left hemispheres of her brain were at war, and the right (nonverbal) side was winning. What did the right side want to do instead of write? Make quilts! Berlo bought an expensive sewing machine and began to piece together wildly colorful bits of fabric into what she called "Serendipity Quilts." These quilts worked in tandem with the talk therapy she began seven months into what was to become an eighteen-month period of depression. The quilting therapy "was mute, kinetic activity in a field of color and pattern. I was reprogramming my brain. Debugging. Brainwashing. It must have worked. When I sat down to work on my Native American art-history book after nine months of quilting, the title and outline for this memoir . . . came out of my pen instead. Different neural patterns had formed, new pathways forged" (Berlo 2001, B12). These new pathways allowed for freer expression of unconscious desires through creativity and pleasure. In the process, Berlo "learned to be more like the artists I was writing about. My own work [became] more like the art I was looking at and writing about in the book: free-wheeling, inventive, open to experimentation, playful" (B13). Instead of the "straightforward, linear, unfolding of a narrative scholarly argument," Berlo's Serendipity Quilts, as well as her new writings, are both playful and complex, involving "multiple patterns held in the eye simultaneously" (B13).

So now I'm thinking that maybe Francie didn't dodge the ethical questions after all. Rather, she juxtaposed pieces of feminist theory into a serendipitous collection of ideas, and then she asked us to play with them.

GWEN GORZELSKY RESPONDS: THE EXPANDING CIRCLE

For me, the debates Francie describes echo scholarship on the ethics of qualitative research. There are three broad strands of this research. The first is a postmodernist concern with whether it's possible to represent others at all, particularly others with less social power than the researcher (e.g., Sullivan 1996; Tyler 1986). The second is a concern with the risks of *not* reporting "bad news" about research subjects, particularly when those subjects may be exerting their power in a way that is detrimental to others (Williams 1996) or when the researcher may be wary of reporting uncomplimentary findings because some research subjects occupy a more powerful position than does the researcher herself (Blakeslee, Cole, and Conefrey 1996). The third strand is concerned with collaborations between researcher and research subjects, collaborations that seek to change the social conditions in which those subjects live (Williams 2004).

As I read Fontia R.'s case, I found all three strands of the argument apply. As I have previously argued (Gorzelsky 2005), Fontia was clearly less socially, politically, and economically powerful than the social workers managing her case or than the well-heeled members of the social circle she occupied before she fell on hard times. At the same time, Fontia was clearly more privileged in all those areas than the thousands in the United States who died of exposure, hunger, and illness during the Great Depression, not to speak of the many more who suffered throughout the world, given the global impact of the Depression. As a researcher, I see it as just as much my ethical obligation to consider how Fontia's privilege—and my own—affects others, as it is my obligation to consider the risks of misrepresenting Fontia and her life. As one who admires quality fabrics and tailoring and has some difficulty obtaining them, I empathize with Fontia's desires. As one who sees it as my ethical responsibility to learn how my patterns of consumption affect the many world citizens less privileged than I, I see it as equally important to understand the ramifications of Fontia's—and my—investment in such consumption. Thus I see the first two strands of scholarship on research ethics in qualitative studies as both relevant to Fontia R.'s case.

As Francie points out, ethics that rely on collaboration between researcher and research subject seem to become unworkable when subjects are deceased, so strand three would seem irrelevant here. But in fact, I think that strand's approach actually subsumes and transforms the concerns raised in the first two strands. I understand Francie's notion of imagin-activation as a way for the living researcher to use archival materials to undertake a dialogue with culturally constructed images, perceptions, beliefs, and investments. For me, this dialogue can produce what Buddhists describe as "right thinking," part of "the noble eight-fold path." I turn to Zen Buddhist ethics here because, as expounded by Vietnamese Zen teacher Thich Nhat Hanh, this thinking provides an approach that offers the only concrete process I've found for working with emotional responses like those Francie cites as the basis of "powerful cultural images" (1999, 17–18). Most importantly, it does so in a way that transforms perceptions to produce "right thinking" by expanding our awareness of larger contexts; others' experiences and how our lives relate to theirs; and our ability to understand with compassion. Nhat Hanh explains that by engaging this process, we begin to recognize the interconnections between our lives and *all* other lives, current, past, and future (133–36, 139). He holds that once we understand these interconnections and others' real motivations, as opposed to our perceptions of those motivations, we cannot help loving them (66–67).

As I read it, Francie's work with Fontia R. produces just such insight, transforming Francie's annoyance with her maternal grandmother into understanding and love. But beyond that, it also allows Francie to show us how our supposedly personal choices about consuming clothes and other goods have implications for others (besides the economic implications). As she demonstrates, these choices expand the power of discourses like eugenics—to the detriment not only of the original targets of these discourses but to that of their proponents, like Fontia herself, who avoids contact with others to hide what she sees as the *dehumanizing* effects of her broken leg. Thus Francie's concept of imagin-activation allows her to make visible not only the way our cultural constructs dehumanize others but the way they dehumanize *us*. It does so by looking with deep compassion at everyone involved. Thus it widens the circle of our inclusiveness and our perceptual base in a way that I see as fundamentally, inherently ethical. The empty Zen circle seems a particularly apt emblem for this process. That circle can be said to symbolize many things, including the totality of images in the Jungian collective unconscious and the wider perception we gain when we move beyond our emotional investment in those images to understand one another and ourselves more deeply.

Researching Literacy as a
Lived Experience

Joanne Addison

Much important work in rhetoric and composition is derived from a specifically feminist orientation. While some of this work focuses on empirical methods and methodologies, outside of case study research we still lack both a strong orientation toward empirical research and a significant body of work from which to draw upon that directly addresses what it means to conduct feminist empirical research in our field. Part of this gap lies in the ongoing struggle of rhet/comp to define itself as a discipline. We are both burdened and energized by our relationship to freshman composition; we are engaged in debates over the relative merits of theory, practice, and praxis and striving to understand our place as a decidedly interdisciplinary field within an institution that more often than not insists on specialization. But it is important that we continue to expand and critique the ways in which feminist rhetoric and empirical research inform one another in writing studies in our ongoing efforts to realize what we can know, how we can know, who can know, and who can speak of what we know.

In approaching the relationship between feminist rhetoric and empirical research from an epistemological perspective, I am suggesting continued movement toward rhetoric and composition as a contextualized human sciences discipline as envisioned by Louise Wetherbee Phelps in *Composition as a Human Science* (1988). Noam Chomsky and others have argued that we cannot move forward in our understanding of the language faculty[1] itself without substantial interdisciplinary efforts (Hauer, Chomsky, and Fitch 2002, 1569). Likewise, we cannot move forward in our understanding of ways the language faculty is operationalized via rhetoric and everyday literacies without drawing on a diversity of scholarly work, providing the friction needed to propel our understandings. I'm drawn to the positioning of composition as a human science as a starting point in articulating feminist methods and methodologies for rhetoric and composition for two reasons. My own work focuses on empirical research and the understanding of literacy as a lived experience; Phelps's positioning of rhetoric and composition as a human science allows for important links between empirical research in our field and other human sciences. Moreover, and most important for our efforts here, the contextualist framework she outlines in arguing for a view of composition as a human science is the very type of framework that can support the work of scholars in our field seeking to articulate the feminist methods and methodologies that guide research in our own discipline and can inform the research of other disciplines.

In *Composition as a Human Science*, a book that represents an important effort to define composition as a discipline, Phelps argues that the model of the human sciences provides us with both the knowledge needed to further our profession and opportunities for us to participate in a larger dialogue about language studies across disciplines (1988, 106). As part of her effort to put forth a view of composition studies as a contextualized discipline, she addresses the myth of natural literacy, instead preferring contextual accounts that are:

> . . . powerful not only in themselves, as exciting and generative for teaching practice, but in their affinities and connections with the work of other fields. The effort to relate language, cognition, writing, and rhetoric in terms of a contextualist framework finds its echo in every human science, especially of course those of language, literature, psychology, and social practices, but also in history, critical theory, philosophy, and many others. For the first time, and not altogether self-consciously at present, composition finds itself in the mainstream of intellectual thought, contributing its own perspective to theoretical and empirical inquires of far-reaching import. Not only is it exploiting ideas from these fields . . . but it is beginning to draw such figures into dialogue with rhetoric and composition. [This] link[s] composition to the more fundamental task being

pursued across the disciplines, namely, to evaluate and balance interpretive (natural or contextualized) approaches with critical and objectivist understandings of human life and experience. (Phelps 1988, 115)

Phelps's consideration of composition studies as a human science within a contextualized framework—akin to developmental psychology wherein the relationship between the individual and her social, cultural, and economic positions is primary—acknowledges the complexity of human experience and the multiple methods and methodologies required to approximate an understanding of the possibilities at hand.

At its core, a contextual framework insists that the context in which any given phenomenon occurs is at least equal to the phenomenon itself at the point of critical interpretation. From the perspective of the philosophy of science, a field upon which my own work draws heavily, contextualism refers more specifically to a methodology wherein a phenomenon acquires meaning only in relation to its context and verifiable empirical measures. Combined, Phelps's argument for composition as a human science within a contextual framework and contextualism as defined within philosophy of science provide strong support for articulating feminist methods and methodologies for rhetoric and composition. With a focus on feminist rhetorical analysis, we might borrow Phelps's last sentence above to state: "a contextualist framework links feminist rhetorical analysis to a more fundamental task being pursued across the disciplines, namely, to evaluate and balance interpretive approaches with critical and objectivist understanding of human life and experience from an explicitly feminist standpoint."

From this perspective, the goal of feminist rhetoric is not primarily to reclaim, establish, or invert but rather to challenge the empirical evidence placed before us and used to further the inequality of women and other subjugated groups of people. Feminist rhetoric allows us to ask questions that have not previously been asked as well as to posit theories and conduct research that would otherwise remain unimagined. As explained by Judy Stamps, a behavioral ecologist at University of California, Davis (UC Davis), the decisions made about the types of empirical data worthy of study are subject to cultural norms and biases:

> For instance, scientists have tended to study species that fit their perceptions of how things should work. Then, when they observe the animals, they often see what they expected to see. An example of this is primate

research. The first species people studied were the ones in which males were fighting, females were scrapping with each other; it was sex and fighting all over the place. Most people didn't go out to look at the most boring primates they could find, the ones who sat around peaceable, with one occasionally looking askance at another, who in turn moved away, and that was it for two weeks in terms of aggressive interactions. So all the studies that came out for awhile stressed the importance of dominance. It's because we selected species that reflected what we thought was interesting. (UC Davis Biological Sciences 1998)

In other words, if the validity of the discourse that constitutes the data isn't challenged, we are likely to seek out data that further inscribes cultural norms.

FEMINIST STANDPOINT THEORY AND STRONG OBJECTIVITY

Feminist standpoint theory began to emerge in the 1970s as both a political theory and research methodology, stated this way by Nancy Hartsock: "A standpoint is not simply an interested position (interpreted as bias) but is interested in the sense of being engaged" (1997, 218). As a political theory it seeks to uncover the relationship between power and knowledge particularly by calling into question Western, scientific, androcentric accounts of reality. As a research methodology it has two primary aims: the critical analysis or revisioning of scientific knowledge in terms of its production, distribution, and material effects;[2] and making accessible phenomenon previously ignored or specifically deemed inaccessible, often by challenging dominant discourses. The most basic assertion upon which feminist standpoint theory rests is that we are socially situated via gender (among other factors) and that this creates epistemological differences that must not only be acknowledged but strongly asserted in our research efforts. Further, beginning research from the standpoint of women allows feminists to challenge the dominant conceptual frameworks in ways that lead to more accurate empirical research and richer theoretical constructs in general.

The enactment of these aims has been a matter of significant discussion. As Donna Haraway put it in *Simians, Cyborgs, and Women: The Reinvention of Nature:* "[the] problem is how to have *simultaneously* an account of radical historical contingency for all knowledge claims and knowing subjects, a critical practice for recognizing our own 'semiotic technologies' for making meanings, *and* a no-nonsense commitment to faithful accounts of a finite freedom, adequate material abundance, modest meaning in suffering, and limited happiness" (1991, 85; emphasis in original). In other words, how do we make sense of the various standpoints from which all of us emerge that are "true" and that result in positive change for all, but especially for those on the margins?

The answer for Haraway and many others is situated knowledge. From this perspective, research subjects or objects of knowledge assert themselves as actors or agents via their own voice or the voice of another. An agent is someone whose particular standpoints are more than lenses through which the objective researcher establishes reality. Rather, the repositioning of research subjects as agents requires, at the very least, an empathetic stance toward research participants or, further, opportunities for research participants to participate directly in the construction of knowledge.

For example, Patricia Gowaty in "Sexual Natures: How Feminism Changed Evolutionary Biology" (2003) argues that the most important way feminism has and will continue to change the field of evolutionary biology is through thoughtfully designed, well-controlled empirical research. In outlining the history of parental investment theory, Gowaty shows how the empathy of feminist researchers has begun to challenge the prevailing hypotheses. The main proponents of parental investment theory argue that the current nature of males and females in most species is the result of an evolutionary selection process that favored females as primary caregivers. The "facts" of "parental care patterns have explained indiscriminate, profligate, competitive, and aggressive males and coy, hesitant, passive, highly discriminating females" (Gowaty 2003, 906), thus reinforcing cultural norms of male and female sexuality and parental roles. But these "facts" are rooted in the seemingly obvious instead of the empirically tested.

In tracing the history of parental investment theory, Gowaty highlights the ways in which feminist theory from a contextual framework not only challenges the prevailing hypotheses but also leads to better empirical research. For example, she points to an article by Natalie Angier, a science writer, who critiques a controlled experiment in which attractive men and women on a college campus approached members of the opposite gender and asked them to have sex. Seventy five percent of the men said "yes" while all of the women said "no." This was used as further support for the choosy female, indiscriminate male parental investment theory. Angier, from a feminist standpoint, simply states that given the current rate of violence against women, perhaps the results had nothing to do with the fact that women are more choosy than men and much to do with the fact that women have more to fear than men (Angier 1999; qtd. in Gowaty 2003, 912–13). It is this very kind of feminist standpoint that can result in more accurate empirical research in that it requires researchers to rethink their conclusions based on the contextualized standpoint of female participants living in a culture in which women regularly experience violence by men in their homes, on the streets, and in the mass media.

In my own experiences as both a researcher and research participant, it has been equally important for feminist researchers to challenge the semiotic technologies of other feminist researchers so that we constantly engage one another in the critical practice required of feminist standpoint theory. For example, in 1994, Susan Hilligoss and I were research participants in an online study of academic women in virtual environments. We did not know each other prior to this research occasion. The general goal of this research was to better understand the experiences of academic women in virtual environments. As Susan and I quickly found out, while much of the discussion among participants focused on oppressive and exclusionary acts against women online, this very group of women engaged in some of these same acts, denying the validity of the standpoint of academic women who are also lesbian. For example, while many participants easily appropriated the term "coming out" to refer to a variety of online activities, including the first posting of an online lurker, the coming out as lesbian by both Susan and myself early in this research project was met with near silence, as were later attempts to relate issues raised by the participants to the uses of the Internet and struggles of GLBT academics. Very quickly our place in this forum was established; most of our conversations occurred outside the domain of the listserv used for the participants' conversations.

Let me make clear that we never have assumed any individual malicious intent on the part of the participants or researchers. Quite the opposite—the researchers readily allowed us to use the data we generated as participants in order to extend their conclusions. Rather, we called attention to the conceptual frameworks that so easily reinscribe the silencing of those on the margin even in progressive settings. In doing so, we relied on a feminist rhetoric of challenge that allowed for data to emerge and conclusions to be drawn that would not have been otherwise.

In our writing about the experience (Addison and Hilligoss 1999), we questioned why it is important that we retell this research from our standpoint in a public forum, as "neither CMC nor feminist theories have offered sufficiently textured or political readings of those silenced in electronic forums. Through our dialogue outside of the research project we were able to build an understanding of our experience in ways that the researchers could not because of the exclusionary practices of the community that lead to an obscuring and even disappearance of our voices" (1999, 27–28). In this case, Susan and I were able to position ourselves as agents capable of asserting a standpoint that challenged the discourse norms of the group and, ultimately, some of the conclusions drawn by the researchers. Feminist rhetoric in the form of a discursive challenge to the empirical evidence placed before the researchers allowed Susan and me to ask questions not prompted by other positionings and to conduct research of our own that would not have otherwise been initiated.

One of the most important undertakings of feminist standpoint theorists in relation to rhetorical analysis is the still too-prevalent conception of objectivity as a scientific endeavor free of the social and political forces that might call its truth value into question. Sandra Harding and others claim that what have been held up as objective scientific methods by Western science are actually quite subjective due to the biases inherent in the conceptual frameworks within which objectivity is operationalized. At many turns, Harding asserts that feminists and others don't criticize objectivity and favor relativity but call for more objective accounts of the world or accounts that acknowledge conceptual biases and apply methods that can result in access to the various standpoints we inhabit. This is often referred to as *strong objectivity:* "Strong objectivity asks us to take a critical look at the conceptual schemes, the frameworks, that *comprise* our social location" (Harding 1987, 18). Further, it asks us to challenge ourselves and others from the limiting perspectives of our conceptual schemes. The result is revised hypotheses and expanded conclusions such as those discussed in the two examples above.

Questions of objectivity are primarily questions of method or the techniques we use to gather data. Dorothy Smith (2004) and Sandra Harding (1987) advocate a broadly conceived notion of method, one that might include the following questions:

- Why are certain phenomena selected for research and not others?

- What are the multiple locations from which the researcher(s) approaches a phenomenon?

- What are the multiple locations from which the "subject" experiences that phenomenon?

- What aspects of the phenomenon are made accessible via this method?

- What aspects of the phenomenon remain inaccessible via this method?

- What theoretical and practical norms govern the researcher's discipline and how might these constructs bias the research?

- How might the researcher's position of dominance bias the research at the same time that it calls her into a position of critical advocacy for others?

- How might this research be disseminated within the academic community and beyond?

It is not enough to simply acknowledge one's position in relation to the research participants, leaving the work of critical analysis to the audience. Instead, it is the researcher's job to critically analyze his or her position in relation to the research participants in an effort to establish strong objectivity.

FEMINIST METHODS

If feminist standpoint theory is a useful methodology for rhetoric and composition, in what ways might it be used to guide research method or the techniques used to gather data about a particular phenomenon?

While I'm not sure that such a thing exists as a purely feminist method, there are ways in which certain types of research and certain methods can be enacted via feminist standpoint theory that lead to improved knowledge of marginalized people. Perhaps one of the most amenable types of research is phenomenological research, particularly empirical phenomenology, in which the subjective or contextualized perspective of the research subjects (or actors from a feminist standpoint) is the starting point for the analysis. One prominent example of empirical phenomenology in our field is the research detailed in Deborah Brandt's book *Literacy in American Lives* (2001).

Brandt states: "Only recently have we begun to accumulate more systematic and direct accounts of contemporary literacy as it has been experienced. Nevertheless, many current debates about literacy education and policy continue to be based largely on indirect evidence, such as standardized test scores or education levels or surveys of reading habits" (2001, 11). In response, Brandt calls for research based on literacy as a lived experience and explains that the purpose of her research is to describe literacy as it has been lived within a particular cultural, historical, and socioeconomic moment.

Feminist standpoint theory can help meet the need for both more empirical phenomenological research and articulations of feminist methods and methodologies in rhetoric and composition. In particular, I am interested in the ways that feminist standpoint theory can lead to more accurate accounts of literacy as it has been experienced within specific cultural, historical, and socioeconomic moments. If we view writing classrooms as the places where we explicitly and implicitly teach students to produce knowledge, help students learn how to control the means of production, and engage in critique, they become interesting places in which to begin understanding how experience sampling methods from a feminist standpoint can inform rhetorical analysis. Understanding how differently positioned students experience literacy through educational institutions via systematic inquiry can lead to improved teaching and research practices and, using experience sampling methods, can easily be extended to other domains.

To this end I have been working with experience sampling methods to better understand how literacy is experienced. This particular set of research methods, currently not in use in composition studies, can form the basis for important contextualized research that informs our understanding of feminist rhetorical practices. Experience sampling methods have been used in various forms since the 1930s and strongly emerged in their current form in the 1970s. This term was popularized by the work of Reed Larson and Mihaly Csikszentmihalyi and refers generally to a technique that allows researchers to gather real-time data about what a specified group of people is doing and how those people feel about what they are doing within everyday settings. In other words, experience sampling methods allow us to empirically sample and begin to understand everyday experiences as they occur. This stands in contrast to research methods such as time-use diaries or narrative reconstructions, which are subject to far more issues related to validity and reliability. "The Experience Sampling Method is one way to understand contextualized behavior. . . . Its main contribution has been to make variations in daily experience, often outside the domain of ready observation, available for analysis, replication, and falsifiability, thereby opening a broad range of phenomena to systematic observation" (Kubey, Larson, and Csikszentmihalyi 1996, 99–100).

In experience sampling research, participants are signaled at either random or event-contingent intervals to complete an experience sampling form (see appendix to this chapter) every day during a set period of time (e.g., one week). For example, in random sampling, a participant might carry a beeper or other device that signals her to complete an experience sampling form at random intervals throughout the sampling period. In a contingent interval study, participants are signaled to complete an experience sampling form when engaged in a specific type of activity (e.g., exercise). The goal is to sample a person's typical activities, record what he or she is doing, and measure how he or she experiences these activities. This method is unique in that it essentially allows a researcher to follow research participants and gather data about their experience at the very moment when they are engaged in the experience, gathering a range and depth of data not possible via other means. When the experience sampling data from each participant is viewed alongside basic demographic data, researchers can begin to identify specific cultural, historical, and socioeconomic trends. Follow-up interviews and analysis of related documents (e.g., extracurricular writing) can be used to establish more accurate accounts of literacy as a lived experience.

I have been gathering data over the last few years within various contexts—online business writing courses, freshman composition classrooms, and writing center tutorials. Much of this data still needs to be entered into a growing analytic database in order to establish a systematic account of the activities and subjective states of our writing students. One branch of this research, in which new teaching assistants and their freshman composition students participate, is aimed at understanding both the experiences of the new teaching assistants and which classroom-based writing activities present high levels of engagement.

For example, one phase of this research focuses on two relatively small and closely related populations: fifty-six students from across five sections of introductory composition and their four new teaching assistants at the University of Colorado at Denver and Health Sciences Center (UCDHSC). UCDHSC, a part of the three-campus University of Colorado system, is a public urban research university that enrolls approximately twelve thousand undergraduate and graduate students each semester. Its mission is to offer programs that serve the needs of the Denver metropolitan area. The freshman population includes graduates of well-funded Denver area schools as well as underserved urban public schools. Thus, beginning students bring with them a wide range of in-school writing experiences. With introductory composition courses capped at twenty-four students, assessing individual student literacy experiences, as well as current course engagement, is a difficult task. The experience sampling methods research project offered teaching assistants and the program an additional means of gathering this important demographic and engagement information.

Even in just this very small part of the project, over the course of one week we captured 152 moments from students and 57 from teaching assistants for a total of 209 responses for analysis. Students were asked to complete an experience sampling response form only during class, while teaching assistants were asked to complete an experience sampling response form any time they were signaled to do so during the course of one week and also while engaged in a literacy activity (broadly defined) or teaching activity (event-contingent).

My goal from the perspective of feminist rhetoric is to begin to uncover the questions that need to be asked from the standpoint of others. Gathering data on what students are actually doing in our classrooms and how they feel about what they are doing (as opposed to what we think we see and assume they feel) is crucial to understanding who is truly engaged in the grand literacy acquisition project in which we all participate. Over time, this research project has become more and more layered, allowing for the collection of data across multiple contexts and within academic, home, and work settings.

Again, while there is much data yet to be analyzed before reaching useful conclusions, some interesting results have arisen to date. It is not surprising that many teachers and students reported being involved in peer group work during their writing classes. Students rank group work as very important to their overall goals, but group work did not score high in terms of challenge and skills, two aspects commonly used to measure student engagement. In other words, many students view the group work ubiquitous in our writing classrooms as necessary but not engaging in those ways that previous research has identified will lead to improved learning. Students do, however, experience high levels of engagement when immersed in individual writing both inside and outside the classroom. The responses of new teaching assistants echo those of their students both when they are teaching and when they are in graduate courses. To date, there has been no statistical difference between the responses of men and women. This fact, however, does not tell us enough. A project not guided by feminist standpoint theory would end when the statistical differences end. Instead, because my project begins from the social location of my participants, this seeming statistical indifference is a call for maximizing objectivity.

As Elizabeth Hirsh and Gary Olson note in their interview with Sandra Harding, "Harding argues that objectivity is maximized not by *excluding* social factors from the production of knowledge—as Western scientific method has purported to do—but precisely by 'starting' the process of inquiry from an *explicitly social* location: the lived experience of those persons who have traditionally been excluded from knowledge production" (1995, emphasis in original). As such, the next step in this process is in-depth interviews designed to illuminate the potential affective dimensions of group work (e.g., peer pressures, linguistic/cultural difference, etc.) that inhibit full engagement with the task at hand.

Because the goal of interviews at this stage in the research is to articulate the situated knowledges from which participants act, the interviews must be non-structured or semi-structured in order to better reflect their meaning structures, especially as they challenge those of the researcher. While experience sampling methods are exceptionally well suited to conducting empirical research that takes as its starting point an *"explicitly social* location," they constitute a research technique that forms the systematic basis for further inquiry and cannot be used as means to an end. Informed by feminist standpoint theory and illuminated by semi-structured interviews, these methods can provide new understandings of the experiences of those often excluded from and struggling to obtain access to dominant discourses.

As feminist rhetorical scholars continue to articulate what it means to engage in feminist rhetorical practices, I urge us to remain in conversation with empirical researchers whose work is informed by theories and practices that challenge what others see, think, and believe about the world. The methodological questions enumerated earlier offer a systematic way of broadening both what we study and how we study it in ways that can lead to more critical and balanced accounts of our lives and the lives of others.

APPENDIX

Experience Sampling Form

adopted from Kubey, Larson, and Csikszentmihalyi 1996

Name _____   Time _____

Date _____

At the time you were beeped, what was the *main* thing you were doing:

____ reading

____ lecture

____ video/internet/tv presentation

____ small groups

____ whole class discussion

___ individual writing

___ group writing

___ talking individually with teacher

___ surfing the internet (class related)

___ checking email

___ daydreaming

___ nothing

___ other _____

To what were you reading and/or writing and/or listening? _____

_____

	Not at all		Somewhat		Very much
How well were you concentrating?	1	2	3	4	5
Was it hard to concentrate?	1	2	3	4	5
How self-conscious were you?	1	2	3	4	5
Did you feel good about yourself?	1	2	3	4	5
Were you in control of the situation?	1	2	3	4	5
Were you living up to your own expectations?	1	2	3	4	5
Were you living up to expectations of others?	1	2	3	4	5

Describe your mood as you were beeped:

Happy	O	O	o	—	o	O	O	Sad
Irritable	O	O	o	—	o	O	O	Cheerful
Strong	O	O	o	—	o	O	O	Weak
Active	O	O	o	—	o	O	O	Passive

Lonely	o	o	o	—	o	o	o	Sociable
Ashamed	o	o	o	—	o	o	o	Proud
Involved	o	o	o	—	o	o	o	Detached
Excited	o	o	o	—	o	o	o	Bored
Closed	o	o	o	—	o	o	o	Open
Clear	o	o	o	—	o	o	o	Confused
Worried	o	o	o	—	o	o	o	Relaxed
Competitive	o	o	o	—	o	o	o	Cooperative

How did you feel about the reading and/or writing in which you were engaged?

	Not at all								Very High
Challenges of the reading and/or writing	0	1	2	3	4	5	6	7	8	9
Your skills in this reading and/or writing	0	1	2	3	4	5	6	7	8	9
Was this reading and/or writing important to you?	0	1	2	3	4	5	6	7	8	9
Was this reading and/or writing important to others?	0	1	2	3	4	5	6	7	8	9
Were you succeeding at what you were doing?	0	1	2	3	4	5	6	7	8	9
Do you wish you had been doing something else?	0	1	2	3	4	5	6	7	8	9
Were you satisfied with how you were doing?	0	1	2	3	4	5	6	7	8	9
How important was this activity in relation to your overall goals?	0	1	2	3	4	5	6	7	8	9

	Not at all									*Very High*

What is the likelihood that 0   1   2   3   4   5   6   7   8   9
this reading and/or writing
will affect your thinking in
relation to this subject?

What is the likelihood that 0   1   2   3   4   5   6   7   8   9
this reading and/or writing
will affect your actions in
relation to this subject?

Any explanation you'd like to add concerning the last 3 questions above?

Other comments?

Rhetorica Online

Feminist Research Practices in Cyberspace

Heidi A. McKee and James E. Porter

The World Wide Web is an important space and media in which people communicate and scholars study the rhetorics of diverse populations. Type, for example, "women's groups online" into Google, and as of May 2008 the number of hits returned will be approximately 150,000. According to a report on the "State of the Blogosphere," over 120,000 new blogs are created every day world wide (Sifry 2006). The number of videos already uploaded to YouTube is in the hundreds of millions. From pregnancy support groups to online chats of Christian activists to the blogs of grrrl gamers and the videos of presidential candidates, rhetoric is out there on the Web to be studied.

But what are the methodological and ethical issues researchers face when seeking to move feminist scholarly practices for print-based or person-based research to Web-based spaces? When is text online text and when is it the communications of living persons for whom a different set of ethical considerations apply? To draw from Gesa Kirsch's work (1999), how should feminist researchers handle the politics of location, interpretation, and publication when working in increasingly networked and mediated online spaces?

In this chapter we examine these and other related questions, as we describe and analyze how researchers are deploying feminist methods and methodologies (both explicitly and implicitly) to study rhetoric online. We focus here on two main research issues: negotiation of informed consent and researchers' approaches for interacting with participants in online spaces.[1] Our discussion is based on research we conducted (McKee and Porter, forthcoming) that explores the ethical issues researchers face when doing "digital writing research."[2] Through interviews with researchers from across the globe, we are working to identify the methodological and ethical dilemmas digital writing researchers face and to propose case-based heuristics researchers may find helpful when planning and conducting studies. Here we will focus on the work of three researchers (of the thirty we interviewed): Janne Bromseth (Norway), Laurie Cubbison (United States), and Yukari Seko (Japan), because in their studies of online rhetoric they raise issues of particular significance to feminist research methodology.[3]

These researchers come from different disciplines—Cubbison works primarily in the field of rhetoric/composition while Bromseth and Seko are working in communications and cultural studies—and often invoke varying vocabularies to describe their methods and aims. We have interviewed numerous researchers working in the fields of communication studies, media and culture, and information technology. Some researchers refer to their methods as feminist, but hardly anyone outside the field of rhetoric/composition frames their methodology as rhetorical. Yet we think much of their research is rhetorical—particularly when it focuses on describing the communication dynamics of online spaces or on the ways that cultures and identities are represented in writing in digital environments.

Yukari Seko studied online suicide groups focusing on the "suicidal murmurs" of one young woman most active in the group. Seko struggled with her relationship and responsibilities to the persons (and communities) she studied. Laurie Cubbison focused her study on how medical patient support groups develop rhetorical strategies for communicating their points of view of illness to others (e.g., doctors, support persons, the general public). As a participant-observer of these communities, Cubbison argued for an ethic of care and respect when studying people's online discourse. Janne Bromseth studied the written expressions of gendered and sexual embodiment in a listserv for lesbian and bisexual women. When deciding how to interact on the list, she had to be especially conscious of issues of power and identity and of the construction of her own ethos. These are complicated rhetorical situations for a researcher, to say the least, especially when the researcher is attempting to adhere to principles for agency and action of feminist research.

Drawing from interviews with these researchers and others, we follow a two-part frame to examine the distinctive ethical issues researchers might face when negotiating access for a research project and interacting with participants in order to collect data. Recognizing the rich tradition feminist rhetorical studies has of person-based research, we focus our discussion on person-based rhetorical studies, but we will also address the particular complexities that online researchers face when determining if their online research involves just text or text and persons.

THE PRINCIPLES OF FEMINIST RESEARCH METHODOLOGY

Of course feminist research is strongly attuned to issues of gender—particularly to power relations among genders and to "gender asymmetry" (Fonow and Cook 2005, 2213). But another key principle of feminist research is methodological reflexivity that "challeng[es] the norm of objectivity that assumes that the subject and object of research can be separated" (2213). Although we think studies of gender still form the core of feminist research, feminist research methodology may be, and often is, applied to a wide range of studies, not just of gender. Many of the tenets of feminist research, particularly feminist, person-based research, have become, we feel, part of what is accepted research practices. For example, many of the underlying or explicitly named principles in key research guidelines and often cited research texts are feminist (see Conference on College Composition and Communication 2003; Kirsch and Mortensen 1996). Thus, we also feel that it is possible for researchers to pursue feminist methodologies without studying gender primarily, although attunement to power in gender relations and to gender asymmetry and gender inequity must certainly be strongly present. We see precisely this quality in the researchers we interviewed. Few cite "feminist methodology" in their approach or characterize their studies as primarily gender-focused but their research perspectives are strongly attuned to issues of gender and their research practices show strong allegiance to feminist methodology. As Laurie Cubbison noted in an e-mail response to a draft of this chapter, "It was interesting that you commented that neither Bromseth nor I specifically mentioned feminist methodology though we were enacting it. I think that, for me, coming out of Purdue's program [in rhetoric/composition], these methods were very nearly self-evident, especially as I attempted to balance the public/private aspects of online discourse."

Understandings of feminist research methodology characterize it as a set of epistemological and ethical dispositions that manifest themselves in methodological choices, and particularly in the reflective and ethical inquiry procedures always involved in methodological choices (Addison and McGee 1999; Fine 1994; Herrington 1993; Porter and Sullivan 1997; Sullivan 1996; Sullivan 2003). As we see it, below are several key qualities characterizing the ethos of the ethical feminist researcher—or, perhaps more simply, of the ethical researcher.[4]

- Committed to social justice and improvement of circumstances for participants. As Sandra Harding and Kathryn Norberg (2005) put it, "The point of good research, for feminists as well as for many conventionalists, has always been to advance social progress" (2012) and to be transformative—to improve participants' lives and/or others' lives. Thus, within the framework of feminist methodology producing knowledge alone without producing an improvement is not a sufficient condition for "good research." "Knowledge" per se, the desired outcome of positivist methodology, is not the ultimate ethical aim of feminist methodology (although it might well be a means toward the end).

- Careful and respectful. For feminist research the welfare and betterment of research participants, both collectively as groups and as individuals, is paramount, taking precedence over research findings, over methodological considerations, over disciplinary or institutional values. But concern/care is only one feature of this quality. Respect for participants means acknowledging their agency, heeding their wishes, consulting their wisdom.

- Critically reflexive. Self reflexivity and critical consciousness about one's own position, gender, and status are key features of feminist thinking. Feminist researchers are continuously attuned to the dynamics of power in all phases of a research project.

- Flexible. Engaging in feminist research requires a willingness to make adjustments in the project, to modify a project protocol as needed to make it more careful, reflexive, dialogic, and ethically rigorous.

- Dialogic. Feminist researchers often consult and consider a variety of viewpoints in making research decisions, including inviting participants to join in the decision-making processes, either in terms of providing feedback at a particular moment or in terms of co-researching collaboratively.

- Transparent. Feminist researchers are committed to making the process and constructed nature of research visible to multiple audiences, to discuss the dilemmas and the process instead of presenting it as a fait accompli.

While this list is not exhaustive, we feel it covers the primary qualities we have seen embodied in feminist research and in the feminist researchers whom we have interviewed. Again, many of the researchers we interviewed did not explicitly identify as feminist researchers, but in their discussions of the reflective, flexible, dialogic research processes they developed and pursued, their ethics certainly align with that of feminist research.

Our own approach to research methodology in this study embraces and enacts several of these principles as well. The ultimate aim of our research is not so much to produce definitive epistemic knowledge about ethical research practices or even to describe empirically what researchers do. Rather, our aim is to improve the quality of ethical decision making for digital researchers. By helping researchers become more well-informed about ethical issues in digital research, we hope to promote more ethical research practice—and that, we hope, will help make research more immediately valuable for the research participants who agree to participate in these studies. Our approach in contacting research participants and in negotiating informed consent has attempted to meet the criterion for "careful and respectful" noted above—although, again, we see this as *sine qua non* of ethical research practice in general, not just feminist research practice. And finally we have attempted to implement the principle of dialogism into our study by sharing with participants what Thomas Newkirk (1996) has called "the rights of co-interpretation." All participants whose experiences we share were given the opportunity to review our write-ups, to provide us with additional clarifications, or even to contest our interpretations. We feel that this kind of dialogism with participants not only shows respect for their agency and for their professional status as researchers, but also makes our own analysis stronger.

interesting

NEGOTIATING ACCESS AS A RESEARCHER

One of the most complex issues for online researchers, particularly researchers working from a feminist research framework, is determining what type of research they are conducting—text-based or person-based—and what ethics of use should apply. Researchers working with print-based materials do not (usually) face this quandary—but the frequent real-time, "conversational" nature of much online communication complicates matters in ways that researchers of rhetoric should consider when seeking to study online. Should researchers treat the material in online spaces such as blogs, discussion forums, or chats as published work by authors that is available to be quoted following fair use and copyright guidelines? Or should such material be treated as communications among persons, which would cast the researcher not so much as a reader but as an observer studying the real-time or archived interactions of persons to which different use ethics apply? Even if it is clear to the researcher that she is an observer studying persons, are those observations in a public space where informed consent is not needed (e.g., a street corner in a face-to-face study)? Or are the observations conducted in a private space for which informed consent might well be needed (such as the face-to-face equivalent of conversations in coffee shops or in homes)?

Some guidelines, such as those of the National Endowment for the Humanities, treat all Internet-based text as "published," and thus as freely available to scholars.[5] However, as numerous researchers have shown, participants in online forums often perceive their postings as private even when those postings are, technically speaking, publicly available on the Web (see, for example, Ess and Association of Internet Researchers 2002; Buchanan 2004; Ess 2001; Frankel and Siang 1999; Hudson and Bruckman 2004). Some scholars such as Joseph Walther

(2001) reject the "expectation of privacy" argument and advocate an open access position that basically asserts that if something is accessible on the Web, then it's public; it is text and no consent is needed. Walther argues: "since the analysis of Internet archives does not constitute an interaction with a human subject, and since it avails itself of existing records, then for IRB purposes, it may be no different than research using old newspaper stories, broadcasts, the Congressional Record, or other archival data, for research." Other online researchers argue for a nuanced decision-making process that takes into consideration such issues as: the explicitly named use guidelines for a space; how users of a particular online space view that space (as public or private); the perceived age of the persons whose writing is being studied (children and teenagers often think of writing in online diaries and blogs as private); and the sensitivity of the topics being discussed (e.g., forums devoted to the grooming of Persian cats should be treated differently from forums where participants give personal accounts of their life with AIDS).

In our interviews, we found that researchers who were working explicitly or implicitly within the theoretical frame of feminist research methodology strongly favored respecting the wishes of the individuals and the community being studied and generally favored treating online postings as person-based rather than text-based research.

For example, for her doctoral research, rhetoric and composition scholar Laurie Cubbison studied the rhetoric of online medical support groups for persons with fibromyalgia and chronic fatigue syndrome (2000). Cubbison explained to us that the argument viewing any texts on the Internet as public "bothers me because it's acting as though communication were public even though it's not on the part of the participants." As a participant herself in these online support groups, Cubbison recognized that her fellow participants, many of whom shared intimate details of their lives with fellow members of the close-knit community, often view their Web conversations as private; thus she did not feel comfortable quoting from the discussions without participants' permission. But because her interest was more "in the big picture and the discourse rather than what individual people were necessarily saying," in her dissertation ("Validating Illness") Cubbison decided not to quote from participants' online discussions. As she told us, "Instead what I did was find the Web sites where members of the group had gone on to publish particular viewpoints and cited it that way. [. . .] Because pretty much everything that I wanted I could find some version of it on a user-created Web site." By seeking other, clearly public sources for her study instead of using posts to the discussion forum, Cubbison felt that she was best protecting and representing the interests of the partici- pants and of the community. In other words, Cubbison distinguished between sites and postings intended for personal conversation and sites and postings intended for broad publication.

Seeking alternative, more public, and clearly published sources for information is just one option for researchers. Another option is to se- cure consent to study and quote online postings. Even though it may be difficult to obtain permission from individuals in online communi- ties, it is not impossible, and researchers can certainly obtain consent to quote from online discussions, as did Janne Bromseth when study- ing the rhetorical negotiations of gender, sexuality, and identity on a Scandinavian mailing list for lesbian and bisexual women. Bromseth developed a number of procedures for obtaining informed consent in ways that she felt were equitable and fair and in ways that we see as rep- resenting the principles of feminist research, particularly being careful and respectful, critically reflexive, flexible, dialogic, and transparent. Bromseth explained:

> I spent almost a year digging myself into theoretical issues—principle issues of ethics actually—of doing research online. [. . .] I was forced to consider it more because the area that I was going to study [lesbian groups] had more of a private character. I also started to look at more closed groups that did not have these public message archives. And then I started to question what is it actually that characterizes privacy? What is private online? You know? I mean the information is so accessible. Even if a mailing list is restricted access, it is rather easy to get access to the list. [. . .] I was also very irritated with people who used that argument that we should not ask for informed consent because it is easy to get into the groups. It is the participants' purpose for being in the group that is important in a way and their feelings about what kind of space this is. It is not as easy as dividing it into restricted access you should ask for con- sent and for public access you should not. [. . .] [That distinction] is a good point of departure, but it's not enough to look at access, how a list is or- ganized, how public the information is. [. . .] So I worked a long time to prepare that [informed consent] process.

Bromseth sought the informed consent of participants because she was not comfortable with determining the status of postings on behalf of her participants; she viewed "the participants' purpose" as having a stronger authority in that decision. As she explained in her dissertation: "Rather than defining a priori that a context is 'public' because of its mediation form, which could be said to be an 'outside-position' of defining the context, I would base my definition on an 'inside-position' and the type of social activity that took place in the group by asking the participants themselves" (Bromseth 2006, 67). As a lesbian herself, Bromseth chose to become a participant observer, and as both a participant and an observer, Bromseth felt that "it was really important for me to feel that the group was supportive of the thought that I would be there to ask questions and participate in the discussions with them with multiple roles, both as researcher and as the participant. I wouldn't do it if there was a lot of suspicion from the participants because then it wouldn't work." Bromseth's keen awareness of the importance of this forum for fellow lesbians made her especially sensitive to what effect her role as a researcher might have. She sought informed consent because "if my presence would imply that some women would stop participating, I would have really big trouble with defending my choice of being there [especially] if the group were really important to that member too. I mean for some of these participants, they live in a place where there are no lesbian communities and there was only this list for the women."

To ensure that her research did not harm participants by exposing their private postings, Bromseth chose to seek consent not only from the individuals in the group, but also from the group itself. But, as she reflected on this practice with us, she noted that she had to work through many questions:

> How would I be sure to reach everyone in the group? That's always an important issue. And how do I ask for consent? Who should consent? Is it each member of the group, or would it be enough that nobody protested? Is it a group decision? So there are so many issues to consider. Is the group working as a group? Are they able to make group decisions? Those kind of things are really important to consider, if you decide that consent at a group level is needed. I decided to ask the group for consent as a group because as a participant observer for a certain amount of time I felt that was right.

To obtain group consent, Bromseth first contacted the listmistress and got permission to contact the group by posting an introductory letter, which she quoted in her dissertation (2006, 75).

In her letter, Bromseth identified herself as a lesbian, explained her research, and invited people to express concerns about her research. She "decided that if no-one had difficulties with my presence and purpose, it would be ethically satisfying to interpret a 'silent agreement' as consent to be present in the group to do research" (2006, 69). Bromseth also made clear to list participants that were she to quote directly from any posts, she would contact those persons for their individual consent. So rather than take the "outsider" perspective that the communications in the list were public information, Bromseth instead chose to ask the listserv administrators, the listserv participants as a group, and then individual participants whom she quotes. All in all, Bromseth's approach is dialogic, reflective, and interactive, following many of the principles of feminist research.[6]

Bromseth was clear about her decision that she was studying the communications of persons and not the published writings of authors, and she was able to shape her interactions with participants and her use of participants' words accordingly. But for many researchers, such decisions are not so clear. At the time we interviewed Yukari Seko in September 2006, she was a student from Japan pursuing a masters of arts in the communications and culture program offered jointly by York and Ryerson Universities in Canada. Her research focuses on the communications in blogs and discussion forums for those with suicidal and self-destructive desires (e.g., cutting). Although she does not specifically use the term "rhetoric" in describing her study, her study is very much a study of rhetoric, particularly in its focus on rhetor-audience interactions, as shown by her explanation of her research:

> Despite its fundamental engagement in the form of individual utterance, the social nature of online communication transforms a traditional blogging into an interactive "murmuring." In other words, a blog, a new mode of online diary, becomes a hybrid entity of personal and public spheres in which individual monologues are exposed under a gaze of anonymous comrades and critics. [. . .] The aim of [my] presented research is thus to analyze the suicidal/SI bloggers' accounts of their self-destructive desire by exploring the ways in which the suicidal/SI bloggers constitute their "threaded" identities. In so doing, I examine (1) how the self-identification

of self-destructive personalities influences the bloggers' autobiographical writing, (2) how the suicidal bloggers define the spaces of utterance in relation to public and private awareness, and (3) how the particular structure of a blog service affects the bloggers' discursive practice and interaction with others. (Seko 2006, 4–7)

In her study, Seko chose to focus on one young woman, whom she calls "Perry," who was both an active participant in an online discussion group and an active blogger. Perry often wrote in her posts and blogs about her desires to hurt herself and her actual acts of cutting herself.

Seko struggled with her decision whether or not to seek informed consent from Perry to quote her blogs and discussion posts. When she asked advice of her thesis advisory committee—composed of scholars who were all themselves experienced Internet researchers—they could not provide Seko with a consensus answer. One committee member advised that she seek consent, another said no consent was needed, and a third said that the answer depended on the particular situation. Seko also sought guidance in published discussions of research ethics. She mentioned to us two scholars in particular, Susannah Stern (2003; 2004), who has published on the ethics of studying youth suicidal bloggers, and Amy Bruckman (2001; 2002), who has published on the ethics of obtaining informed consent from online participants. In her extended and thoughtful analysis of the dilemmas she faced, Seko raised issues important for online researchers, particularly researchers of rhetoric, to consider:

> I kind of want to raise a comment about Susannah Stern and Amy Bruckman, especially Amy Bruckman about the chatroom research, she mentioned something so interesting about the definition of space—how it depends on the researcher's articulation and the user's articulation. If I think of Perry's comments as the letter for the editors, I don't have to get any informed consent, but if I think of it as personal conversation, I have to get informed consent. And again, it's totally related to my articulation of blog. I think of blog as a hybrid entity between monological and interactive discursive practice. And the monological discursive practice— autobiographical, monological—is what I'm so fascinat[ed by], because compared to communal space such as chatroom or discussion board, or listserv, blog is more self-conscious, self-focus [. . . but] the space is public because Perry doesn't have the space by herself. Provider can remove her blog whenever the provider decided to, so again, she doesn't own her

space. But her discourse herself is diary, so her intellectual property, her discourse herself is her property. So there's a lot of focal points and point of view I can approach.

For the MA thesis level, I think I'm not going to take informed consent, because I'm still working on the Internet research ethics issues for research. If I do right now—I don't know. The other reason I'm not going to take informed consent is my way of approaching the blog is I'm defining the blog, the blog-in-practice, as social performance, not as a reflection of internal reality. So basically I'm trying to look at Perry's discursive practice as data. Of course I have a lot of dilemma inside. If I qualify my position—I'm looking for her discursive practice as social action. Maybe it's another excuse not to obtain informed consent. I'm not sure. It's again about Bruckman's difference and articulation of space and articulation of practices. So I articulate Perry's discursive practice as social, not private. [. . .] Everything is so mixed up. It has a lot of aspects. Blogs are problematic sphere. It's a private diary, in the meantime it's a discussion board, in the meantime it's a community. [. . .] . In the paper [Seko 2006] I suggest maybe her usage of public community space is like an invitation board to her personal diary because in her personal diary she gave more detailed information. So in the public discussion she sort of say "I have an urge, I really want to cut, I do something" and she put the link, an automatic link, to her personal blog. [. . .] So she actually sometimes express her blog to be cued, to be peeked, to be lurked.

[. . .] But on her profile page she put in her personal email address and her msn and im and also she mentioned her birthdate, address. So I know where she is and how old she is, like everything. So I feel kind of guilty about it because she doesn't know my existence, she doesn't know being studied. Although I did—I used some quote from her personal blog—at most, the longest one is like 10 lines—right now I'm working on making a map of her friends network map, her commentators and her and her relationships and friends. It is actually significant part for my MA thesis research. So I'm still wondering should I obtain consent or not.

In this reflection, Seko makes it clear that influencing part of her decision is concern about the status of a blog: despite monological aspects, Seko also recognizes that blogs are interactive and constitute a kind of social performance or social action. (This makes them different, for instance, from closed e-mail-based listservs such as the forum Bromseth studied.)

To complicate matters further, Seko mentioned to us that Perry identifies herself as being seventeen years old, which means that were Seko to seek informed consent, she would actually need to seek assent from Perry and consent from one or both of Perry's legal guardians—because according to Canada's code of ethics, as in the United States,[7] minors involved in human subjects research cannot give informed consent. Perry's online writings indicated that Perry did not have a good relationship with her parents; thus Seko felt that seeking parental consent would cause Perry greater harm than Seko's simply being a lurking, observing researcher because it potentially could cause Perry to stop using the online space to communicate with a community that is important to her. As Seko explained when reflecting on the importance of online writing communities for young women with suicidal and self-destructive tendencies, "They need a space to shout, actually." And for Seko, at the point in her research when we interviewed her, the "shouts" she read from these young women bloggers were shouts out to a public of which Seko (uneasily) included herself as researcher as part.

RESEARCHER INTERACTIONS WITH PARTICIPANTS

Obviously the decision about whether and how to seek informed consent influences a researcher's subsequent interactions with participants. But there are other particular issues of interaction that online researchers may need to negotiate throughout the study. First is a question all online researchers need to consider: what kind of ethos to establish in an online, often text-based community? Second is the question of crisis intervention, an issue that comes up particularly for those studying youth communications online: When and how should a researcher intervene? Again, when studying print-based documents—for example, women's nineteenth-century diaries—a researcher may come upon disturbing information such as suicidal thoughts or reports of spousal abuse, but the question of whether to intervene to potentially save the life of this long-dead person is not an issue. For researchers studying online communications of living persons, the question of intervention is another matter.

One key issue for online researchers is what kind of presence and identity to maintain vis-à-vis online participants.[8] Both Bromseth and Cubbison spoke at length about the importance of establishing a credible online researcher ethos. As Bromseth moved "from outside to the inside" over several months, she cautiously negotiated the transition from a "lurking position" to a participating position in the online community called Sapfo. She decided early on to be fully visible as a researcher on the list, which allowed list participants "to join in, and contest my interpretations" (Bromseth 2006, 71). But she was not present on the list only as a researcher. Another important facet of establishing her credibility was, as she says, "Creating a culturally appropriate image of myself through an intersection of subject positions as woman/lesbian/researcher, both initially when asking for consent, and afterwards, trying to 'get on the inside' and establish a dialogue" (74).

In short, Bromseth established a hybrid identity on the list. In face-to-face situations, participants can make assumptions about the researcher's gender based on her embodiment (presence of the physical body, performance, dress), but in online environments that rely only on text, how does the researcher achieve embodiment? Bromseth addressed this issue by "making everything explicit in text" (2006, 74), that is, by self identifying as a lesbian and by sharing her experiences as such. In this way, she established credibility with the group.

Establishing such credibility takes time, effort, patience, and commitment to the group as well as to the research project. Cubbison stressed the importance of belonging to a community as a critical requirement for studying it, as she explained in her interview with us: "It is unrealistic to expect us to be totally divorced from the topic that the research focuses around. Not only is it unrealistic, I would say it's bad scholarship. In order to be a part of the community and observe the community, we have to have a preexisting relationship with that community in order for the research to even begin to take place." Cubbison recommends that a researcher has a "pre-existing relationship" with the community she plans to study—making sure that her list identity as a "knowledgeable engaged participant" is stronger than her researcher identity. Having this kind of relationship helps the participant researcher establish "street cred":

> There's a sense among online communities at this point I think that a researcher who just drops in and says I'm going to write about you is in effect an invader and does not understand the values, the discourses, the discourse conventions of that community. Is a blunderer in a lot of ways.

[. . .] I think the participant observer needs to establish some street cred within the community or you just become some other researcher who is honing in on our territory. You really need to establish yourself in the community even before you start doing research. [. . .] you have to be a known quantity to members of the community. Not as a researcher so much, although you acknowledge that part of yourself, you acknowledge the academic side of yourself, but to be, it's more important to them that you be a knowledgeable engaged participant in the activity or otherwise you're just another onlooker who will get flamed to a crisp if you just come in and say I want to write a paper about you guys. You won't last long in at least one of the groups I'm on if that's how you enter.

Cubbison questions whether it is ethical to lurk at all in a community you are studying. She strongly stresses "the participant aspect" of the participant researcher role: "This is the case where the participant observer really depends on the participant aspect. Sure you could follow it, sure you could lurk in a forum for months and then do your write up and they may or may not ever find out about it, but it's still not respectful of the group." For both Bromseth and Cubbison, it is important to acknowledge explicitly one's researcher persona in the online community—but for both it is also critical to be a truly and fully engaged participant in the community, to have a personal and/or political stake in the community agenda. In their published writings, it is clear that Cubbison (2000) and Bromseth (2006) see this position as arising out of the theoretical frame of feminist research methodology. But, interestingly, in their interviews with us, neither researcher explicitly mentioned their views as informed by "feminist research." Rather, both researchers articulated their positions in terms of the criteria for good research in general. However, we see their approaches as following many of the principles for feminist research we have discussed. What we heard from a variety of researchers—including Bromseth and Cubbison—was the importance of being forthright to the group about multiple roles of researcher, participant, and observer in order to maintain personal and research credibility when studying online discussion groups and virtual worlds.

In addition to establishing a persona, online researchers often need to decide whether to intervene. Sometimes the intervention is simply to provide technical support to an online community (see Sapienza 2007) but sometimes when studying online rhetoric the issues can be even more serious. Seko's research in/on suicidal bloggers, for example, raised many ethical dilemmas.

Seko points out that in studying online postings, researchers might well encounter distressing information such as "farewell messages (or death notes), detailed descriptions of self-injury, and appointments for group suicides" (2006). A significant question for the researcher studying such groups, then, is whether and how to intervene when it appears that someone may be seriously considering suicide (see, for example, Stern 2004). Of course researchers working directly with participants could encounter such experiences, too, but what makes the online situation more problematic, according to Seko, is that it is hard "to correctly judge the 'seriousness' and 'urgency' of the suicidal individuals in online environments" (2006, 29).

At one point in her research, Seko encountered posts by Perry who, in despair over a conflict with her boyfriend, expressed repeatedly (in a community thread on LiveJournal.com) her desire to harm herself—and then later that same day reported that she actually did injure herself by cutting her wrist "5 times in the toilet" (2006, 21). However, while Perry was contemplating and actually injuring herself, she was also posting to the blog and interacting with others who responded to her postings (expressing sympathy and understanding for her situation). In one exchange, another participant ("Anne") responded with a "compassionate message" indicating a high degree of sympathy for Perry's situation: "me and you are twins seriously" (24). No one in this exchange tried to talk Perry out of her action, they "simply addressed their compassions with her depression instead of trying to prevent her [self-injury] action" (26).

The deep ethical issue for the researcher studying this interaction is of course the question of whether to respond, and how. Is some kind of intervention warranted in an effort to help the blogger, particularly when the blogger identifies as seventeen years old? Should Seko have contacted Perry or perhaps Perry's Internet Service Provider so they could track her hometown and contact information?[9] Seko contemplated whether and how to act, but ultimately decided against it. In her interview with us, she explained her rationale:

Yukari Seko: As a community member I'm allowed to contact her. So I could post to her blog actually, but I never do that [. . .] I'm not sure. Isn't it weird if you are a prospective suicide and you suddenly get some contact from people you don't know at all? I don't know—that could be kind of harmful I think. Maybe she thinks she is under surveillance or something. Or like she was monitored.

Heidi McKee: And then she might stop using this space?

Yukari Seko: Or maybe she just kill herself because she might be like "Oh my god, this world is so cruel, this world is so scary." Because I can't judge the impact of my reaction on her. So basically I've tried to be invisible for her. [I] have never contacted her [. . .] The only thing I can do is try to protect her space.

Seko, while concerned for Perry's health and welfare, also recognized the limitations of what she, as a researcher, can actually know or do in an online space. Seko's decision to respect Perry's privacy and agency in this situation was also based on her understanding of the discursive conventions of blogging—how such spaces can be both personal and public at the same time, and how Perry may be using those spaces to seek social support that she does not have in her face-to-face life.

Few researchers studying online communications will encounter situations as potentially dire as suicidal ideations, but all researchers of online communications need to decide how to interact and participate in a community. Janne Bromseth's, Laurie Cubbison's, and Yukari Seko's experiences are just a few examples of the complexity of choices online researchers face. Making ethical decisions about how to present oneself and how to interact with participants online requires that researchers understand the distinct rhetorical dynamics of online spaces and especially the particularities of the contexts in which they seek to study.

REFLECTION

The researchers we have studied and interviewed evidence a good deal of concern, care, and respect for the participants whose writings they are studying and whose actions they are observing. Their research practices evidence strong allegiance to what we think of as the key tenets of feminist methodology—particularly their considerations for recognizing participants' agency.

When a person's writing is perceived less as an object apart from that person ("a text") but instead more as an expression and an action of a person rather than an author, researchers are more likely to view studies of online communication as person-based—and, thus, to seek informed consent. However, what we also observed is that researchers are critically reflexive in deciding this question. If the topic is not a personal or sensitive one, or, as with Seko's research, if the writing is already on broad public display and identified as such by the writer (for example, how Perry used her posts to invite others to read her blog), then the presumption can tip the other way, toward regarding the writing as published and, thus, as usable/quotable without informed consent. However even in those cases, these researchers tend to view writing more as embodied expression of self (a feminist view) rather than as disembodied object (a masculinist and logocentric view). Importantly as well, the researchers often do not make this call by themselves; they consult and negotiate with others in a dialogic process.

The relationship between researcher and participant in online research is often based on a strong bond of shared identity. That does not mean that the researchers become intimate or friendly with their research participants—Kirsch (2005) warns against moving to this level of relationship with participants. What it means, though, is that the researchers belong to the community as participants, even when, at the same time, they are careful to maintain a distinct and visible researcher role. Cubbison and Bromseth are active participants in the communities they are studying; in a sense, they share the goals of the community—which in all cases involved some form of transformation (improvement) in the lives of the participants (greater self-awareness of sexual identity, political or institutional change, greater understanding of a disease and how to cure it). And yet they are careful to maintain the visibility and transparency of their researcher roles so that the participants do not misunderstand their presence or mistake their intentions.

stay transparent

These researchers also exhibit deep respect for the autonomy and agency of the participants and communities being studied. Even in situations involving crisis, the researchers are reluctant to intervene. They do not see their role as being saviors, heroes, superwomen, or regulatory agents. It is not that these researchers would never intervene to help a research participant in need of help. Not at all. Rather, their ethical presumption tips in the direction of humility rather than the arrogance of assuming that one can know best for others.

humility

Another quality is certainly appreciation and understanding of the rhetorics of cyberspace. These researchers understand that online digital writing operates according to very different rhetorical dynamics from print-based and face-to-face rhetorical dynamics—and, consequently, that there are different ethical principles involved. Researchers also understand that cyberspace is not just one kind of space but rather a wide variety of digital forums with a variety of distinctive dynamics and rhetorical ethics involved. Just because a listserv discussion group archives its postings does not mean that those postings can necessarily be treated like books in a library. Several of the researchers noted the hybrid nature of the online communities they were studying. Bromseth, for example, noted that Sapfo is both a forum for political discussion and a place where individuals explore their sexual identities in an intimate and personal way. The critically reflexive researcher is aware of how online forums have distinct characters requiring distinct ethical judgments.

The researchers we interviewed were willing not only to make their researcher role visible to participants but also to make their ethical decision-making process visible to participants, to peer scholars, and other researchers. Transparency is a key operating principle for these researchers. They agreed to be part of our study and, in the case of everyone cited in this chapter, to use their own names. They were willing to present their process of decision making, including the difficulties of the decisions they faced, how they sometimes modified their position from one study to another, and how they worried (and still worry) about the decisions they made. We admire them for their forthrightness and courage in discussing their research processes. We see the willingness to acknowledge and make visible the complexities of the process of research—and not just to report results as if they were revealed truth—as another key quality of feminist research.

For feminist scholars seeking to study the overwhelming amount of rhetoric on the Web, the processes of planning and conducting research are certainly complicated, but not impossible. It is our hope that in reading about the experiences and decision-making processes of these three researchers, readers might have a richer sense of some of the issues to consider when setting out to research rhetorica in cyberspace.

Three

Pedagogical Postscript

Writing as Feminist Rhetorical Theory

Laura R. Micciche

What would it mean to read feminists as rhetorical theorists of writing, rather than predominately as social theorists? What can this sort of directed reading teach us about writing and rhetoric? And what can we do with what we learn? These questions lead me to explore a method for engaging with feminist work that emphasizes writing as a conceptual and imaginative process of vital importance to feminist rhetorical theory. In a reciprocal exchange, seeing writing as central to feminist rhetorics promises to expand what writing can mean as a tool for knowledge-making and remaking and for instructional methods. Embedded in feminist rhetorics are theories of writing—or guiding principles explaining what writing is, what it does—for, after all, writing constitutes a core materiality of feminist work. That is, in addition to oratory and social action—both of which entail putting language to work for social change—writing is essential to feminist projects, particularly for those projects that critique oppressive practices and discourses, articulate strategies for change and collective action, identify and describe how rituals of the ordinary are, in actuality, problems, and generally depict the expansive multiplicity of women's and others' realities.

In the context of rhetorical theory, feminist writing practices have effectively expanded the traditional canon of rhetoric, especially as revisionist accounts of rhetorical history and theory have encouraged ongoing reconsiderations of what counts as rhetoric and invited new possibilities for reading women's writing as enactments of rhetorical theory. Joy Ritchie and Kate Ronald's anthology *Available Means* (2001) illustrates that the category of women rhetors includes not only philosophers and linguists—those most often associated with producing rhetorical theory—but also fiction writers, poets, anthropologists, and critical theorists, among other diverse practitioners. Indeed, Ritchie and Ronald hope that their choices of inclusion pose the following questions: "What do we have available to us in the body of women's writing that we might consider as rhetorical theory? What qualities might a work of women's writing need to possess in order for us to consider it as rhetorical theory? And finally, what blinders are preventing us from reading more of women's rhetoric as theory?" (xxx).

Taking a cue from Ritchie and Ronald, we might read feminist rhetoric as writing theory in action and, by doing so, gather new insights to inform and otherwise invigorate writing pedagogy. A starting point in this effort is to make visible how a number of feminists conceptualize writing as a rhetorical act, in order not to neglect the ideological and political content of feminist rhetorical theory but to position this content as woven into writing practices. From here, we can extract pedagogical methods that capitalize on the fruitful intersections among feminist writing practices and feminist rhetorical theory. Methods, using Sandra Harding's work as a guide (1987), are techniques or ways of gathering evidence, and methodology, "a theory and analysis of how research does or should proceed" (3). Whereas methods encompass practical ways of doing that can be extracted from feminist rhetorical theory and applied to writing instruction, methodology locates *doing* in a larger context, explaining the underlying theory that informs it. Feminist methods are inventional sources that create openings for pedagogy; feminist methodologies form the theoretical grounding through which these openings attain explanatory power and politicized significance.

To illustrate the sort of openings I have in mind, I turn to Donna Haraway's "A Manifesto for Cyborgs" (1990) in order to foreground *play* as an under-explored yet highly suggestive rhetorical and pedagogical element in feminist writing projects. Play encourages dissonance, reminding us that writing is an imaginative, world-building activity. This claim works against a generalized conception of play as frivolous and extra-rhetorical, in excess of the literacy skills frequently deemed important in expository, analytical, and argument-based writing courses. Such presumptions, as this provisional reading suggests, limit approaches to writing and restrict methods of reading feminist rhetorical theory as an inventive site for pedagogy. Haraway's work, in contrast, reminds us that writing is a technology of power, agency, and, not to be underestimated, irreverence. Writing, understood in this light, requires rhetorical intent, or control and choice-making, and does not shy away from play as a strategic, potentially vigorous function of critical discourse.

As Michaela Meyer indicates, intent can consist of playful methods, such as intentional ambiguity, the goal of which is "to purposefully use ambiguity in a way that *creates a space for discourse that did not exist before.* In creating that space, the ambiguity delivers an invitation to audience members to participate in the newly created discourse. . . . "intentional ambiguity would allow the rhetor *a degree of control* over the message" (2007, 11; emphasis in original). Intentionality and control are important aspects of feminist rhetorics, for they signal the responsibility necessary to construct and enact agency. Instances of purposeful discursive acts abound within the context of feminist rhetorical theory. For instance, in the introduction to *Teaching Rhetorica*, Kate Ronald and Joy Ritchie describe how women rhetors—I would sharpen this to signify feminist rhetors—have revised traditional rhetorical concepts through an explicitly gendered and, quite frequently, feminist lens. They write that women's rhetorical practices model an ethos marked not by objectivity and distance but rather by a desire to "len[d] specificity to material differences." This desire insists "on the inextricable links between experience and rhetoric, language and action" (2006, 9). Feminist methodologies indeed require a writerly ethos sensitive to situatedness, empathic connections to research subjects, and a view of knowledge as always partial and in process. This construction of ethos is at odds with definitions that tend to crowd writing textbooks, the cornerstones of which include certainty and credibility, not doubt and wonder. The latter signify crucial ingredients for conceptualizing and proposing altered realities, common goals of feminist rhetorics. The rhetorical tradition places almost exclusive importance on definitions of ethos that privilege the individual speaking or writing well, while feminist constructs of ethos often emphasize collective identity and collaboration as significant to knowledge building and to the development of credibility. For example, Sonja Foss and Cindy Griffin identify a primary goal of feminist rhetoric to be the creation of spaces for rhetors to "develop models for cooperative, nonadversarial, and ethical communication" (1995, 15).

In addition to re-crafting rhetorical concepts (to which I return later in my discussion of play and invention), feminist methods of research and writing also highly value questions in knowledge building and in the performance of writing. Questions necessitate intentionality and assertions of agency—even, perhaps, a willingness to be disobedient in the long shadow of tradition. Along these lines, questions often take the form of critique. A function of feminist critique is to question what passes as ordinary, often as a cover for maintaining the assumed value of intellectual inheritance, in order to unsettle the ground upon which norms hold sway. Feminist critique reveals how it is that we come to be orientated[1] in one direction and not another, emphasizing the ideological, historical, and cultural effects of directionality on women's lives as well as on the lives of those who are disadvantaged by imbalances of power. Sara Ahmed argues that acts of orientation are partly the result of "lines" we follow and create: "The lines that direct us, as lines of thought as well as lines of motion, are in this way performative: they depend on the repetition of norms and conventions, of routes and paths taken, but they are also created as an effect of this repetition" (2006, 16). Feminism's directional disturbance generates alternatives to an established line, often interrupting the repetition of norms in order to draw new lines of possibility. Feminist rhetoric, borrowing from Ronald and Ritchie's description of the uses of women's rhetoric, "challenges dominant epistemologies, asserts new topoi/contexts from which to argue, places material experience—especially that of women, women of color, sexual minorities, and other nonmainstream groups—at the center of knowledge formation, and it reconnects language/rhetoric to action and change" (2006, 11). A feminist orientation to writing creates lines of deviation rather than lines of obedience.

Not surprisingly, then, feminist rhetorics foreground writing as a political, imaginative act through which to reenvision reality. Feminists remind us that writing is not a transparent reproduction of what is; it is an active construction that reflects and refracts, creates and distorts, imagines and displaces. How we choose to position writing reflects larger configurations of meaning and power; in short, writing is fertile material for doing feminist rhetorical work because it establishes links between language, action, and consequences.

For Lynn Worsham, writing "produces a sense of defamiliarization vis-à-vis unquestioned forms of knowledge." Following this logic, writing "would become an indispensable agency for making the world strange and infinitely various" (2003, 120). But how is it that writing makes strange or reconjugates reality? In one sense, writing brings us close to a subject by trying to approximate an idea, sense, or feeling. Writing, simultaneously, produces distance, a relentless example of how language can never get close enough, can never adequately render experience or thought faithfully into words. This tension between proximate and distant meanings marks writing as a strange encounter that charms and frustrates at alternative strokes.

Because writing often moves in fits and starts, it has the potential to be an interruptive technique, both intentional and unintentional. The intentional variety desires interruption as a political tool, the goal of which is to unstick normative conventions from fixed locations, making possible a questioning of what is in order to make claims for what might be. Nedra Reynolds describes interruption as a rhetorical strategy that "offers a tactical, practical means toward discursive agency" (1998, 72). Reynolds argues that in both speech and writing, interruption can derail dominant frames of intelligibility, increasing the rhetor's capacity to change the lines of direction in a given context. Unintentional interruptions are perhaps most familiar to writers during an early draft stage or to inexperienced writers who are as yet unaccustomed to developing cohesion strategies. In these cases, writing is less a political interruption than a cognitive and emotional one. Writing reveals idiosyncrasies and breaks in consistency that interrupt meaning and purpose—a familiar dissonance to teachers of writing at all levels. It's important to distinguish between intentional and unintentional interruption so as not to romanticize interruption as an always empowering strategy. One way to underscore this distinction is to speak about, on one hand, interruption as a rhetorical device aimed at creating certain effects and, on the other, a consequence of writing through doubt, without awareness of how and where one's text interrupts itself or those of others.

Interruption creates a pause in discourse, often allowing for seemingly tangential ideas to move to the center, whereas disruption, another of writing's capabilities, breaks discourse apart, creating fault lines through which new meanings can emerge. Charlotte Perkins Gilman's "The Yellow Wallpaper" ([1892] 1997) is a good example of the latter. The story dramatizes how scientific discourse has historically othered women through massive dismissals of the body, effectively generating a rupture in medical discourse. Writing the story of a postpartum woman's mental and physical struggle creates a transformative lens through which to understand the intersections of illness, gender, motherhood, and writing. Writing is figured as a healing mechanism for the narrator, and yet she is forbidden from writing by her husband John, a doctor, who worries that it will generate "fancies" of the imagination, further agitating her fragile state. Gilman's narrative disrupts interpretations of the female body and of "feminine illnesses," usually attributed to hysteria, by granting her narrator a voice through which to tell her story. She occupies more than the object status that women typically held in medical discourse of the late 1800s, when Gilman was writing. The story might be read as a truncated history and critique of the biology of writing, long demarcated as a male province, not suited to women's bodily comportment (see Woolf [1929] 1989). This history is furiously challenged and mocked by Helene Cixous, who names writing "*the very possibility of change*, the space that can serve as a springboard for subversive thought, the precursory movement of a transformation of social and cultural structures" (1991, 337, emphasis in original). But how is it that writing has this capacity? What is it about word-work that enables "subversive thought"? These questions begin to suggest that when we think of writing as something other than a reflection of reality, it takes on awesome social and cultural significance, particularly because writing is an act of inscription that can disrupt commonplaces, as Cixous contends, just as it can entrench them.

Some tentative responses to these questions emerge in Toni Morrison's "Nobel Lecture in Literature." In her parable about language, an old blind woman is approached by a group of young people who challenge her to say whether the bird in one group member's hand is living or dead. This encounter functions as the basis for Morrison's reading of the bird as language, and the woman as a writer. She goes on to describe distinctions between living and dead language, with the former representing "an act with consequences." Dead language, in contrast, is "unyielding" and characterized by "exclusivity and dominance." "Unreceptive to interrogation," dead language "cannot form or tolerate new ideas, shape other thoughts, tell another story, fill baffling silences" (2001, 418). Morrison equates dead language with "oppressive language," which "does more than represent violence; it is violence; does more than represent the limits of knowledge; it limits knowledge" (419). Language needs to be cared for, in her account, lest its power becomes perverted by the will to neglect and thereby marginalize differences. On this point, Morrison writes, "Word-work is sublime . . . because it is generative; it makes meaning that secures our difference, our human difference—the way in which we are like no other life" (420). Thus, language—and writing—can generate subversive thought by refusing the mystification of reality wrought by evacuated language that serves stasis; in the presence of such language, fears rupture.

For feminists, writing is always political because language reflects and deflects power relations. It is freighted with a long history of inequality—gendered, raced, classed, and more—which bears down during the act of putting words together. Trinh T. Minh-ha characterizes this weight by evoking clichés about who is authorized to write within the context of inequitable social arrangements: "Writing, reading, thinking, imagining, speculating. These are luxury activities, so I am reminded, permitted to a privileged few, whose idle hours of the day can be viewed otherwise than as a bowl of rice or a loaf of bread less to share with the family" (1989, 7). Women must be "language-stealers" in her account (19), for writing is crucial to women's agency: "Shake syntax, smash the myths, and if you lose, slide on, *unearth* some new linguistic paths. Do you surprise? Do you shock? Do you have a choice?" (20, emphasis in original). These "new linguistic paths" are analogous to Ahmed's lines of orientation. In both instances, writing becomes a means for invention, not only of ideas but also of alternative realities and their etchings on and in language.

Writing documents and makes visible those experiences and ways of knowing that require unearthing because they have been buried in the shit of oppressive discourses. Writing commemorates. It celebrates and honors—acts that are particularly relevant to feminist recoveries of muffled or silenced voices whose emergence reorganizes what we have come to identify as "tradition" (see Glenn 1997; Jarratt 1991). In another sense, as Minh-ha explains, women (particularly French feminists) "have attempted to render noisy and audible all that had been silenced in phallocentric discourse" (1989, 37). Indeed, Cixous champions laughter as the ultimate subversion of man-made language. In her inimitable style, she writes, "laughs exude from all our mouths; our blood flows and we extend ourselves without ever reaching an end; we never hold back our thoughts, our signs, our writing; and we're not afraid of lacking" (1991, 336). Laughter constitutes defiance, a refusal of obedience to the law of the father. Laughter obliterates silence and locates pleasure in women's bodily excess.

As Cixous demonstrates, writing circulates within an affective economy. Writing reminds us of women's long-standing exclusion from knowledge building, a history of alienation and objectification that cannot fail to conjure strong feelings. This explains why for writers like Morrison, Alice Walker, and Gloria Anzaldúa, among others, writing entails caring for others, for histories, for words and writing. Virginia Woolf expresses this beautifully as she urges upcoming women writers to resuscitate Shakespeare's sister. "Drawing her life from the lives of the unknown who were her forerunners . . . she will be born. As for her coming without that preparation, without that effort on our part, without that determination that when she is born again she shall find it possible to live and write her poetry, that we cannot expect, for that would be impossible. But I maintain that she would come if we worked for her, and that so to work, even in poverty and obscurity, is worthwhile" ([1929] 1989, 114). Throughout the essay, Woolf's anger at the male dominion over writing is unmistakable, as is her fury at women's marginal presence in the stacks of her fictional Oxbridge library. This affective context informs Woolf's call for women to write, regardless of interruption and despite less than adequate material conditions.

Caring also informs feminist research practices, as Jacqueline Jones Royster makes clear in her description of afrafeminist models of intellectual work. She characterizes her research standpoint as rooted in affective attachments to African American women's rhetorical practices, and she sees her responsibility as a researcher in terms of a collective good: "[African American women intellectuals] . . . are accountable ultimately to the merging of the interests of mind, body, and soul as part and parcel of the wholeness of the knowledge-making enterprise, which includes accounting for our own social obligations as members of the group" (2000, 224). As both participant in and observer of African American women's rhetorical scenes, Royster is keenly aware of the "bifocal standpoint," as she calls it, that distinguishes her research orientation (225). Operating in service of both community and academic discipline, she describes her research as "caring" and as guided by "passionate attachments" (225). Woolf and Royster illustrate, in different ways, that writing is an affective investment in a way of seeing the world. Writing can function as feeling work; it creates an affective economy around concepts like voice, recovery, subjectivity, and agency, all of which are embedded in feminist writing projects. Writing is feminist machinery and play is one of its gears.

How might play constitute a deliberate and valuable method influencing writing pedagogy? What is the relationship between play and writing? Can play be serious, critical, rhetorical? One of the more playful feminist texts available is Donna Haraway's widely influential "A Manifesto for Cyborgs" (1990). Originally published in 1985, it has been frequently anthologized in feminist readers. A feminist scientist, socialist, postmodernist, and myth-maker, Haraway offers the cyborg as a hybrid creature that blurs boundaries between human, animal, and machine, signifying radical subjectivity. The cyborg is an imaginative resource through which Haraway imagines a post-gender world, one bereft of origin stories. Absent a need for genesis as an explanation for how the world came into being, "the cyborg does not expect its father to save it through a restoration of the garden, that is, through the fabrication of a heterosexual mate, through its completion in a finished whole, a city and cosmos. The cyborg does not dream of community on the model of the organic family" (192). According to Haraway, this is no cause for "faithlessness" (194); instead, the cyborg represents possibility and imaginative play. For Haraway, an inessential identity is important to the cyborg figure because she dreams of coalition politics built upon something other than identity and identification; she wonders how politics could be altered by foregrounding "partial, contradictory, permanently unclosed constructions of personal and collective selves" (199). In this account, transgressions of identity boundaries inspire and give pleasure, and subversion of a collective "we" fatally refuses wholeness and actively courts contradiction.

Writing, and its power as a signifying tool, is central to Haraway's cyborgian figure: "Cyborg writing must not be about the Fall, the imagination of a once-upon-a-time wholeness before language, before writing, before Man. Cyborg writing is about the power to survive not on the basis of original innocence, but on the basis of seizing the tools to mark the world that marked them as other" (1990, 217). Seizure amounts to textual performances and rhetorical tropes that enact possession through writing: irony, manifesto, myth, and story. A deliberate playfulness, akin to the intentional ambiguity Meyer suggests (2007), develops as Haraway merges vocabularies of various (often competing) frameworks: feminism, science/technology, socialism, postmodernism, science fiction, secularism. This merging of perspectives illustrates that the very language we use to define and name women, experience, and the political (among other things) needs to be multidimensional, even multispecies. In Haraway's vision, writing is both serious play and a tool for making inscriptions on the world. She appropriates rhetorical methods—story, myth, theory—for the creation of an explicitly socialist feminist vision. Haraway's ethos turns more on possibility than on credibility, exemplifying a feminist twist on a traditional rhetorical concept. Obedient to none of the traditions from which she writes, whether socialism or science, Haraway performs disobedience as a viable strategy—perhaps even a necessary strategy—for a feminist writing project.

What would it mean to conceive Haraway's cyborgian writing model as a feminist methodology for writing theory and pedagogy? For starters, important descriptors of writing would have to include *play*; *imagination*, a resource too often reserved for "creative" writing; and explicit attention to the *political* function of writing, a difficult, uncomfortable modifier. Here I focus only on play, leaving the others for a longer work-in-progress.[2] Play is not in excess to writing. Writing as play means that fictional elements are valid aspects of critical writing. Play involves performance, critical engagement with texts, considerable rhetorical skill, audience awareness, capacity to negotiate voice and tone, and an understanding of social relations—pragmatic, rhetorical knowledge, in other words. In addition, though, play entails wonder, curiosity, idealism, hyperbole, and imaginative leaps—an expansive horizon that purposefully exceeds predetermined limits.

Haraway's project uses writing to imagine a world based on the one we know but different from it in substantial, unpredictable, even heretofore unthought ways. Haraway's playfulness is not at the expense of rigor. Imaginative exploration of possibility is crucial to the cyborgian model of writing; closure, cohesion, and unity are subordinate traits, ones less likely to reimagine boundaries and identities than would a more fluid configuration of writing. Thus, the highly valued commodities of many writing classrooms—thesis statements, inductive reasoning, Toulmin argumentation methods—get challenged and construed as overly anxious in light of the exploratory writing performed by Haraway.

Yet play does not connote non-seriousness, or at least it doesn't have to. It's more akin to a serious effort to organize meaning around a logic of one's own making rather than one provided or assumed. Such an effort embraces assertions of agency and intention. Play is difficult, risky business when it comes to writing because the possibilities are endless. If we ask students to develop a mythology organized around an inventional figure—a kind of play with reality, history, and social relations—then we expect students to go beyond "word-play," or silly hypotheticals. For students to write a mythology would require them to engage in research, experimentation with form and genre, demanding acts of invention, and argumentation. In other words, the skills necessary for this kind of writing are not markedly distinct from those already valued in the context of academic writing practices. The framing of the skills and the very conception of writing to which these skills are linked, however, constitutes new territory.

I anticipate charges that these ideas are ignorant to the realities of academic writing courses, specifically composition courses, and that this is theory-ungrounded, rhetoric-unchecked. The fact that conceptions of writing beyond those transparently in service of a "skill set" remain unthinkable in writing classrooms not designated as sites for creative writing is one indication of the failure of radical politics, including feminism, to produce substantive change in how we think about writing. Critical pedagogies, eco-criticism, Marxism and post-Marxism, and queer theory, for example, depend upon hope, change, imagination, and utopian ideals. Whereas some of these values have significantly influenced classroom arrangements and pedagogical practices, they have been far from influential on conceptions of writing. Can we design writing activities that insist upon invention as a centerpiece of critical writing and thinking? How might invention itself be reinvented through feminist rhetorics that place a high premium on play as serious critical work? I seek to generate not so much a linear path from Haraway to pedagogical applications as a set of openings through which to imagine writing as a feminist practice that foregrounds play. Thus, the following assignment sketches are just that—hardly complete or lockstep; intended, instead, as heuristics for adaptation in a variety of contexts. They seek to approximate the spirit of play inspired by Haraway's cyborgian writing model and the feminist rhetoric it embraces. The content of the assignments is not necessarily focused on feminist issues. This is intentional, as I hope to present instructional methods and concepts of writing that adapt feminist thinking to a wide variety of content areas. My goal is to describe ways of *doing* feminist rhetorics in writing courses, or ways to integrate feminist methods into the conception and performance of writing. I imagine feminist rhetorical theory as a source that can productively infiltrate pedagogical methods, not prescribe content, and thereby begin to change how we think of writing and its purposes.

ASSIGNMENT I: PARODY AND DISCOURSE

Goals:

- To experiment with writing parody and manipulating ethos in order to construct counter-stories that make strange the familiar.

- To produce both a playful account of and critical commentary on a given issue (in this example, disciplinarity).

Description:

Write a parody of disciplinary discourses that illuminates how thinking is shaped by language as well as by research protocols and methodological conventions. Construct stories about these disciplinary differences. The purpose of this assignment is to get a feel for what language makes possible and impossible when used through varying frames of reference. Jordan Smoller's 1986 essay "The Etiology and Treatment of Childhood"[3] is a marvelous example. In a spoof of disciplinary thinking that demonstrates Smoller's thorough, and decidedly playful, understanding of the interactive relationship between rhetorical conventions and knowledge construction, Smoller reviews how a number of disciplines explain the "causes of childhood." The sociological viewpoint advocates "assimilat[ing] children into mainstream society," though with the understanding that "some victims are so incapacitated by their childhood that they are simply not competent to work" (1986, 6). The biological model is chiefly responsible for the view that "childhood is usually present from birth," which "has led some to speculate on a biological contribution" (7). The essay continues in this fashion, complete with invented sources to heighten the parody, as is the case with a source entitled "Spontaneous Remission of Childhood" published in *New Hope for Children and Animals* (11). Sometimes bordering on the absurd, the essay illustrates awareness of how sociology or biology sees and responds to a problem, while performing that awareness through a subversion of typical codes of conduct.

ASSIGNMENT 2: INVENTIONAL ARGUMENT

Goals:

- To generate intentional ambiguity and engage with rhetorical innovation.
- To expose and revise a tacitly agreed upon "story" that circulates within a particular disciplinary context.

Description:

- Start with vocabulary: What are the key terms in a particular disciplinary conversation? What explanatory functions do they serve?
- Redefine, refine, build: What aspects of these terms do you reject, question, challenge? What aspects do you accept, seek to enlarge, wish to amplify? What terms, concepts, or figures do you need to invent?
- Create an inventional argument: What kind of "story" can you construct with your redefined and invented terms? A mythology, a utopian manifesto, a tragedy? What kind of world are you describing, and why?
- Identify connections and ruptures: Which voices help you make this world? Which ones must you address? Which ones repudiate?

These tasks essentially outline the organizing structure of "A Manifesto for Cyborgs." This is argument—complete with claims, support, evidence, refutation—but argument that dreams up alternative ways of being in response to unsatisfactory existing ones. Argument that is not obedient to form and tradition. It is utopian argument, designed for imaginative thinking beyond the parameters of already established lines of thought. One of its central affective orientations is that of wonder. Ahmed describes wonder as a critical rhetorical positioning that "allows us to see the surfaces of the world *as made*, and as such wonder opens up rather than suspends historicity. Historicity is what is concealed by the transformation of the world into 'the ordinary,' into something that is already familiar, or recognizable" (2004, 179). She continues, "Wonder is about learning to see the world as something that does not have to be, and as something that came to be, over time, and with work. As such, wonder involves learning" (180). An inventional argument of this sort necessitates a critical stance that both engages and plays with the madeness of everyday life in order to imagine other possible makings.

ASSIGNMENT 3: CREATING INTERRUPTIONS

Goals:

- To practice asking questions that change the course of a conversation or debate.

- To assert agency as a writer and thinker in order to think in critical ways alongside as well as against source material.

Description:

Like a dialogue of sources assignment, in which students create a conversation among secondary sources to arrive at a better understanding of what's at issue in a given debate, the interruptive paper creates a dialogue—but of a different sort. Its purpose is to put sources in conversation in order to interrupt them, moving tangential ideas to the center, if warranted, in order to put pressure on the center of debate or discussion. What happens, for instance, when the center of debates about sexism in advertising turns from women's bodies to women's emotions? How might this move alter the conversation, lead somewhere other than to the conclusion that "sex sells," introduce new insights about the consequences of sexist advertising on women's subjectivities? How does our thinking change or create openings that take us in unexpected and potentially fruitful directions? Does putting emotion at the center orientate us differently to advertising, to sexism?

Whereas a dialogue of sources paper typically asks students to insert their own voices alongside those of their sources, gauging where they "fit" into the conversation, the interruptive paper desires no such fit. The goal is not integration into already established lines of thought but assertions of agency that court disintegration if and when necessary. In addition, the interruptive paper looks for normative claims and common sense associations in order to investigate what counts as normal within a particular context. Students are invited to reject the pretense of polite, consensual dialogue so as to allow contradictions and questions to surface, potentially changing the surface as well as the deep structure of debate.

In the context of feminist rhetorical theory, the cornerstones of these three assignments—parody, invention, and interruption—are writing modes as well as politicized acts that aim for movement of some kind. Movement is a synecdoche for feminism; it denotes both a critical mass of people and demonstrable shifts in thought and action. Likewise, the assignments described above seek to position writing as a site of movement, a place where writers not only perform what they know about familiar rhetorical concepts (i.e., ethos, audience, purpose, invention, argument, and situation) but also develop counterperformances to underscore their own agency, power, and imaginative potential in relation to a living rhetorical tradition that resists stasis.

GETTING THERE

Reading feminists as rhetorical theorists of writing offers a new vocabulary for talking about and theorizing writing, one that assigns political, social, and intellectual value to imaginative, often oppositional, writing. Not immediately pragmatic in the way that writing a proposal or offering a solution might appear to be—although, considering that such tasks are often delineated within the parameters of classrooms, and frequently culled from mass-produced textbooks, I put stress on the *seeming* pragmatics of such assignments—the kinds of assignments described above have pragmatic value, admittedly less quantifiable or measurable than that associated with more recognizable genres.

What's valuable is the aspirational as well as willful thinking inspired by such assignments, affective dispositions of great importance to thoughtful, seeking writing as well as to a thriving democracy. Ahmed offers another way to say this when she says that feminist pedagogy invites "the affective opening up of the world through the act of wonder, not as a private act, but as an opening up of what is possible through working together" (2004, 181). For her, wonder involves "a reorientation of one's relation to the world" (183). I think writing can do the same; writing and rhetoric teachers must unearth ways to make this possible and desirable for our students.

Notes

FOREWORD

1. My profound gratitude to Lisa Suter, who graciously shared her research notes with me. Lisa is a doctoral candidate in rhetoric and composition at Miami University. Her dissertation is titled *The Rhetor(ic)on: The Iconography of Rhetoric and the Rhetoric of Iconography*. See also her "When Rhetoric was a Woman."

2. Readers can quite easily find these images of Rhetorica online. Simply search for "Rhetorica," "Lady Rhetorica," or "Dame Rhetorica." The "Seven Sisters (or Ladies) of the Liberal Arts" will also yield images of Rhetorica.

3. See Swearingen (1991, 227–28) for a more detailed catalogue of Rhetorica's incarnations through rhetorical history.

INTRODUCTION

1. The image of Rhetorica on the cover of *Reclaiming Rhetorica,* edited by Andrea Lunsford, is a plate from *Die Tarocchi,* the tarot, of Rhetorica XXIII, attributed to the painter Mantegna. It depicts a queen with a sword and two heralds.

2. See also the "Transnational Feminist Rhetorics" special issue of *College English,* which contains essays by Hesford and Schell (2008, 461–60), Queen (2008, 471–89), Dingo (2008, 490–505), Kulbaga (2008, 506–21), Bahri (2008, 522–28), and Min-Zhan Lu (2008, 529–34).

3. For a useful survey of the history of feminist rhetorics in communication studies, see "Feminist Perspectives in Rhetorical Studies: A History" in Foss, Foss, and Griffin 1999.

4. Many thanks to Lynn Worsham, who spent hours helping me think through the challenges and opportunities of feminist research.

5. See also the introduction to *Feminism and Methodology* where Sandra Harding argues that there is not a "distinctive feminist method of research," but three distinctive features of feminist research: a "[r]ecognition of the im-

portance of using women's experience as resources for social analysis" with the proviso that there is no universal woman and that "class, race, and culture" are "always categories within gender" (1987, 7); a focus on the idea that feminist inquiry has the goal of "provid[ing] for women explanations of social phenomena that they want and need" (8); and the idea that the researcher "must be placed in the same critical plane as the subject matter, thereby recovering the entire research process for scrutiny in the results of the research" (9).

6. For more on debates and discussion of feminist research in the social sciences, see DeVault 1999 and Naples 2003.

7. For a useful bibliographic essay on feminist research methodologies that address historical rhetoric, see Tasker and Holt 2008.

8. For a discussion of essentialism in feminist composition studies, see Ritchie 2003 and Looser 1993.

REFIGURING RHETORICA

1. Davis writes, "There is probably no area of contemporary life in which some idea of a norm, mean, or average has not been calculated." Further, "The concept of a norm . . . implies that the majority of the population must or should somehow be part of the norm" and "with the concept of the norm comes the concept of deviations" (1995, 23, 29).

2. Rosemarie Garland-Thomson defines the normate as "the constructed identity of those who, by way of the bodily configurations and cultural capital they assume, can step into a position of authority and wield the power it grants them" (1996a, 8).

3. The British social model of disability focuses on how social barriers and structures disenable; it often separates the idea of impairment (understood at the bodily level) and disability (understood as a social phenomenon). The postmodern approach, which we take here, argues that there is no neat dividing line between nature and culture, bodily impairment and social disability; even what is deemed a bodily impairment is produced in and through cultural norms. Some disability studies scholars approach the body through phenomenology, considering the ways that our bodies, through the process of embodiment, extend into the surrounding environment to include objects (Iwakuma 2002, 79) and receive corporeal reinforcement from others (Price and Shildrick 2002). Prosthetic and cyborg theories, while differently founded, both challenge the idea of a simple divide between a "natural" and artificially supplemented body (Wills 1995, Serlin 2004). Other postmodern approaches see the body as materialized through discourses such as Foucault's biopower (Tremain 2005, Price and Shildrick 2002) and extend Butler's theory of performativity of sex/gender to include the performativity of ability/disability (Kuppers 2003).

4. Elizabeth Grosz explains how the disabled body, through the "defiance of the structure of binary oppositions that govern [us] . . . confirms the viewer as

bounded, belonging to a 'proper' social category." Disability becomes "all that must be ejected or abjected from self-image to make the bounded, category-obeying self possible" (1996, 57, 65).

5. Haraway writes: "This self-invisibility is the specifically modern, European, masculine, scientific form of the virtue of modesty. This is the form of modesty that pays off its practitioners in the coin of epistemological and social power." Freed "from his biasing embodiment" this modest witness "is endowed with the remarkable power to establish the facts" (1997, 23–24).

6. Shelley Tremain provides a Foucauldian analysis of this process of medicalization: "The modern body was created as the effect and object of medical examination.... The doctor's patient had come to be treated in a way that had at one time been conceivable only with cadavers. The passivity of this object resulted from the procedure of clinical examination, where the investigative gaze fixed and crystallized as 'the body' that which it perceived" (2002, 35).

7. See the Web site of the Disability History Museum, "Disability History Museum Library," http://www.disabilitymuseum.org/lib/?c.

8. Krista Ratcliffe's "rhetoric of listening" (2005) or Cheryl Glenn's "rhetoric of silence" (2004) might be two examples of alternative senses serving to suggest alternative ways of knowing and making meaning.

9. Vivian May and Beth Ferri write that many leading feminist thinkers respond to the attribution of physical and mental inferiority to women by dismantling the false construction of woman-as-disabled without challenging the construction of disability as a biological fact. They argue that "by definitively asserting that women are not disabled by their sex, many feminists have simply replaced one subject-object dualism (male vs. female) with another: woman vs. disability" (2005, 120).

10. We realize, of course, that not all students with disabilities might self-disclose because of perceived stigmas, but the next iteration of the survey will include this category/label.

11. The disability studies critique of normativity also has potentially important contributions to make to debates about standards, standardized testing, and other assessment issues in composition and rhetoric. We cannot in this space develop this line of critique, but merely note that the focus on "standards" in the teaching of writing has always centered on error (error within writing, but more importantly located within specific groups of writers), not on rhetorical fluency. Further, the history of composition as a sorting-gate course, as a means of remediation, with cultural and corporeal biases fused to such functions, lead us to believe that this history can be read as a legacy of norming and making abnormal. Histories of composition therefore never fail to turn up disability metaphors, institutional processes of gazing and enfreakment, and intersecting oppressions grounded in perceptions of lack and defect. Further attention to these trends is necessary.

I would like to thank the following people for their feedback: Lois Agnew, Margaret Himley, and especially Eileen Schell, whose extensive comments transformed this into a chapter.

1. Credit is due, of course, to Judith Butler's work, especially her ground-breaking *Gender Trouble* (1999), which provides the groundwork for theorizing gender in this way. I will not restate her argument here, but suffice it to say that Butler's work is pandemic to any gender analysis and theorizing that I do in this chapter.

2. A short list of this work includes: Glenn (1997), Logan (1999), Lunsford (1995), Mattingly (2000), Royster (2000), and Wertheimer (1997).

3. It is worth noting that this problem is not only faced by feminist rhetoricians, but plagues much historical recovery work—identity categories are rarely as fixed as we create them in retrospective scholarship.

4. Stryker (2008, 22) offers the following definition of cisgender: "the prefix *cis*- means 'on the same side as' (that is, the opposite of *trans*) . . . 'cisgendered' or 'cissexual' names the usually unstated assumption of nontransgender status contained in the words 'man' and 'woman.'"

5. To offer brief contextualization: Patrick Califia is an activist, sex radical, and author of *Sex Changes: The Politics of Transgenderism* (1997) and many other works; Mark Anthony Neal is a black male feminist academic and author of the important feminist work *New Black Man: Rethinking Black Masculinity* (2005); John (Radclyffe) Hall is the author of *The Well of Loneliness* (1990) who lived openly as an "invert" in the early twentieth century.

6. Again, to offer brief contextualization of these writers/activists: Leslie Feinberg is the author of several books including *Stone Butch Blues* (1993) and *TransLiberation: Beyond the Pink and Blue* (1998); Kate Bornstein is the author of *Gender Outlaw: On Men, Women, and the Rest of Us* (1994) and other books; Emi Koyama hosts the Web site www.eminism.org, which has a vast amount of resources examining the connections between transgender/transsexuality and feminism; Virginia Prince is a longtime transgender activist who is credited with coining the term *transgenderist*, the precedent to *transgender*.

7. For those who are unfamiliar, "sie" or "ze" is a gender-neutral pronoun that grammatically replaces he or she. The other commonly used gender-neutral pronoun is "hir," which replaces him or her.

8. For a book-length extrapolation of this claim, see Prosser 1998, which explores the tropes of transsexual narratives and would provide interesting inroads to transgender theory for rhetorical scholars.

9. For further introduction to transgender theory, see Bornstein 1994, Feinberg 1998, Wilchins 2004.

1. Among the other excursions represented are: a trip to Ciudad Juárez, Mexico, to address the murders of women, especially maquiladora workers, in the Juárez desert; a 1994 trip to Bedford Hills Correctional Facility, where she worked with female inmates and where child molestation emerged as a common experience among the incarcerated women; a visit to Sri Lanka in 2004 after the tsunami in which she explores grief; a trip to New Orleans nine months after Hurricane Katrina; and an interview with anti-Iraq war activist Cindy Sheehan.

2. I use the term *context* as a broader framing term that encompasses historical context, cultural context, and political climate. My use of the term *public sphere* retains its correlation with acts of communication. Thus the terms *context* and the *public sphere* are not interchangeable.

3. Social theorists use the term *opportunity structures* in ways that parallel rhetoricians' use of the term kairos. Similar to the methodology of Kirk and Sikkink, my methodological emphasis on social, cultural, and political frames shares concerns with constructionists in international relations theory and social movement theory.

4. See, for example, Bahir 2004, Hesford and Kulbaga 2003, Hesford 2006, Lu 2004, Schell 2006, and Hesford and Schell 2008, especially the essays by Rebecca Dingo, Theresa Kulbaga, and Mary Queen.

5. Biemann indicated to me that she is narrating, but she also noted, "it's not one authorial voice, it's many theoretical voices that speak through me, not that I'm merely quoting, but it's all shared knowledge somehow." Biemann's intentions were expressed to me in personal correspondence from 2008. All of the direct quotes and statements from Biemann in this chapter are drawn from that correspondence.

6. For further discussion of Biemann's construction of gender in transnational spaces see Berelowitz 2001, Biemann 2000.

GROWING ROUTES

1. The conversations and e-mails I exchanged with the following individuals contributed to this work: Thi Kieu Trang Hoang (January 2005–September 2007); Thi Thu Chung Le (January–September 2007); Khanh Chi Nguyen (January 2005–September 2007); Tu Mai Dinh (February 2007); Nguyen Tuan (February 2007), Kim Tran (June–September 2007).

1. This question is made more complicated given the various conversations about the status of rhetorical studies, identified by some as interdisciplinary, even pan-disciplinary.

2. I don't mean to belittle Royster's point that as an African American woman, she must find her way into a collection that leaves this group out. Instead, I mean to emphasize that we must all, as researchers, find ways into our research.

3. For the collections that formed the basis of my study, see Campbell 1989, Lunsford 1995, Phelps and Emig 1995, Logan 1995, Wertheimer 1997, Ritchie and Ronald 2001, and *Rhetoric Society Quarterly's* special issues in feminist historiography in rhetoric, edited by Susan Jarratt in 1992 and Patricia Bizzell in 2002.

4. It was at this point that I started shaping my choice of readings, ruling out the body of texts that focused primarily on composition pedagogy and feminism since I felt comfortable with my understanding of feminist composition pedagogy and since rhetorical studies wasn't always an explicit part of these texts—though Ronald and Ritchie 2006 is an example of composition pedagogy and feminist rhetorical studies coming together explicitly. Also, it was simply a practical way to focus my research topically.

5. Dialogic exchange in the feminist rhetorics community is evidenced by acknowledgments to collections, conferences like Feminism(s) and Rhetoric(s), organizations like the Coalition of Women Scholars in the History of Rhetoric, and my observations of the privileging of community and dialogue in the framing texts of edited collections.

RHETORICS OF POSSIBILITY

1. With Flores's help, this work was published as "In Our Own Image?!: A Rhetorical Criticism of *Latina Magazine*" (Calafell 2001).

2. I am grateful to Davis as well as to Marsha Houston for introducing me to black feminist and womanist perspectives. I am also indebted to Davis for demonstrating to me the possibilities of a woman of color challenging the rhetorical canon by locating our space in it, as well as modeling the possibilities of bringing together performance and rhetorical studies as a space of potential.

3. Literature about Malintzin by Chicana feminist writers includes, but is not limited to, Alarcón 1981, Blea 1992, Castillo 1994, Cota-Cardenas 2000, and del Castillo 1977. For examples of literature about Malintzin by others, see Anaya 1984, Díaz de Castillo 1956, and Paz 1961.

4. The texts I later chose to examine included, for example, the photograph book *Americanos: Latino Life in the United States*. See Calafell and Delgado 2004.

5. For examples of performance scholars, see Conquergood 1991, Madison

1998 and 1999, and Corey 1998 and 2006. For examples of rhetoric scholars, see Ono and Sloop 1995. For examples of feminists of color, see Moraga 1983, Anzaldúa 2002, Collins 2000, and Christian 1990.

MINING THE COLLECTIVE UNCONSCIOUS

1. All information in this chapter about the details of the life of "Fontia R." are taken from case file #133 in the Hannan Foundation Archives, Walter P. Reuther Library, Wayne State University.

2. Just before this article went to press, Gesa E. Kirsch and Liz Rohan published *Beyond the Archives: Research as a Lived Process* (2008), which addresses the role of serendipity, location, personal connections of researchers and their research subjects, and politics with the processes of archival research.

RESEARCHING LITERACY AS A LIVED EXPERIENCE

1. Hauser, Chomsky, and Fitch define the faculty of language "in the broad sense (FLB) . . . [to] include a sensory-motor system, a conceptual system, a conceptual-intentional system, and the computational mechanisms for recursion, providing the capacity to generate an infinite range of expressions from a finite set of elements" with the later being the only uniquely human component (2002, 1569).

2. In the 1970s, standpoint theorists were concerned primarily with the social sciences and since then have become increasingly concerned with the natural sciences.

RHETORICA ONLINE

1. Issues of publication (e.g., working with avatars, preserving anonymity, protecting a community, etc.) have also become increasingly complex for those studying online environments, but given space constraints we do not discuss those issues in this chapter.

2. This larger study is titled *The Ethics of Internet Research: A Rhetorical, Case-Based Process* (McKee and Porter, forthcoming). In another work, we stated: "By 'digital writing research' we mean research that focuses on (1) computer-generated, computer-based, and/or computer-delivered documents; (2) computer-based text production; and (3) the interactions of people who use computerized technologies to communicate through digital means" (McKee and Porter 2008, 739).

3. The three researchers cited in this chapter were interviewed either face-to-face or online via Skype between March 2006 and February 2007. All interviews were conducted in English, although English is not the first-language for Janne Bromseth (Norwegian) or Yukari Seko (Japanese). All three granted us

permission to use their real names. All statements by these researchers in this chapter are derived from these interviews, unless otherwise attributed.

4. For further discussion of ethical qualities for cyber-researchers, see De-Pew 2007; Hine 2000; Sapienza 2007; Smith 2007; Porter 1998; and Sullivan and Porter 1997.

5. When Amy Bruckman (2001) queried the National Endowment for the Humanities (NEH) to determine their guidelines for human subjects approval, she received this response: "Multiple mid- and senior-level NEH officers I emailed and spoke with all said the same thing: the NEH has always interpreted the human subjects regulations as not applying to them. (All asked not to be named or directly quoted.)" (12).

6. Not all online communities are as cohesive and as connected as the online group that Bromseth researched. Some online spaces, such the virtual world Second Life, and multiplayer online games, such as *World of Warcraft*, are massive, sprawling, ever-changing communities with thousands or even millions of participants. For someone conducting research in these massive online worlds, issues of informed consent are complicated further because of the virtual, role-playing nature of the worlds (see McKee and Porter, forthcoming).

7. Canada's code of ethics is governed by the Tri-Council Policy Statement Ethical Conduct for Research Involving Humans, MRC, NSERC, SSHRC, 1998. In the United States, the Code of Federal Regulations (45CFR46) is similar.

8. For a more extensive discussion of researcher ethos in online communities, see Sapienza 2007. Sapienza analyzes researcher and participant relations when conducting participant observer ethnographies of online communities. Drawing from his experience in the transnational community "Virtual Russia," Sapienza focuses on three overlapping and interrelated roles that researchers may be called on to assume: the role of technologist, the role of participant (insider), and the role of scholar.

9. In her interview with us in 2006, Yukari Seko explained that since the "net group suicide" in Japan, Internet service providers have been strongly encouraged to report any user who posts suicidal intentions to public authorities.

WRITING AS FEMINIST RHETORICAL THEORY

1. See Sara Ahmed's fascinating discussion of *orientation* and *being orientated* in *Queer Phenomenology* (2006). For example, in her introduction, she writes, "orientations involve different ways of registering the proximity of objects and others. Orientations shape not only how we inhabit space, but how we apprehend this world of shared inhabitance, as well as 'who' or 'what' we direct our energy and attention toward" (3).

2. The longer project related to this chapter explores further the significance of feminist thought for composition by extrapolating concepts of writing

usable in first-year writing classrooms from feminist rhetorical theories. While feminist scholarship in composition and rhetoric has proven instrumental in redirecting thinking about writing, gender, and other categories of identity, it has not produced an explicit theory of writing inflected by feminist principles, a major goal of my study.

3. Thanks to my colleague Kathy Rentz for passing along this irreverent and instructive essay. Also, I benefited greatly from the wise and generous responses to an earlier draft offered by Jonathan Alexander, Russel Durst, and Lucille Schultz.

References

Addison, Joanne, and Susan Hilligoss. 1999. Technological fronts: Lesbian lives "on-the-line." In *Feminist cyberscapes: Mapping gendered academic spaces,* ed. Pamela Takahashi and Kristine Blair, 21–40. Stamford: Ablex.

Addison, Joanne, and Sharon James McGee, eds. 1999. *Feminist empirical research: Emerging perspectives on qualitative and teacher research.* Portsmouth, NH: Boynton/Cook.

Ahmed, Sara. 2004. *The cultural politics of emotion.* New York: Routledge.

———. 2006. *Queer phenomenology: Orientations, objects, others.* Durham: Duke Univ. Press.

Alarcón, Norma. 1981. Chicana feminist literature: A revision through Malintzin/or Malintzin: Putting flesh back on the object. In Moraga and Anzaldúa, 1981, 182–90.

Alcoff, Linda Martín. 1991–92. The problem of speaking for others. *Cultural Critique* 20:5–32.

———. 2003. Introduction. In *Singing in the fire: Stories of women in philosophy,* ed. Linda Martín Alcoff, 1–14. Lanham, MD: Rowman & Littlefield.

Alcoff, Linda Martín, and Satya P. Mohanty. 2006. Reconsidering identity politics: An introduction. In *Identity politics reconsidered,* ed. Linda Martín Alcoff, Michael Hames-Garcia, Satya P. Mohanty, and Paula M. L. Moya, 1–9. New York: Palgrave.

Alexander, Jacqui. 2005. *Pedagogies of crossing: Meditations on feminism, sexual politics, memory, and the sacred.* Durham: Duke Univ. Press.

Anaya, Rudolfo. 1984. *The legend of La Llorona.* Berkeley: Tonatiuh-Quinto Sol International.

Angier, Natalie. 1999. *Woman: An intimate geography.* Boston: Houghton Mifflin.

Anzaldúa, Gloria. 1999. *Borderlands/La frontera: The new mestiza.* 2nd ed. San Francisco: Aunt Lute Books.

———. 2002. Now let us shift . . . the path of *conocimento* . . . Inner work, public acts. In *This bridge we call home: Radical visions for transformation,* ed. Gloria Anzaldúa and Ana Louise Keating, 540–78. New York: Routledge.

Arendt, Hannah. 1963. *On revolution*. New York: Viking Press.

Aristotle. 1926. *Nicomachean ethics*. Trans. H. Rackham. Loeb Classical Library. Cambridge, MA: Harvard Univ. Press.

Association of Internet Researchers (Ethics Working Committee). 2002. *Ethical decision-making and internet research: Recommendations from the AOIR ethics working committee*. November 27. http://www.aoir.org/reports/ethics .pdf.

Atwill, Janet M. 1998. *Rhetoric reclaimed: Aristotle and the liberal arts tradition*. Ithaca: Cornell Univ. Press.

———. 2002. Introduction: Finding a Home or Making a Path. In Atwill and Lauer 2002, xi-xxi.

Atwill, Janet M., and Janice M. Lauer, eds. 2002. *Perspectives on rhetorical invention*. Knoxville: Univ. of Tennessee Press.

Bahri, Deepika. 2004. Terms of engagement: Postcolonialism, transnationalism, and composition studies. In *Crossing borderlands: Composition and postcolonial studies*, ed. Andrea Lunsford and Lahoucine Ouzgane, 67–83. Pittsburgh: Univ. of Pittsburgh Press.

———. 2008. Response: A world of difference. *College English* 70 (5): 522–27.

Ballif, Michelle.1992. Re/dressing histories: Or, on recovering figures who have been laid bare by our gaze. *Rhetoric Society Quarterly* 22 (1): 91–99.

Barnard, Ian. 2004. *Queer race: Cultural interventions in the racial politics of queer theory*. New York: Peter Lang.

Barthes, Roland. 1988. The old rhetoric: An *aide-mémoire*. In *The semiotic challenge*. Trans. Richard Howard, 11–93. New York: Hill and Wang.

Bassett, E. H., and Kathleen O'Riordan. 2001. Ethics of internet research: Contesting the human subjects research model. In *Internet research ethics*. http:// www.nyu.edu/projects/nissenbaum/ethics_bassett.html.

Baumlin, James. 2005. Rereading/misreading Jung: Post-Jungian theory. *College Literature* 32:177–86.

Bawarshi, Anis S. 2003. *Genre and the invention of the writer: Reconsidering the place of invention in composition*. Logan: Utah State Univ. Press.

Baxandall, Rosalyn F., and Linda Gordon, eds. 2000. *Dear sisters: Dispatches from the women's liberation movement*. New York: Basic Books.

Baynton, Douglas C. 1997. Bringing disability to the center: Disability as an indispensable category of historical analysis. *Disability Studies Quarterly* 1 (Summer): n.p.

Berelowitz, Jo-Anne. 2001. A journey shared: Ursula Biemann's *Been there and back to nowhere:* Gender in transnational spaces. *Genders* 33:1–7.

Berlo, Janet Catherine. Quilting to save my life. *Chronicle of Higher Education,* March 30, 2001, B11–B13.

Berthoff, Ann. 1982. *The Making of Meaning*. Montclair, NJ: Boynton-Cook.

Biemann, Ursula. 2000. *Been there and back to nowhere: Gender in transnational space: Postproduction documents 1988–2000*. Berlin: b books.

———. 2001a. Female geobodies: Resignifying the economic within sexual difference. *n.paradoxa* (July):1–6.

———. 2001b. dir. *Remote sensing: experimental documentary*. Digital video. Women Make Movies.

———. 2001c. dir. *Writing desire*. Digital video. Women Make Movies.

———. 2004. Remotely sensed: A topography of the global sex trade. *Feminist Review* 70 (2002): 75–88.

Biesecker, Barbara. 1992. Coming to terms with recent attempts to write women into the history of rhetoric. *Philosophy and Rhetoric* 25 (2): 140–61.

Bizzell, Patricia. 1992. Opportunities for feminist research in the history of rhetoric. *Rhetoric Review* 11 (1): 50–58.

———. 1997. Foreword. In *Constructing knowledges: The politics of theory-building and pedagogy in composition,* by Sidney Dobrin, 1–4. Albany: SUNY Press.

———. ed. 2002. Feminist historiography in rhetoric. Special issue, *Rhetoric Society Quarterly* 32 (1).

———. 2003. Feminist methods of research in the history of rhetoric: What difference do they make? In Kirsch, Maor, Massey, Nickoson-Massey, Sheridan–Rabideau 2003, 194–205.

Bizzell, Patricia, and Bruce Herzberg, eds. 2001. *The rhetorical tradition: Readings from classical times to the present*. 2nd ed. Boston: Bedford/St. Martins.

Blair, Carole, Julie R. Brown, and Leslie A. Baxter. 1994. Disciplining the feminine. *Quarterly Journal of Speech* 80:383–409.

Blakeslee, Ann M., Caroline M. Cole, and Theresa Conefrey. 1996. Constructing voices in writing research: Developing participatory approaches to situated inquiry. In Mortensen and Kirsch 1996, 134–54.

Blea, Irene I. 1992. *La chicana and the intersections of race, class and gender*. New York: Praeger.

Bloom, Harold. 1994. *The Western canon: The books and schools of the ages*. New York: Harcourt.

Bornstein, Kate. 1994. *Gender outlaw: On men, women, and the rest of us*. New York: Vintage.

Bourdain, Anthony. 2001. *A cook's tour: Global adventures in extreme cuisine*. New York: HarperCollins.

Brandt, Deborah. 2001. *Literacy in American lives*. Cambridge: Cambridge Univ. Press.

Bromseth, Janne C. H. 2006. Genre trouble and the body that mattered: Negotiations of gender, sexuality and identity in a Scandinavian mailing list community for lesbian and bisexual women. PhD diss., Norwegian Univ. of Science and Technology.

Bruckman, Amy. 2001. Studying the amateur artist: A perspective on disguising data collected in human subjects research on the Internet. In *Internet research ethics*. http://www.nyu.edu/projects/nissenbaum/ethics_bruckman.html.

———. 2002. Ethical guidelines for research online. http://www.cc.gatech
.edu/-asb/ethics.

Buchanan, Elizabeth A., ed. 2004. *Readings in virtual research ethics: Issues and controversies*. Hershey, PA: Information Science Publishing.

Buchanan, Lindal. 2005. *Regendering delivery: The fifth canon and antebellum women
rhetors*. Carbondale: Southern Illinois Univ. Press.

Buell, Frederick. 1994. *National culture and the new global system*. Baltimore: Johns
Hopkins Univ. Press.

Butler, Judith. 1993. *Bodies that matter: On the discursive limits of "sex."* New York:
Routledge.

———. 1999. *Gender trouble: Feminism and the subversion of identity*. New York:
Routledge.

Calafell, Bernadette Marie. 2001. In our own image?!: A rhetorical criticism
of *Latina Magazine*. *Voces: A Journal of Chicana and Latina Studies* 3 (1–2):
12–46.

———. 2005. Pro(re-)claiming loss: A performative pilgrimage in search of Malintzin Tenépal. *Text and Performance Quarterly* 25:43–56.

———. 2007a. *Latina/o communication studies: Theorizing performance*. New York:
Peter Lang.

———. 2007b. Mentoring and love: An open letter. *Cultural Studies Critical
Methodologies* 7:425–41.

Calafell, Bernadette Marie, and Fernando Delgado. 2004. Reading Latina/o
images: Interrogating Americanos. *Critical Studies in Media Communication*
21:1–21.

Calhoun, Cheshire. 1992. Emotional work. In Cole and Coultrap-McQuin 1992,
117–24.

Califia, Patrick. 2003. *Sex changes: The politics of transgenderism*. 2nd ed. San Francisco: Cleis Press.

Campbell, Karlyn Kohrs. 1973. The rhetoric of women's liberation: An oxymo-
ron. *Quarterly Journal of Speech* 59: 74–87.

———. 1989. *Man cannot speak for her: A critical study of early feminist rhetoric*.
2 vols. New York: Greenwood Press.

———. 1993. Biesecker cannot speak for her either. *Philosophy and Rhetoric* 26
(2): 153–59.

———. 2001. Rhetorical feminism. *Rhetoric Review* 20 (1–2): 9–12.

———. 2002. Consciousness raising: Linking theory, criticism, and practice.
RSQ 32 (1): 45–64.

Castillo, Ana. 1994. *Massacre of the dreamers: Essays on Xicanisma*. Albuquerque:
Univ. of New Mexico Press.

Cherryholmes, Cleo H. 1999. *Reading pragmatism*. Vol. 24 of *Advances in contemporary educational thought*. New York: Teachers College Press.

Chodorow, Joan, ed. 1997. *Jung on active imagination*. Princeton: Princeton Univ.
Press.

Christian, Barbara. 1990. The race for theory. In *Making face, making soul: Haciendo caras*, ed. Gloria Anzaldúa, 335–45. San Francisco: Aunt Lute.

Cisneros, Sandra. 1989. *The house on mango street*. New York: Vintage Books.

Cixous, Hélène. 1991. The laugh of the medusa. In *Feminisms: An anthology of literary theory and criticism*, ed. Robyn Warhol and Diane Price Herndl, 334–49. New Brunswick: Rutgers Univ. Press.

Clare, Eli. 2003. Gawking, gaping, staring. *GLQ* 9 (1–2): 257–61.

Clark, Donald Lemen. 1957. *Rhetoric in Greco-Roman education*. New York: Columbia Univ. Press.

Clifford, James. 1988. *The predicament of culture: Twentieth-century ethnography, literature, and art*. Cambridge: Harvard Univ. Press.

———. 1991. Traveling cultures. In *Cultural studies*, ed. Lawrence Grossberg, Cary Nelson, and Paula A. Treichler, 96–111. New York and London: Routledge.

Code, Lorraine. 1991. *What can she know? Feminist theory and the construction of knowledge*. Ithaca: Cornell Univ. Press.

Cole, Eve Browning, and Susan Coultrap-McQuin, eds. 1992. *Explorations in feminist ethics: theory and practice*. Bloomington: Indiana Univ. Press.

Collins, Patricia Hill. 2000. *Black feminist thought: Knowledge, consciousness, and the politics of empowerment*. New York: Routledge.

Conference on College Composition and Communication. 2003. Guidelines for the ethical conduct of research in composition studies. CCCC position statement. http://www.ncte.org/cccc/resources/positions/ethicalconduct.

Conquergood, Dwight. 1991. Rethinking ethnography: Towards a critical cultural politics. *Communication Monographs* 59:179–94.

———. 2002. Performance studies: Interventions and radical research. *Drama Review* 46:145–56.

Corey, Frederick C. 1998. The personal: Against the master narrative. In *The future of performance studies: Visions and revisions*, ed. Sheron J. Dailey, 249–53. Annandale, VA: National Communication Association.

———. 2006. On possibility. *Text and performance quarterly* 26:330–32.

Corker, Mairian, and Tom Shakespeare, eds. 2002. *Disability/postmodernity: Embodying political theory*. London: Continuum.

Cota-Cardenas, Margarita. 2000. *Puppet: A Chicano novella*. Albuquerque: Univ. of New Mexico Press.

Couser, G. Thomas. 2001. Conflicting paradigms: The rhetorics of disability memoir. In *Embodied rhetorics: Disability in language and culture*, ed. James C. Wilson and Cynthia Lewiecki-Wilson, 78–91. Carbondale: Southern Illinois Univ. Press.

———. 2004. *Vulnerable subjects: Ethics and life-writing*. Ithaca: Cornell Univ. Press.

Crawford, Ilene. 2005. Playing in traffic: A timely metaphor for postmodern ethnography and composition studies. *Composition Studies* 33 (2): 11–23.

———. 2007. The emotional effects of literacy: Vietnamese women negotiating the shift to a market economy. In *Women and literacy: Inquiries for a new century*, ed. Beth Daniell and Peter Mortenson, 229–42. New York: Routledge.

Crow, Barbara A., ed. 2000. *Radical feminism: A documentary reader*. New York: New York Univ. Press.

Crowley, Sharon. 1999. Afterword: The material of rhetoric. In *Rhetorical bodies*, ed. Jack Selzer and Sharon Crowley, 357–66. Madison: Univ. of Wisconsin Press.

Crowley, Sharon, and Debra Hawhee. 2004. *Ancient rhetorics for contemporary students*. 3rd ed. New York: Pearson Longman.

Cubbison, Laurie. 2000. Validating illness: Internet activism in response to institutional discourse. PhD diss., Purdue University.

Currah, Paisley, Richard M. Juang, and Shannon Price Minter, eds. 2006. *Transgender rights*. Minneapolis: Univ. of Minnesota Press.

D'Angelo, Frank J. 1984. The evolution of the analytic *topoi*: A speculative inquiry. In *Essays of classical rhetoric and modern discourse*, ed. Robert K. Connors, Lisa S. Ede, and Andrea A. Lunsford, 50–68. Carbondale: Southern Illinois Univ. Press.

Davis, Lennard J. 1995. *Enforcing normalcy: Disability, deafness, and the body*. New York: Verso.

Davis, Olga. 1998. A black woman as rhetorical critic: Validating self and validating the space of otherness. *Women's Studies in Communication* 21:77–89.

del Castillo, Adelaida R. 1977. Malintzin Tenepal: A preliminary look into a new perspective. In *Essays on La mujer*, ed. Rosaura Sanchez and Rosa Martinez Cruz, 124–49. Los Angeles: Chicano Studies Center.

Delgado, Fernando. 1997. The dilemma of the minority scholar: Finding a (legitimized) voice in an intellectual space. In *Conference proceedings of the National Communication Association's 1997 summer conference on racial and ethnic diversity in the 21st century: A communication perspective*. National Communication Association.

———. 1998. When the silenced speak: The textualization and complications of Latina/o identity. *Western Journal of Communication* 62:420–38.

DePew, Kevin. 2007. Through the eyes of researchers, rhetors, and audiences: Triangulating data from the digital writing situation. In McKee and DeVoss 2007, 49–69.

DeVault, Marge. 1999. *Liberating method: Feminism and social research*. Philadelphia: Temple Univ. Press.

Dewey, John. 1997. *Experience and Education*. 1938. New York: Touchstone.

Díaz de Castillo, Bernal. 1956. *The discovery and conquest of Mexico 1517–1521*. Trans. A. P. Maudslay. New York: Farrar, Straus, and Cudahy.

Dingo, Rebecca. 2008. Linking transnational logics: A feminist rhetorical analysis of public policy networks. *College English* 70 (5): 490–505.

Dobrin, Sidney I. 1997. *Constructing knowledges: The politics of theory-building and pedagogy in composition*. Albany: SUNY Press.

Dolmage, Jay. 2005a. Between the valley and the field: Metaphor and the construction of disability. *Prose Studies* 27 (1): 108–19.

———. 2005b. Disability studies pedagogy, usability and universal design. *Disability Studies Quarterly* 25 (4). http://www.dsq-sds-archives.org/_articles_html/2005/fall/dolmage.asp.

———. 2006. Breathe upon us an even flame: Hephaestus, history and the body of rhetoric. *Rhetoric Review* 25 (2): 119–40.

———. 2007. Disabled upon arrival: Difference as defect. Paper presented at the Conference on College Composition and Communication, March, New York, NY.

———. 2008. Mapping composition: Inviting disability in the front door. In Lewiecki-Wilson, Brueggemann, and Dolmage 2008, 14–27.

———. 2009. Metis, metis, Medusa, mestiza: Rhetorical bodies across rhetorical traditions. *Rhetoric Review* 28 (1): 1–28.

———. 2009 (forthcoming). Disability, usability and universal design. In *Rhetorically Re-Thinking Usability*, ed. Shelley Rodrigo and Susan Miller, 167–90. New York: Hampton Press.

Donawerth, Jane, ed. 2002. *Rhetorical theory by women before 1900: An anthology*. Lanham, MD: Rowman & Littlefield.

Downey, John K. 2003. Suffering as common ground. In *Constructing human rights in the age of globalization*, ed. Mahmood Monshipouri, Neil Englehart, Andrew J. Nathan, and Kavita Philip, 308–28. New York: M. E. Sharpe.

Ensler, Eve. 2006. *Insecure at last: Losing it in our security obsessed world*. New York: Villard.

Ess, Charles. 2001. Introduction. In *Internet research ethics*. http://www.nyu.edu/projects/nissenbaum/ethics_ess.html.

Ess, Charles, and the Association of Internet Researchers. 2002. Ethical decision making and Internet research. http://aoir.org/reports/ethics.pdf.

Eyerman, Ron. 2001. *Cultural Trauma: Slavery and the formation of African American identity*. New York: Cambridge Univ. Press.

Fahnestock, Jeanne, and Marie Secor. 2002. Rhetorical analysis. In *Discourse studies in composition*, ed. Ellen Barton and Gail Stygall, 177–200. Cresskill, NJ: Hampton Press.

Feinberg, Leslie. 1993. *Stone butch blues*. Ithaca, NY: Firebrand Books.

———. 1998. *TransLiberation: Beyond the pink and blue*. Boston: Beacon.

Fetterley, Judith. 1981. *The Resisting Reader: A feminist approach to american fiction*. Bloomington: Indiana Univ. Press.

Fine, Michelle. 1994. Working the hyphens: Reinventing self and other in qualitative research. In *Handbook of qualitative research*, ed. Norman K. Denzin and Yvonna S. Lincoln, 70-82. Thousand Oaks, CA: Sage.

Flores, Lisa A. 1996. Creating discursive space through a rhetoric of difference:

Chicana feminists craft a homeland. *Quarterly Journal of Speech* 82:142–56.

Flynn, Elizabeth. 1988. Composing as a woman. *College Composition and Communication* 47:423–35.

Fonow, Mary Margaret, and Judith A. Cook, eds. 1991. *Beyond methodology: Feminist scholarships as lived research.* Bloomington: Indiana Univ. Press.

———. 2005. Feminist methodology: New applications in the academy and public policy. *Signs: Journal of Women in Culture and Society* 30: 2211–36.

Foss, Karen A., Sonja K. Foss, and Cindy L. Griffin. 1999. *Feminist rhetorical theories.* Thousand Oaks, CA: Sage Publications.

———. 2004. *Readings in feminist rhetorical theory.* Thousand Oaks, CA: Sage Publications.

Foss, Sonja. 2004. *Rhetorical criticism.* 3rd ed. Long Grove, IL: Waveland Press.

Foss, Sonja, and Cindy Griffin. 1995. Beyond persuasion: A proposal for an invitational rhetoric. *Communication Monographs* 62:2–18.

Foucault, Michel. 1990. *The history of sexuality.* Vol. 1. Trans. Robert Hurley. New York: Vintage.

Fox, Ellen L. 1992. Seeing through women's eyes: The role of vision in women's moral theory. In Cole and Coultrap-McQuin 1992, 111–16.

Fox Keller, Evelyn. 1985. *Reflections on gender and science.* New Haven: Yale Univ. Press.

Fox Keller, Evelyn, and Christine R. Grontkowski. 1999. The mind's eye. In *Feminism and science*, ed. Evelyn Fox Keller and Helen E. Longino, 187–202. New York: Oxford Univ. Press.

Frankel, Mark S., and Sunyin Siang. 1999. Ethical and legal aspects of human subjects research in cyberspace: A report of a workshop. American Association for the Advancement of Science. http://www.aaas.org/spp/sfrl/projects/intres/report.pdf.

Fraser, Nancy. 2005. Reframing justice in a globalizing world. *New Left Review* 36:69–88.

Fredal, James. 2006. *Rhetorical action in ancient athens.* Carbondale: Southern Illinois Univ. Press.

Friedman, Susan Stanford. 2001. Locational feminism: Gender, cultural geographies, and geopolitical literacy. In *Feminist locations: Global and local, theory and practice,* ed. Marianne DeKoven, 13–36. New Brunswick: Rutgers Univ. Press.

Freire, Paulo. 1984. *Pedagogy of the Oppressed.* Trans. Myra Bergman Ramos. New York: Continuum.

Frye, Marilyn. 1983. *The politics of reality: Essays in feminist theory.* Trumansburg, NY: Crossing Press.

Fuss, Diana. 1989. *Essentially speaking: Feminism, nature, and difference.* New York: Routledge.

Gale, Xin. 2000. Historical studies and postmodernism: Rereading Aspasia of Miletus. *College English* 62:53–78.

Garland-Thomson, Rosemarie. 1996a. *Extraordinary bodies*. New York: Columbia Univ. Press.

———. 1996b. Introduction: From wonder to error—a genealogy of freak discourse in modernity. In *Freakery: Cultural spectacles of the extraordinary body*, ed. Rosemarie Garland Thomson, 1–19. New York: New York Univ. Press.

———. 2005. Feminist disability studies. *Signs* 30 (2): 1557–87.

Gilligan, Carol. 1982. *In a different voice: Psychological theory and women's development*. Cambridge: Harvard Univ. Press.

Gilman, Charlotte Perkins. [1892] 1997. *"The yellow wallpaper" and other stories*. New York: Dover.

Glenn, Cheryl. 1994. Sex, lies, and manuscript: Refiguring Aspasia in the history of rhetoric. *College Composition and Communication* 45 (2): 180–99.

———. 1995. Remapping rhetorical territory. *Rhetoric Review* 13:287–303.

———. 1997. *Rhetoric retold: Regendering the tradition from antiquity through the renaissance*. Carbondale: Southern Illinois Univ. Press.

———. 2000. Comment: Truth, lies, and method: Revisiting feminist historiography. *College English* 62 (3): 387–89.

———. 2004. *Unspoken: A rhetoric of silence*. Carbondale: Southern Illinois Univ. Press.

Goggin, Maureen Daly. 1995. The disciplinary instability of composition. In *Reconceiving writing, rethinking writing instruction*, ed. Joseph Petraglia, 27–48. Mahwah, NJ: LEA.

Gorzelsky, Gwen. 2005. *The language of experience: Literate practices and social change*. Pittsburgh: Univ. of Pittsburgh Press.

Gowaty, Patricia. 2003. Sexual natures: How feminism changed evolutionary biology. *Signs: Journal of Women in Culture and Society* 28 (3): 901–22.

Greene, Graham. [1955] 1977. *The quiet American*. Penguin.

Grewal, Inderpal. 2005. *Transnational America: Feminisms, diasporas, neoliberalisms*. Durham: Duke Univ. Press.

Grewal, Inderpal, and Caren Kaplan. 2000. Postcolonial studies and transnational feminist practices. *Jouvert* 5 (1). http://english.chass.ncsu.edu/jouvert/v5i1/grewal.htm.

Grosz, Elizabeth. 1994. *Volatile bodies: Toward a corporeal feminism*. Bloomington: Indiana Univ. Press.

———. 1996. Intolerable ambiguity. In *Freakery: Cultural spectacles of the extraordinary body*, ed. Rosemarie Garland Thomson, 55–68. New York: New York Univ. Press.

Gupta, Akhil, and James Ferguson. 1997. Beyond 'culture': Space, identity, and the politics of difference. In *Culture, power, place: Explorations in critical anthropology*, ed. Akhil Gupta and James Ferguson, 33–51. Durham: Duke Univ. Press.

Hall, John Radclyffe. 1990. *The well of loneliness*. New York: Anchor Books.

Hannerz, Ulf. 1990. Cosmopolitans and locals in world culture. *Theory, Culture, and Society* 7:237–51.

Haraway, Donna. 1990. A manifesto for cyborgs: Science, technology, and socialist feminism in the 1980s. In *Feminism/Postmodernism*, ed. Linda J. Nicholson, 190–233. New York: Routledge.

———. 1991. *Simians, cyborgs, and women: The reinvention of nature*. New York: Routledge.

———. 1997. *Modest-witness@second-millennium.Femaleman-meets-oncomouse: Feminism and technoscience*. New York: Routledge.

Harding, Sandra. 1987. Introduction: Is there a feminist method? In *Feminism and methodology: Social science issues*, ed. Sandra Harding, 1–14. Bloomington: Indiana Univ. Press.

Harding, Sandra, and Kathryn Norberg. 2005. New feminist approaches to social science methodologies: An introduction. *Signs: Journal of Women in Culture and Society* 30: 2009–15.

Hartsock, Nancy C. M. 1997. The feminist standpoint: Developing the ground for a specifically feminist materialism. In *The second wave: A reader in feminist theory,* ed. Linda Nicholson, 216–37.

Hauser, Marc, Noam Chomsky, and W. Tecumseh Fitch. 2002. The faculty of language: What is it, who has it, and how did it evolve? *Science* 298 (5598): 1569–79.

Hawhee, Debra. 2005. *Bodily arts*. Austin: Univ. of Texas Press.

Hawisher, Gail E., and Cynthia L. Selfe. 1997. The edited collection: A scholarly contribution and more. In *Publishing in rhetoric and composition*, ed. Gary A. Olson and Todd W. Taylor, 103–18. Albany: SUNY Press.

Hayles, N. Katherine. 1999. *How we became posthuman: Virtual bodies in cybernetics, literature, and informatics*. Chicago: Univ. of Chicago Press.

Held, Virginia. 2004. Care and justice in the global context. *Ratio Juris* 17: 141–55.

Herrington, Anne J. 1993. Reflections on empirical research: Examining some ties between theory and action. In *Theory and practice in the teaching of writing: Rethinking the discipline,* ed. Lee Odell, 40–70. Carbondale: Southern Illinois UP.

Hesford, Wendy S. 2006. Global turns and cautions in rhetoric and composition studies. *PMLA* 121 (3): 787–801.

Hesford, Wendy S., and Theresa Kulbaga. 2003. Labored realisms: Geopolitical rhetoric and Asian American and Asian (im)migrant women's (auto)biography. *JAC* 23 (1): 77–107.

Hesford, Wendy S., and Eileen E. Schell. 2008. Configurations of transnationality: Locating feminist rhetorics. *College English* 70 (5): 461–70.

Hine, Christine. 2000. *Virtual ethnography*. Thousand Oaks, CA: Sage.

Hirsh, Elizabeth, and Gary Olson. 1995. Starting from marginalized lives: A conversation with Sandra Harding. *JAC: A Journal of Composition Theory* 15 (2): 193–225.

Holbrook, Sue Ellen. 1991. Women's work: The feminizing of composition. *Rhetoric Review* 9 (2): 201–29.

Holling, Michelle A., and Bernadette M. Calafell. 2007. Identities on stage and staging identities: *ChicanoBrujo* performances as emancipatory practices. *Text and Performance Quarterly* 27:58–83.

hooks, bell. 1992. *Black looks: Race and representation*. New York: South End Press.

———. 1994. Homeplace: A site of resistance. In *The woman that I am: The literature and culture of contemporary women of color*, ed. D. Soyini Madison, 448–53. New York: St. Martin's Press.

———. 1999. *Remembering rapture: The writer at work*. New York: Owl Books.

———. 2000. *Feminist theory: From margin to center*. 2nd ed. London: Pluto Press.

Horner, Winifred Bryan. 1988. Preface to *Rhetoric in the Classical Tradition*, ed. Winifred Bryan Horner, ix–xii. New York: St. Martin's.

Hudson, James M., and Amy Bruckman. 2004. "Go away": Participant objections to being studied and the ethics of chatroom research. *Information Society* 20:127–39.

Iwakuma, Miho. 2002. The Body as embodiment: An investigation of the body by Merleau-Ponty. In Corker and Shakespeare 2002, 76–87.

Jaggar, Allison. 1983. *Feminist politics and human nature*. Totowa, NJ: Rowman & Allenheld.

Jarratt, Susan C. 1991. *Rereading the Sophists: Classical rhetoric refigured*. Carbondale: Southern Illinois Univ. Press.

———. 1992. Performing feminisms, histories, rhetorics. *Rhetoric Society Quarterly* 22 (1): 1–6.

———. 2000. Comment: Rhetoric and feminism: Together again. *College English* 62:390–93.

———. 2002. Sappho's memory. *Rhetoric Society Quarterly* 32 (1): 11–41.

Jarratt, Susan C., and Rory Ong. 1995. Aspasia: Rhetoric, gender, and colonial ideology. In *Reclaiming Rhetorica: Women in the rhetorical tradition,* ed. Andrea Lunsford, 9–24. Pittsburgh: Univ. of Pittsburgh Press.

Jarratt, Susan C., and Lynn Worsham, eds. 1998. *Feminism and composition studies: In other words*. New York: MLA.

Kant, Immanuel. 1949. *Critique of practical reason and other writings in moral philosophy*. Trans. and ed. Lew White Beck. Chicago: Univ. of Chicago Press.

Kaplan, Caren. 1996. *Questions of travel: Postmodern discourses of displacement*. Durham: Duke Univ. Press.

———. 2001. Hillary Rodham Clinton's orient: Cosmopolitan travel and global feminist subjects. *Meridians* 2 (1): 219–40.

Keck, Margaret E., and Kathryn Sikkink. 1998. *Activists beyond borders: Advocacy networks in international politics*. Ithaca: Cornell Univ. Press.

Kirsch, Gesa E. 1993. *Women writing the academy: Audience, authority and transformation*. Carbondale: Southern Illinois Univ. Press.

———. 1999. *Ethical dilemmas in feminist research: The politics of location, interpretation, and publication*. Albany: SUNY Press.

————. 2005. Friendship, friendliness, and feminist fieldwork. *Signs: Journal of Women in Culture and Society* 30: 2163–72.

Kirsch, Gesa E., and Peter Mortensen. 1996. Introduction. In Mortensen and Kirsch 1996, xix–xxxiv.

Kirsch, Gesa E., and Liz Rohan, eds. 2008. *Beyond the Archives: Research as lived process*. Carbondale, Ill.: Southern Illinois Univ. Press.

Kirsch, Gesa E., and Patricia A. Sullivan, eds. 1992. *Methods and methodology in composition research*. Carbondale: Southern Illinois Univ. Press.

Kirsch, Gesa E., Faye Spencer Maor, Lance Massey, Lee Nickoson-Massey, and Mary P. Sheridan-Rabideau, eds. 2003. *Feminism and composition: A critical sourcebook*. Boston: Bedford/St. Martins.

Kubey, Robert, Reed Larson, and Mihaly Csikszentmihalyi. 1996. Experience sampling method applications to communication research questions. *Journal of Communication* 46 (2): 99–120.

Kulbaga, Theresa A. 2008. Pleasurable pedagogies: *Reading Lolita in Tehran* and the rhetoric of empathy. *College English* 70 (5): 506–21.

Kuppers, Petra. 2003. *Disability and contemporary performance: Bodies on edge*. London and New York: Routledge.

Kuusisto, Stephen. 2008. Teaching by ear. In Lewiecki-Wilson, Brueggemann, and Dolmage, 2008, 124–29.

Langellier, Kristin M. 1998. Voiceless bodies, bodiless voices: The Future of personal narrative performance. In *The future of performance studies: Visions and revisions,* ed. Sheron J. Dailey, 207–13. Annandale, VA: National Communication Association.

Lauer, Janice. 1984. Composition studies: Dappled dscipline. *Rhetoric Review* 3 (1): 20–29.

————. 2002. Rhetorical invention: The diaspora. In Atwill and Lauer 2002, 1–15.

Lauter, Estella, and Carol Schreier Rupprecht, eds. 1985. *Feminist archetypal theory: Interdisciplinary re-visions of jungian thought*. Knoxville: Univ. of Tennessee Press.

LeFevre, Karen Burke. 1987. *Invention as a social act*. Carbondale: Southern Illinois Univ. Press.

Lerner, Gerda. 1997. *Why history matters: Life and thought*. New York: Oxford Univ. Press.

Lewiecki-Wilson, Cynthia, and Brenda Jo Brueggemann, with Jay Dolmage, eds. 2008. *Disability and the teaching of writing: A critical sourcebook*. New York: Bedford/St. Martin's.

Lindgren, Kristin. 2004. Bodies in trouble: Identity, embodiment and disability. In *Gendering disability*, ed. Bonnie G. Smith and Beth Huchinson, 145–65. New Brunswick: Rutgers Univ. Press.

Linton, Simi. 1998. *Claiming disability: Knowledge and identity*. New York: New York Univ. Press.

Logan, Shirley Wilson. 1995. *With pen and voice: A critical anthology of nineteenth-*

century African American women. Carbondale: Southern Illinois Univ. Press.

———. 1999. *"We are coming": Nineteenth-century black women's persuasive discourse.* Carbondale: Southern Illinois Univ. Press.

Looser, Devoney. 1993. Composing as an 'essentialist?': New directions for feminist composition theories. *Rhetoric Review* 12 (1): 54–69.

Lorde, Audre. 1984. *Sister outsider.* Freedom, CA: The Crossing Press.

Lowe, Lisa. 1996. *Immigrant acts: On Asian American cultural politics.* Durham: Duke Univ. Press.

Lu, Min-Zhan. 2004. Composing postcolonial studies. In *Crossing borderlands: Composition and postcolonial studies,* ed. Andrea Lunsford and Lahoucine Ouzgane, 9–32. Pittsburgh: Univ. of Pittsburgh Press.

———. 2008. Review: Knowledge making within transnational connectivities. *College English* 70 (5): 529–34.

Lugones, Maria. 1987. Playfulness, "world" traveling, and loving perception. *Hypatia* 2:3–19.

Lunsford, Andrea, ed. 1995. *Reclaiming Rhetorica: Women in the rhetorical tradition.* Pittsburgh: Univ. of Pittsburgh Press.

Lunsford, Andrea, and Lisa Ede. 2006. Crimes of writing and reading. In Ronald and Ritchie 2006, 13–30.

Madison, D. Soyini. 1998. Performance, personal narrative, and the politics of possibility. In *The future of performance studies: Visions and revisions,* ed. Sheron J. Dailey, 276–86. Annandale, VA: National Communication Association.

———. 1999. Performing theory/embodied writing. *Text and Performance Quarterly* 19:107–24.

Manning, Rita. 1992. Just caring. In Cole and Coultrap-McQuin 1992, 45–56.

Marsden, Jean I. 2002. Beyond recovery: Feminism and the future of eighteenth century literary studies. *Feminist Studies* 28 (3): 657–62.

Mattingly, Carol. 2000. *Well-tempered women: Nineteenth-century temperance rhetoric.* Carbondale: Southern Illinois Univ. Press.

———. ed. 2001. *Water drops from women writers: A temperance reader.* Carbondale: Southern Illinois Univ. Press.

May, Vivian M., and Beth A. Ferri. 2005. Fixated on ability: Questioning ableist metaphors in feminist theories of resistance. *Prose Studies* 27 (1–2): 120–40.

Maynard, Mary, and June Purvis. 1994. *Researching women's lives from a feminist perspective.* Bristol, PA: Taylor and Francis.

McKee, Heidi A., and Dànielle Nicole DeVoss. 2007. *Digital writing research: Technologies, methodologies, and ethical issues.* Cresskill, NJ: Hampton.

McKee, Heidi, and James E. Porter. 2008. The ethics of digital writing research: A rhetorical approach. *College Composition and Communication* 59:711–49.

———. forthcoming. *The ethics of internet research ethics: A rhetorical, case-based process.* New York: Peter Lang.

McRuer, Robert. 2003. As good as it gets: Queer theory and critical disability. *GLQ* 9 (1–2): 79–105.

————. 2006. *Cultural signs of queerness and disability*. New York: New York Univ. Press.

McRuer, Robert, and Abby Wilkerson. 2003. Cripping the (queer) nation. *GLQ* 9 (1–2): 1–23.

Meyer, Michaela D. E. 2007. Women speak(ing): Forty years of feminist contributions to rhetoric and an agenda for feminist rhetorical studies. *Communication Quarterly* 55 (1): 1–17.

Micciche, Laura. 2001. The role of edited collections in composition studies. *Composition Forum* 12 (2): 101–24.

Mill, John Stuart. 1965. *Mill's ethical writings*. New York: Collier Books.

Miller, Carolyn R. 2002. Foreword. In *Rhetoric and kairos: Essays in history, theory, and praxis*, ed. Phillip Sipiora and James S. Baumlin, xi–xiv. Albany, NY: SUNY Press.

Miller, Susan. 1991. The feminization of composition. In *The politics of writing instruction: Postsecondary,* ed. Richard Bullock and John Trimbur, 39–53. Portsmouth, NH: Boynton/Cook.

Minh-ha, Trinh T. 1989. *Woman, native, other: Writing postcoloniality and feminism*. Bloomington: Indiana Univ. Press.

Mitchell, David, and Sharon Snyder. 2001. *Narrative prosthesis: Disability and the dependence of discourse*. Michigan: Univ. of Michigan Press.

————. 2006. *Cultural locations of disability*. Chicago: Univ. of Chicago Press.

Mohanty, Chandra Talpade. 2003. *Feminism without borders: Decolonizing theory, practicing solidarity*. Durham: Duke Univ. Press.

Moi, Toril. 2002. *Sexual/textual politics: Feminist literary theory*, 2nd ed. New York: Routledge.

Moraga, Cherríe. 1983. *Loving in the war years: Lo que nunca pasó por sus labios*. Boston: South End Press.

Moraga, Cherríe, and Gloria Anzaldúa, eds. 1981. *This bridge called my back: Writings by radical women of color*. New York: Kitchen Table.

Morrison, Toni. 2001. The Nobel lecture in literature. In *Available means: An anthology of women's rhetoric(s)*, ed. Joy Ritchie and Kate Ronald, 416–23. Pittsburgh: Univ. of Pittsburgh Press.

Mortensen, Peter, and Gesa E. Kirsch, eds. 1996. *Ethics and representation in qualitative studies of literacy*. Urbana, IL: NCTE.

Murdoch, Iris. 1970. *On "God" and "good": The sovereignty of good*. London: Ark Paperbacks.

Mutua, Makau. 2001. Savages, victims, and saviors: The metaphor of human rights. *Harvard International Law Journal* 42:201–45

Mydans, Seth. 2002. A fallen Saigon rises again in the West. *New York Times*. April 5. http://travel2.nytimes.com/mem/travel/article-page.html?res=9C0C E4DA1F3AF936A35757C0A9649C8B63.

Naples, Nancy A. 2003. *Feminism and method: Ethnography, discourse analysis, and activist research*. New York: Routledge.

Neal, Mark Anthony. 2005. *New black man: Rethinking black masculinity*. New York: Routledge.

Newkirk, Thomas. 1996. Seduction and betrayal in qualitative research. In Mortensen and Kirsch 1996, 3–16.

Nhat Hanh, Thich. 1999. *The heart of the Buddha's teaching: Transforming suffering into peace, joy, and liberation; The Four Noble Truths, The Noble Eightfold Path, and other basic Buddhist teachings*. New York: Broadway.

Noddings, Nel. 1984. *Caring, a feminine approach to ethics and moral education*. Berkeley: Univ. of California Press.

Nussbaum, Martha. 1995. *Poetic justice: The literary imagination and public life*. Boston: Beacon Press.

———. 1996. *For love of country: Debating the limits of patriotism*. Boston: Beacon Press.

———. 1997. *Cultivating humanity: A classical defense of reform in liberal education*. Cambridge: Harvard Univ. Press.

Ong, Aihwa. 1999. *Flexible citizenship: The cultural logics of transnationality*. Durham: Duke Univ. Press.

Ono, Kent A. 1997. A letter/essay I've been longing to write in my personal/academic voice. *Western Journal of Communication* 61:114–25.

Ono, Kent A., and John M. Sloop. 1995. The critique of vernacular discourse. *Communication Monographs* 62:19–46.

Paz, Octavio. 1961. *The labyrinth of solitude: Life and thought in Mexico*. Trans. Lysander Kemp. New York: Grove.

Pelias, Ronald J. 2005. Performative writing as scholarship: An apology, an argument, an anecdote. *Cultural Studies, Critical Methodologies* 5:415–24.

Petruzzi, Anthony P. 2001. Kairotic rhetoric in Freire's liberatory pedagogy. *JAC* 21 (2): 349–81.

Phelps, Louise Wetherbee. 1988. *Composition as a human science: Contributions to the self-understanding of a discipline*. New York: Oxford Univ. Press.

Phelps, Louise Wetherbee, and Janet Emig, eds. 1995. *Feminine principles and women's experience in American composition and rhetoric*. Pittsburgh: Univ. of Pittsburgh Press.

Plain, Gill, and Susan Sellers, eds. 2007. *A history of feminist literary criticism*. Cambridge Univ. Press.

Pollock, Della. 1998. Performative writing. In *The ends of performance*, ed. Peggy Phelan and Jill Lane. New York: New York Univ. Press.

Porter, James E. 1998. *Rhetorical ethics and internetworked writing*. Greenwich, CT: Ablex.

Price, Janet, and Margrit Shildrick. 2002. Bodies together: Touch, ethics and disability. In Corker and Shakespeare 2002, 62–75.

Price, Margaret. 2008. Writing from normal: Critical thinking and disability in the composition classroom. In Lewiecki-Wilson, Brueggemann, and Dolmage 2008, 56–73.

Prosser, Jay. 1998. *Second skins: The body narratives of transsexuality*. New York: Columbia Univ. Press.

Queen, Mary. 2008. Transnational feminist rhetorics in a digital world. *College English* 70 (5): 71–89.

The Quiet American. 2002. Dir. Philip Noyce. Perf. Michael Caine, Brendan Fraser, and Do Thi Hai Yen. Miramax.

Ranney, Frances J. 1999. Posner on legal texts: Law, literature (economics), and "welcome harassment." In *Undisciplining literature: Literature, law, and culture*, ed. Kostas Myrsiades and Linda Myrsiades, 94–116. New York: Peter Lang Publishing.

———. 2000. Beyond Foucault: Toward a user-centered approach to sexual harassment policy. *Technical Communication Quarterly* (Winter): 9–28.

———. 2005. *Aristotle's ethics and legal rhetoric: An analysis of language beliefs and the law*. Burlington, VT: Ashgate Press.

———. Forthcoming. A case study in difference: Fabricating a feminine self in a man-made era. In *Affirming difference*, ed. Elizabeth A. Flynn, Ann Brady, and Patty Sotirin.

———. Forthcoming. Down but not out in Detroit: One woman makes a moral (fashion) statement. *Women's Studies: An Interdisciplinary Journal*.

Ranney, Frances J., Ruth Ray, and Gwen Gorzelsky. Case studies in the rhetoric(s) of need: An invitation to feminist archival research. Panel Presentation at the Feminism(s) and Rhetoric(s) Conference sponsored by the Coalition of Women Scholars in the History of Rhetoric and Composition. October, Michigan Technological University, Houghton, MI.

Ratcliffe, Krista. 1996. *Anglo-American feminist challenges to the rhetorical traditions: Virginia Woolf, Mary Daly, Adrienne Rich*. Carbondale: Southern Illinois Univ. Press.

———. 2006. *Rhetorical listening: Identification, gender, whiteness*. Carbondale: Southern Illinois Univ. Press.

Ray, Ruth. 2000. *Beyond nostalgia: Aging and life-story writing*. Charlottesville: Univ. Press of Virginia.

———. 2008. *Endnotes: An intimate look at the end of life*. Cornell Univ. Press.

Reynolds, Nedra. 1998. Interrupting our way to agency: Feminist cultural studies and composition. In Jarratt and Worsham 1998, 58–73.

Rich, Adrienne. 1986. Notes toward a politics of location. In *Blood, bread, and poetry: Selected prose, 1979–1985*, 210–31. New York: W. W. Norton & Company.

Ritchie, Joy S. 2003. Confronting the "essential" problem: Reconnecting feminist theory and pedagogy. In Kirsch, Maor, Massey, Nickoson-Massey, and Sheridan–Rabideau 2003, 79–102.

Ritchie, Joy S., and Kathleen Boardman. 2003. Feminism in composition: Inclusion, metonymy, and disruption. In Kirsch, Maor, Massey, Nickoson-Massey, and Sheridan–Rabideau 2003, 7–26.

Ritchie, Joy, and Kate Ronald, eds. 2001. *Available means: An anthology of women's rhetoric(s)*. Pittsburgh: Univ. of Pittsburgh Press.

Romain, Dianne. 1992. Care and confusion. In Cole and Coultrap-McQuin 1992, 27–37.

Ronald, Kate. 2008. Feminist perspectives on the history of rhetoric. In *The Sage handbook of rhetorical studies*, ed. Andrea Lunsford, Kirt H. Wilson, and Rosa Eberly, 139–52. Thousand Oaks, CA: Sage Publications.

Ronald, Kate and Joy Ritchie, eds. 2006. *Teaching Rhetorica: Theory, pedagogy, practice*. Portsmouth, NH: Boynton/Cook.

Rorty, Richard. 1990. Feminism and pragmatism. Tanner Lecture on Human Values. December, University of Michigan, Ann Arbor.

Rose, Martha L. 2003. *The staff of Oedipus: Transforming disability in ancient Greece*. Ann Arbor: Univ. of Michigan Press.

Rose, Shirley K., and Irwin Weiser. 2002. Introduction to *The writing program administrator as theorist: Making knowledge work*, ed. Shirley K. Rose and Irwin Weiser, 1–6. Portsmouth, NH: Boynton/Cook.

Rowland, Susan. 2002. *Jung: A feminist revision*. Cambridge: Polity Press.

Royster, Jacqueline Jones. 1995. In search of ways in. In *Feminine principles and women's experience in American composition and rhetoric*, ed. Louise Wetherbee Phelps and Janet Emig, 385–91. Pittsburgh: Univ. of Pittsburgh Press.

———. 2000. *Traces of a stream: Literacy and social change among African American women*. Pittsburgh: Univ. of Pittsburgh Press.

———. 2003. Disciplinary landscaping, or contemporary challenges in the history of rhetoric. *Philosophy and Rhetoric*. 36 (2): 148–67.

———. 2005. Marking trails in the studies of race, gender, and culture. In *Calling cards: Theory and practice in the study of race, gender, and culture*, ed. Jacqueline Jones Royster and Ann Marie Mann Simpkins, 1–14. Albany: SUNY Press.

Royster, Jacqueline Jones, and Ann Marie Mann Simpkins, eds. 2005. *Calling cards: Theory and practice in the study of race, gender, and culture*. Albany: SUNY Press.

Ryan, Kathleen J. 2006. Recasting recovery and gender critique as inventive arts: Constructing edited collections in feminist rhetorical studies. *Rhetoric Review* 25 (1): 22–40.

Sandahl, Carrie. 2003. Queering the crip or cripping the queer? Intersections of queer and crip identities in sole autobiographical performance. *GLQ* 9 (1–2): 25–56.

Sandoval, Chela. 2000. *Methodology of the oppressed*. Minneapolis: Univ. of Minnesota Press.

Sapienza, Fil. 2007. Ethos and research positionality in studies of virtual communities. In McKee and DeVoss 2007, 89–106.

Scaltas, Patricia Ward. 1992. Do feminist ethics counter feminist aims? In Cole and Coultrap-McQuin 1992, 15–26.

Schell, Eileen E. 2006. Gender, rhetorics, and globalization: Rethinking the spaces and locations of women's rhetorics. In Ronald and Ritchie 2006, 160–73.

Schiebinger, Londa L. 1993. *Nature's body: Gender in the making of modern science.* Boston: Beacon Press.

Serlin, David. 2004. *Replaceable you: Engineering the body in postwar America.* Chicago: Univ. of Chicago Press.

Seko, Yukari. 2006. Analyzing online suicidal murmurs. Paper presented at the annual conference of Internet Research 7.0: Internet Convergences. September, Brisbane, Australia.

Showalter, Elaine. 1999. *A literature of their own: British women novelists from Brontë to Lessing.* Expanded ed. Princeton: Princeton Univ. Press.

Shugart, Helene A., 2003. An appropriating aesthetic: Reproducing power in the discourse of critical scholarship. *Communication Theory* 13:275–303.

Siegfried, Charlene Haddock. 1996. *Pragmatism and Feminism: Reweaving the social fabric.* Chicago: Univ. of Chicago Press.

Sifry, David. 2006. State of the blogosphere, February 2006: Part 1: On blogosphere growth. Sifry's alerts: David Sifry's musings. http://www.sifry.com/alerts/archives/000419.html.

Slagle, Anthony R. 2006. Ferment in LGBT studies and queer theory: Personal ruminations on contested terrain. *Journal of Homosexuality* 52:309–28.

Smith, Beatrice. 2007. Researching hybrid literacies: Methodological explorations of "ethnography" and the practices of the cybertariat. In McKee and DeVoss 2007, 127–49.

Smith, Bonnie G., and Beth Huchinson, eds. 2004. Gendering fisability. New Brunswick: Rutgers Univ. Press.

Smith, Dorothy. 2004. Women's perspective as a radical critique of sociology. In *The feminist standpoint theory reader,* ed. Sandra Harding, 21–34. New York: Routledge.

Smoller, Jordan W. 1986. The etiology and treatment of childhood. In *Oral sadism and the vegetarian personality: Readings from the journal of polymorphous perversity,* ed. Glenn C. Ellenbogen, 3–13. New York: Ballantine.

Snyder, Sharon L., Brenda Jo Brueggemann, and Rosemarie Garland-Thomson. 2002. *Disability studies: Enabling the humanities.* New York: MLA.

Spelman, Elizabeth V. 1997. Fruits of sorrow: Framing our attention to suffering. Boston: Beacon Press.

Spivak, Gayatri. 1987. *In other worlds: Essays in cultural politics.* London: Methuen.

Stahl, William Harris, Richard Johnson, and E. L. Burge, trans. 1977. *The marriage of philology and mercury.* Vol. II of *Martianus Capella and the seven liberal arts.* New York: Columbia Univ. Press.

Stern, Susannah R. 2003. Encountering distressing information in online research: A consideration of legal and ethical responsibilities. *New Media and Society* 5:246–66.

————. 2004. Studying adolescents online: A consideration of ethical issues. In *Readings in virtual research ethics: Issues and controversies,* ed. Elizabeth Buchanan, 274–87. Hershey, PA: Information Science Publishing.

Stiker, Jacques. 1999. *A history of disability.* Ann Arbor: Univ. of Michigan Press.

Stryker, Susan. 2008. *Transgender history.* Berkeley: Seal Press.

Sullivan, Patricia A. 1996. Ethnography and the problem of the "other." In Mortensen and Kirsch 1996, 97–114.

————. 2003. Feminism and methodology in composition studies. In Kirsch, Maor, Massey, Nickoson-Massey, and Sheridan-Rabideau 2003, 124–39.

Sullivan, Patricia, and James E. Porter. 1997. *Opening spaces: Writing technologies and critical research practices.* Greenwich, CT: Ablex.

Suter, Lisa. 2003. When rhetoric was a woman. Paper presented at Feminism(s) and Rhetoric(s) Conference. October, Ohio State University, Columbus.

Sutherland, Christine Mason, and Rebecca Sutcliffe, eds. 1999. *The changing tradition: Women in the history of rhetoric.* Calgary: Univ. of Calgary Press.

Swearingen, C. Jan. 1991. *Rhetoric and irony: Western literacy and Western lies.* New York: Oxford Univ. Press.

Tasker, Elizabeth, and France B. Holt-Underwood. 2008. Feminist research methodologies in historic rhetoric: An overview of scholarship from the 1970s to present. *Rhetoric Review* 27 (1): 54–71.

Thayer, Millie. 2000. Traveling feminisms: From embodied women to gendered citizenship. In *Global ethnography: Forces, connections, and imaginations in a postmodern world,* ed. Michael Burawoy et al., 203–34. Berkeley: Univ. of California Press.

Tomm, Winnie. 1992. Ethics and self-knowing: The satisfaction of desire. In Cole Coultrap-McQuin 1992, 101–10.

Tong, Rosmarie. 1993. *Feminine and feminist ethics.* Belmont, CA: Wadsworth.

Tremain, Shelley. 2002. On the subject of impairment. In Corker and Shakespeare 2002, 32–47.

————. 2005. *Foucault and the government of disability.* Ann Arbor: Univ. of Michigan Press.

Trent, James W. 1994. *Inventing the feeble mind: A history of mental retardation in the United States.* Berkeley: Univ. of California Press.

Tyler, Stephen A. 1986. Post-modern ethnography: From document of the occult to occult document. In *Writing culture: The poetics and politics of ethnography,* ed. James Clifford and George E. Marcus, 122–40. Berkeley: Univ. of California Press.

UC Davis Biological Sciences. 1998. *Feminism prompts new perspectives in biology.* Newsletter. http://biosci.ucdavis.edu/alumni/newsletter/spring98/feminism.html.

Vico, Giambattista. 1990. *On the study methods of our time.* Trans. Elio Gianturco. Ithaca: Cornell Univ. Press.

Vonnegut, Kurt. 1988. *Slaughterhouse-five or The children's crusade: A duty-dance with death.* New York: Laurel.

Walther, Joseph B. 2001. Research ethics in Internet-enabled research: Human subjects issues and methodological myopia. In *Internet research ethics.* http://www.nyu.edu/projects/nissenbaum/ethics_walther.html.

Warner, Michael, ed. 1993. *Fear of a queer planet: Queer politics and social theory.* Minneapolis: Univ. of Minnesota Press.

Wehr, Demaris S. 1987. *Jung and feminism: Liberating archetypes.* Boston: Beacon Press.

Weil, Simone. 1977. *The Simone Weil reader.* Ed. George A. Panichas. New York: McKay.

Weiser, Irwin, and Shirley K. Rose. 2002. Theorizing writing program theorizing. In *The writing program administrator as theorist: Making knowledge work,* ed. Shirley K. Rose and Irwin Weiser, 183–95. Portsmouth, NH: Boynton/Cook.

Wertheimer, Molly Meijer, ed. 1997. *Listening to their voices: Essays on the rhetorical activities of historical women.* Columbia: Univ. of South Carolina Press.

West, Robin. 1997. *Caring for justice.* New York: New York Univ. Press.

Wilchins, Riki. 2004. *Queer theory, gender theory: An instant primer.* New York: Alyson Books.

Williams, Bronwyn T. 2004. Changing directions: Participatory-action research, agency, and representation. In *Ethnography unbound: From theory shock to critical praxis,* ed. Stephen Gilbert Brown and Sidney I. Dobrin, 241–57. Albany: SUNY Press.

Williams, Cheri L. 1996. Dealing with the data: Ethical issues in case study research. In Mortensen and Kirsch 1996, 40–57.

Williams, Patricia. 1991. *The alchemy of race and rights.* Cambridge: Harvard Univ. Press.

Wills, David. 1995. Prosthesis. Stanford: Stanford Univ. Press.

Wilson, James C. 2002. (Re)Writing the genetic body-text: Disability, textuality, and the human genome project. *Cultural Critique* 50:23–39.

Wilson, James C., and Cynthia Lewiecki-Wilson, eds. 2001. *Embodied rhetorics: Disability in language and culture.* Carbondale: Southern Illinois Univ. Press.

———. 2002. Constructing a third space: Disability studies, the teaching of English, and institutional transformation. In *Disability studies: Enabling the humanities,* ed. Sharon L. Snyder, Brenda Jo Brueggemann, and Rosemarie Garland-Thomson, 296–307. New York: MLA.

Wilson, Rob. 1998. A new cosmopolitanism is in the air: Some dialectical twists and turns. In *Cosmopolitics: Thinking and feeling beyond the nation,* ed. Pheng Cheah and Bruce Robbins, 351–61. Minneapolis: Univ. of Minnesota Press.

Woolf, Virginia. [1929] 1989. *A room of one's own.* New York: Harcourt.

Worsham, Lynn. 1998. After words: A choice of words remains. In Jarratt and Worsham 1998, 329–56.

———. 2002. Living and learning in a post-traumatic age. Paper presented at the annual Conference on College Communication and Composition, March, Chicago.

———. 2003. Writing against writing: The predicament of écriture féminine in composition studies. In Kirsch, Maor, Massey, Nickoson-Massey, Sheridan-Rabideau 2003, 103–23.

Wu, Hui. A comment on "Historical studies and postmodernism: Rereading Aspasia of Miletus." *College English* 63 (1): 102–5.

Contributors

JOANNE ADDISON is an associate professor in the English Department at the University of Colorado Denver. She writes about empirical methods and methodologies in literacy studies with a focus on the use of digital technologies in understanding literacy as it is lived. In addition to her work using experience sampling methods, she and Sharon James McGee are also engaged in a study of writing in high schools and colleges across the United States that is funded by CCCC.

BERNADETTE M. CALAFELL is an assistant professor in the Department of Human Communication Studies at the University of Denver. She has published articles in various journals such as *Text and Performance Quarterly*, *Critical Studies in Media Communication*, *Cultural Studies = Critical Methodologies*, *Communication Review*, and the *Journal of International and Intercultural Communication*. She is also the author of *Latina/o Communication Studies: Theorizing Performance* (2007).

ILENE WHITNEY CRAWFORD is an associate professor of English and women's studies at Southern Connecticut State University. Her work has appeared in *Composition Forum*, *JAC*, *Academic Writing: Interdisciplinary Perspectives on Communication Across the Disciplines* and the collection *A Way to Move: Rhetorics of Emotion and Composition Studies,* edited by Laura R. Micciche and Dale Jacobs.

JAY DOLMAGE is the coordinator of the first-year writing program at West Virginia University. His research looks at the intersections of rhetoric, disability studies, and pedagogy. His essay "Breathe Upon Us an Even Flame: Hephaestus, History, and the Body of Rhetoric" was the *Rhetoric Review* Theresa Enos Award Winner in 2006; the essay "Metis, Mestiza, Medusa: Rhetorical Bodies across Rhetorical Traditions" is the lead essay in the January 2008 issue of the same journal. His work has also appeared in *JAC*, *CCC*, *College English*, *Prose Studies*, and several edited collections.

GWEN GORZELSKY is associate professor in the Department of English at Wayne State University. She has recent and forthcoming articles on literacy, pedagogy, and research methods in *College Composition and Communication* and *Socially Progressive Research Methodologies for the Study of Writing and Literacy*. She is the author of *The Language of Experience: Literate Practices and Social Change* (2005).

WENDY HESFORD, associate professor of English at The Ohio State University, is the author of *Framing Identities: Autobiography and the Politics of Pedagogy* (1999), coeditor with Wendy Kozol of *Haunting Violations: Feminist Criticism and the Crisis of the "Real"* (2000) and *Just Advocacy? Women's Human Rights, Transnational Feminisms, and The Politics of Representation* (2005), and coauthor with Brenda Jo Brueggemann of *Rhetorical Visions: Reading and Writing in a Visual Culture* (2006). Hesford's second single-authored book, *Spectacular Rhetorics: Human Rights, Feminisms, and the Transnational Imaginary*, is forthcoming. She is the recipient of numerous awards and grants, including a NEH Summer Seminar fellowship, 2007 Visiting Scholar at Columbia University's Center for the Study of Human Rights, OSU Seed Grant, OSU Research Enhancement Grant, several FTAD Seed Grants, and most recently the MLA 2005 Florence Howe essay award. She has published essays in various journals, including *PMLA, Biography, College English, JAC,* and *TDR: Journal of Performance Studies,* among others.

CYNTHIA LEWIECKI-WILSON is professor of English and director of graduate studies at Miami University. Her research interests include feminist and disability rhetoric and composition studies. She has authored and coedited articles, chapters, and books, including *Embodied Rhetorics: Disability in Language and Culture* (2001) with James C. Wilson and *Disability and the Teaching of Writing: A Critical Sourcebook* (2008) with Brenda Jo Brueggemann and Jay Dolmage. New projects include a study of disability discourses in civic debates and a forthcoming collection, *Disability and Mothering: Intersections of Cultural Embodiment*, coedited with Jen Cellio.

HEIDI A. MCKEE is an assistant professor of English at Miami University, where she serves on the institutional review board. She also serves as cochair of the national Qualitative Research Network. She has published numerous articles on digital writing studies, and she is coeditor with Dànielle Nicole DeVoss of the collection *Digital Writing Research: Technologies, Methodologies, and Ethical Issues*, which won the Computers and Writing award for Best Book of 2007. With James Porter, she coauthored the forthcoming *The Ethics of Internet Research: A Rhetorical, Case-Based Approach*.

LAURA R. MICCICHE is associate professor of English and director of composition at the University of Cincinnati, where she teaches writing, rhetoric, and pedagogy courses. A longstanding interest of hers is how writing becomes a frequent site of political, economic, and affective contestation. Her scholarly work includes *Doing Emotion: Rhetoric, Writing, Teaching* (2007), *A Way to Move:*

Rhetorics of Emotion and Composition Studies (2003, edited with Dale Jacobs), and articles in journals such as *College English, College Composition and Communication,* and *JAC.*

JAMES E. PORTER is a professor of English and interactive media studies at Miami University, where he also directs the first-year composition program. Porter's research focuses on digital rhetoric, particularly on how the rhetorical topics of invention, delivery, audience, and ethics are changed in digital environments. His forthcoming book, coauthored with Heidi McKee, is titled *The Ethics of Internet Research: A Rhetorical, Case-Based Approach.*

FRANCES J. RANNEY is associate professor of English and director of women's studies at Wayne State University. Her past publications focus on legal language, especially in areas of law significant to women. In *Aristotle's Ethics and Legal Rhetoric* (2005) Dr. Ranney argues that beliefs about the relationship of law to justice are rooted in theories about the nature of language. Closely examining one sexual harassment case from the perspectives of economic and literary approaches to law, she argues for a rhetorical method that enables intervention in legal discourse. Dr. Ranney's forthcoming publications concern everyday practices by which individuals establish gender identity, especially through the rhetoric and theory of fashion and the body. Two such articles provide the case study of an elderly Detroit woman who used fashion choices to make a moral statement compatible with the Progressive Era discourses among which she grew up. Dr. Ranney's current research, in gender and technology studies, uses constructs from object-relations psychology to understand how we establish relations with each other through technologically mediated interactions, including particularly our interactions through mundane domestic technologies.

RUTH E. RAY is professor of English and faculty associate in gerontology at Wayne State University in Detroit. Her current projects include an edited book on old women in the Great Depression and an auto/biographical book on reading and writing old women's lives as a feminist. She is the author of *Beyond Nostalgia: Aging and Lifestory Writing* (2000) and *Endnotes: An Intimate Look at the End of Life* (2008).

K. J. RAWSON is a PhD candidate in the Composition and Cultural Rhetoric Program at Syracuse University, where he is completing a dissertation entitled "Archiving Transgender: Affects, Logics, and the Power of Queer History." K. J.'s article titled "Accessing Transgender // Desiring Queer(er?) Archival Logics" appears in the Fall 2009 issue of *Archivaria.* K. J.'s research interests include queer, feminist, and transgender studies/theories/rhetorics.

KATE RONALD is Roger and Joyce L. Howe Professor of English at Miami University in Oxford, Ohio. She is director of the Howe Writing Initiative, a joint venture of the Department of English and the Richard T. Farmer School of Business. She is the author and coeditor of many books and articles, including *Available Means: An Anthology of Women's Rhetoric(s)* (2001), coedited with Joy Ritchie; *Teaching Rhetorica* (2006), coedited with Joy Ritchie, and *Farther Along: Transforming Dichotomies in Rhetoric and Composition* (1989), coedited with Hepzibah Roskelly.

KATHLEEN J. RYAN is an assistant professor of English and the director of composition at the University of Montana. She currently teaches graduate courses in composition pedagogy and undergraduate courses in rhetoric and composition. Her research agenda focuses on feminist rhetorical studies and writing program administration. Her publications have appeared in *Rhetoric Society Quarterly, Composition Studies, Rhetoric Review, WPA: Journal of the Council of Writing Program Administrators*, and *Feminist Teacher*. "Theorizing Feminist Pragmatic Rhetoric as a Communicative Art for the Composition Practicum," coauthored with Tarez Graban, is forthcoming from *College Composition and Communication*.

EILEEN E. SCHELL is associate professor of writing and rhetoric and chair and director of the writing program at Syracuse University. She is also a faculty affiliate in women's and gender studies and in the Gerontology Studies Center at Syracuse University. Her first book is a feminist analysis of labor politics in composition studies, *Gypsy Academics and Mother-teachers: Gender, Contingent Labor, and Writing Instruction* (1998). She is coeditor, with Patricia Lambert Stock, of *Moving a Mountain: Transforming the Role of Contingent Faculty in Composition Studies and Higher Education* (2001), which won the 2003 Conference on College Composition and Communication Best Book Award. She is also coauthor of *Rural Literacies* (2007, with Kim Donehower and Charlotte Hogg) in the Studies in Writing and Rhetoric Series. She has authored many articles in composition studies, feminist studies, and rhetorical studies in *College Composition and Communication, College English, Dialogue: A Journal for Writing Specialists, JAC, Workplace: A Journal of Academic Labor,* and *WPA: The Journal of Writing Program Administration*.

Index

academic women in virtual environments, 141–42
active imagination, 128–30
affirmative action model of history, 13
Afrafeminist research methods, 4
African American women, 11, 32
agency, defining as means of enacting, 100
agents, research subjects as, 140
agent/victim binary, 63–64
Ahmed, Sara, 186, 188, 196n1
ambiguity, intentional, 175
anachronistic labeling, 49
analysis: gendered, 40; intersectional, 14–15; of power dynamics, 49; rhetorical, 96; of travel, 76
Angier, Natalie, 140–41
anthologies of recovered women rhetors, 45
anti-immigration rhetoric of early twentieth century, 30
Anzaldúa, Gloria, 48, 105, 113
archival research, 121, 122, 129–30
Aspasia, 15
assignment sketches: creating interruptions, 186–87; inventional argument, 185–86; parody and discourse, 184–85; pragmatic value of, 187–88
attunement, 99
Atwill, Janet, 90
Available Means (Ritchie and Ronald), 11, 44–45, 95–96, 173–74

Ballif, Michelle, 13
Barnard, Ian, 46
Barthes, Roland, 72
basic writers, 80
Baynton, Douglas, 33

Berlo, Janet Catherine, 132–33
Biemann, Ursula, 55, 61–68, 193n5
Biesecker, Barbara, 12–13, 44, 94–95
bifocal standpoint, 181
Bizzell, Patricia, 4, 15, 97
blindness, students with, 25, 28
blogs, 152, 161–64
Bornstein, Kate, 192n6
Bourdain, Anthony, 73
Brandt, Deborah, 144
Bromseth, Janne, 153, 159–61, 164–65, 169
Bruckman, Amy, 162, 196n5
Bustamante, Maris, 68–69

Calhoun, Cheshire, 125
Califia, Patrick, 47, 192n5
Campbell, Karlyn Kohrs, 12–13, 44, 94–95
Campbell-Biesecker exchange, 44, 94–95
canonization, 39, 42–44
canons: feminist rhetorical, 39–40, 42–46; of invention and arrangement, 93, 100
capitalism: expansion of, and English language acquisition, 71
care, alternatives to, 125–26
care ethic, 122–23, 155
care/justice relationship, 123–24
chatroom research, 162
Chodorow, Joan, 128
Chomsky, Noam, 136–37
cisgender, defined, 192n4
Cixous, Helene, 178, 180
Clifford, James, 84
Clinton, Hillary, 53
collective unconscious, 129, 132
college experience, whiteness of, 108
composition: courses in, 146, 183; disability metaphors in histories of, 191n1;

composition: *(cont.)*
   feminist scholarship in, 9–10; as feminized field, 5; as human science, 136–38
Composition as a Human Science (Phelps), 136–37
connections: literacy as means for, 79–80; need for, 111; in Zen Buddhism, 135
Conquergood, Dwight, 114–15
"Constructing a Third Space" (Wilson and Lewiecki-Wilson), 26
Constructing Knowledges (Dobrin), 97
contextual framework, 137–38, 193n2
contingent interval studies, 145
control, as aspect of feminist rhetorics, 175
Cook, Judith, 7–8
Cook's Tour, A (Bourdain), 73
cosmopolitan, as term, 54
cosmopolitan feminist rhetorical analytics, 65
cosmopolitan identifications, and global justice, 58
cosmopolitanism, 54–55, 59
cosmopolitan travel, 53
Couser, G. Thomas, 36–37
Crawford, Ilene, 7
"Creating Discursive Space Through a Rhetoric of Difference" (Flores), 109
crip, as term, 36
crisis intervention, 164
critical anthropology, 84
critical consciousness, 155
critical pedagogies, 183
critical reflection, 91
critical rhetoric, 114
critical rhetorical scholarship, disciplinary practices in, 107
critical writing, as rhetorical analysis, 96
"Critique of Vernacular Discourse" (Ono and Sloop), 114
Csikszentmihalyi, Mihaly, 145
Cubbison, Laurie, 153–55, 158–59, 164–66, 169
Cultivating Humanity (Nussbaum), 54
cultural amnesia, 19
cultural logics, 29
cultural outsiders in the academy, 108–9
cyborgian writing model, 182
cyborgs, 181–82

Davis, Barney and Hiram, 32
Davis, Olga, 109–10, 194n2 (Rhetorics of Possibility)

dead language, 178–79
definition, as critical theoretical act, 100
Delgado, Fernando, 106–7
dialogism, 156–57, 194n5 (Making Pathways)
dialogue of sources papers, 186
digital route/root systems, 81–82
digital writing research, 153, 159–64, 170, 195n2 (Rhetorica Online)
Diogenes, 54
directional disturbances, feminism's, 176
disabilities, euphemisms for, 35
disabilities, oppression of people with, 29
disability: ableist perspective in stories about, 36–37; British social model vs. postmodern approach to, 190n3; construction of meanings of, 36; as deviance, 25; hierarchy of, 32–33; history of, 30–31; intersectional understanding of, 33; lack of challenge to construction of, 191n9; medicalizing of, 35; reframing of, 23–24; as stigma, 33–34; universalization of, 34; use of, as rhetorical power, 27
disability studies: benefits of, 38; critique of normativity, 191n11; embodied foundation for, 27–28; feminist rhetorical methods as foundation for, 23; and methods for new rhetorical futures, 24; and normativities, 17
disabled body, 190–91n4
disablement, role of social arrangements in, 35
disciplinarity, as landscaping, 102
disciplinary territoriality, as aspect of male paradigm, 107
discipline, traditional definition of, 101–2
disembodied rhetorical history, 27
disobedience, as strategy for feminist writing projects, 182
disruptions in writing, 177–78
Dobrin, Sidney, 97
documentary techniques, 65–66
Dolmage, Jay, 26–28, 30
double-entry notes, 94
Dreaming of Double Woman (Berlo), 132–33

edited collections, 11, 94–95
embodied rhetorical action, identity as, 63
embodiment, in disability studies theory, 27–28
emotion, role in feminist historiography, 15
empirical data worthy of study, 138–39
empirical phenomenology, 144

empirical research, feminist standpoint in, 140–41
English language acquisition, capitalism's expansion and, 71
Ensler, Eve, 55–60
epistemology, as framework in feminist studies, 8
epistemology, defined, 3
essentialism in feminist scholarship, 12
Ethical Dilemmas in Feminist Research (Kirsch), 8–9
ethical paralysis, 128
ethical researchers, qualities of, 155–56
ethic of care, 121–23, 155
ethics: feminist, 121–22, 126–27; in Internet research, 159–64; qualitative research, 133–34; of research, 120; Zen Buddhist, 135
ethnographic knowledge, paradoxical nature of, 84
ethnography, feminist rhetorics as complement to, 84
ethos, construction of, in feminist rhetorics, 164–65, 175
"Etiology and Treatment of Childhood" (Smoller), 184–85
eugenics, early twentieth-century, 30, 35, 119–20, 130
euphemisms for disabilities, 35
everyday life, lack of attention to, in rhetorical scholarship, 110
evolutionary biology, 140
experience sampling form, 148–51
experience sampling methods, 144–45, 146–48

Feinberg, Leslie, 48, 192n6
female embodiment, in rhetoric traditions, 23
female genital mutilation, 57
feminine ethics, 126
feminist academics, challenges of, 4–5
feminist cosmopolitanism, 54–55
feminist critique, functions of, 176
feminist ethical project, 121, 127, 131–32
feminist ethics, 122, 126–27
feminist historiography, 10–11, 15
feminist methods, 174
feminist orientalism, 56
feminist orientation to writing, 176
feminist philosophers, 127
feminist post-Jungian work, 129

feminist pragmatism, 90
feminist recovery method, critics of, 44
feminist research: branches of inquiry in, 10; in evolutionary biology, 140; features of, 4, 189–90n5; innovations of, 128; major paths of, in rhetoric and composition, 9; principles for, 7–9; and rhetorical research, 2; trends, debates, and dilemmas in, 8
feminist research methodologies, 154–56, 174–75
feminist rhetorical canon, 39–40, 42–46
feminist rhetorical methods, as movement, 6–7
feminist rhetorical normativity, 42–43
feminist rhetorical recovery scholarship, 10–11, 13, 40, 45–47
feminist rhetorical studies: challenges of, 89–90; defined, 90; disciplinary status of, 95, 102; methods and methodologies in, 7–16, 96; nationalist vs. transnationalist emphasis, 61–62
feminist rhetorical theorizing, and analysis of power dynamics, 49
feminist rhetorical theory, 40, 173, 175, 184–87
feminist rhetorics: alignment of, with developments in feminism and gender theory, 52; of challenge, 142; as complement to critical anthropology, 84; debate over evidence in histories of, 15; goal of, 138, 175–76; methodological approaches to, 40; relationship between, and empirical research, 136; as writing theory in action, 174
feminists, as rhetorical theorists of writing, 187
feminists, postmodern, 129
feminist scholarship, 12, 78
feminist standpoint theory, 139, 140–41, 142, 143–44
feminist writing practices, 173–74
Ferguson, James, 75
flexibility, as quality of ethical feminist researcher, 156
Flores, Lisa, 109
Flynn, Elizabeth, 5
Fonow, Mary, 7–8
Fontia R. (case #133), 119, 122, 124–25, 130, 134
Fox, Ellen L., 126
framing/shaping, as theorizing, 99

framing texts, for edited collections, 94–95
Franks, Lucinda, 53
freakification, 32
freak shows, 31–32
Freud, Sigmund, 123
Fruits of Sorrow (Spelman), 60
Fuss, Diana, 12

Gale, Xin, 15
Garland-Thomson, Rosemary, 11–12, 31–32, 190n2
gender, 46, 49–50
gender critique, 91, 96
gendered analysis, 40, 49
gender expression advocacy, 47–48
gender-neutral pronouns, 192n7
gender normatives, 46, 51
gender oppression, 48
gender relations, commercialized, on the Internet, 66–67
gender theory, alignment of feminist rhetorics with developments in, 52
gene research, rhetoric in support of, 30
Gilligan, Carol, 122–23
Gilman, Charlotte Perkins, 178
GLBT academics, and uses of the Internet, 141–42
Glenn, Cheryl, 15, 49–51, 191n8
global feminism, in rhetorical studies, 53
global feminist citizenship, 58
global rhetorical studies, internationalist focus of, 69
global sex industry, 63–68
Gorzelsky, Gwen, 118–19, 133–35
Gowaty, Patricia, 140
greater good justification, 122
Greene, Graham, 73
Grewal, Inderpal, 60
Grontowski, Christine R., 29–30
Grosz, Elizabeth, 190–91n4
group consent, 160–61
group work, student ranking of, 147
growing routes, as methodology, 71, 76
Gupta, Akhil, 75

Hall, John (Radclyffe), 47, 192n5
Hannan Foundation, 118–19
Haraway, Donna, 139–40, 174–75, 181–83, 191n5
Harding, Sandra, 2–3, 143
Hephaestus, 27–28
Hilligoss, Susan, 141–42

Holbrook, Sue Ellen, 5
homeplaces, 105–6, 109, 116–17
hooks, bell, 112, 115, 116
human rights internationalism, 54
human rights violations against women, 56
human sciences model, 137
human subjectivity model, 13
human subject research, 164, 196n5

identification, visual rhetoric of, 53
identity, 63, 181–82, 192n3
identity politics, 105
imagin-activation, 126, 129–32, 134–35
imagination, 75
impersonal abstraction, as aspect of male paradigm, 107
In a Different Voice (Gilligan), 123
individual writing, student ranking of, 147
informed consent issue, 159–61, 162–64
inner space, 126, 131
inner teaching, 131
Insecure at Last (Ensler), 56, 59–60
intentionality, as aspect of feminist rhetorics, 175
interactionist dialectical process, 29–30
interarticulations, 60, 65
interconnections, in Zen Buddhism, 135
interdisciplinary research, 6
Internet: ethical issues in research, 159–64; gender relations on, 66–67; uses of, and struggles of GLBT academics, 141–42
interruption, as rhetorical strategy, 177–78
interruptions, creating (assignment sketch), 186–87
interruptive papers, 186
intersectional analysis, 14–15
intersectionality, 14, 32–34
intertextuality, 62
interviews, 147–48, 195–96n2 (Rhetorica Online)
intuition, operation of, in inner spaces, 131
invention, 91–92, 101
inventional argument (assignment sketch), 185–86
invention studies, 91

Jarratt, Susan C., 10, 15, 40
Johnson, William, 31–32
journey narrative, 59, 110–12, 116. *See also* travel
Jung, Karl, 129
Jung on Active Imagination (Chodorow), 128

justice, conceptions of, 123
justice/care relationship, 123–24

kairos, 55–56, 62–63, 69, 193n3
Kant, Immanuel, 120
Keller, Evelyn Fox, 29–30
Kirsch, Gesa E., 8–9, 195n2 (Mining the Collective Unconscious)
Kolodny, Annette, 1
Kuusisto, Stephen, 28

labeling, anachronistic, 49
labels, history of, 35
language, distinctions between living and dead, 178–79
language choices, implications of, 37–38
language faculty, 80, 137, 195n1 (Researching Literacy)
language practices, reflections on, 35–38
Larson, Reed, 145
Lauer, Janice, 5
laughter, as subversion of man-made language, 180
"Letter/Essay I've Been Longing to Write in My Personal/Academic Voice" (Ono), 114
Lewiecki-Wilson, Cynthia, 25–26
Literature of Their Own, A (Showalter), 43
Linton, Simi, 35–36
listening, 49, 191n8
listservs, 153
literacy, 79–80, 144
Literacy in American Lives (Brandt), 144
literacy narratives, 71, 76–77
literacy sponsors, concept of, 82–83
Logan, Shirley Wilson, 11
Lunsford, Andrea, 1

mail-order bride market, 66–67
male paradigm, in scholarship, 107
La Malinche, 104
Malintzin, Doña Marina, 104, 110–12, 116
Man Cannot Speak for Her (Campbell), 12, 44
"Manifesto for Cyborgs" (Haraway), 174, 181–83, 186
Manning, Rita, 125
man/woman binary, destabilization of, 50
Marsden, Jean, 10–11
master narrative, disruption of, 112
Maynard, Mary, 128
McRuer, Robert, 34

medical model, 29–31, 191n6
memory, role in shaping perspective, 75
methodological homeplace, 116–17
methodological reflexivity, 154
methodology, 2, 174
methods, 174
metis, rhetorical value of, 27–28
Micciche, Laura, 95
Miller, Susan, 5
Minh-ha, Trinh T., 179–80
minority voices, 106–7
minors in human subject research, 164
mobility, privileged, 58
Mohanty, Chandra, 77–78
Moi, Toril, 43
Moraga, Cherríe, 105, 108
moral activity, paradigms for, 125
Morrison, Toni, 178–79
movement: feminist rhetorical methods as, 6–7; in feminist rhetorical theory, 40; physical, 78–79, 82, 84; as synecdoche for feminism, 187; theory of, 76
multicultural rhetoric, 60
multimodal scholarship, 5
Murdoch, Iris, 126

Naples, Nancy, 127–28
National Endowment for the Humanities (NEH), 157, 196n5
natural literacy myth, 137
Neal, Mark Anthony, 47, 192n5
Nhat Hanh, Thich, 135
"Nobel Lecture in Literature" (Morrison), 178–79
Noddings, Nel, 124
norm, concept of, 190n1
normal, critique of, in queer theory, 41–42
normal, demystifying, 24–26
normate, 24–25, 190n2
normativities: and disabilities as stigma, 33; disability studies and, 17, 191n11; feminist rhetorical, 42–43; and the scientific gaze, 31; sexual and gender, 45–46
note-taking practices, 92–94, 99
Noyce, Philip, 74
Nussbaum, Martha, 54

objectification of the Other, 30–32
objective research methodologies, 32
objectivity, 32, 142–43, 147
online communities, 152–53, 164, 196n6, 196n8

online digital writing, rhetorical dynamics of, 158–60, 170
online ethos, 164–65
online forums, 157–60
Ono, Kent A., 114
open access position, 158
opportunity structures, 193n3
oppositional logics, 64
oppression: epistemologies and methodologies of, 14; people with disabilities and, 29, 32–33
oppressive language, as violence, 179
ordering experiences, as conceptual acts, 99
organizational research strategies, 94
orientations, 176, 196n1
Other voices, challenges in engaging, 107

paradigms for moral activity, 125
Pareiyo, Agnes, 57
parental investment theory, 140
parody and discourse (assignment sketch), 184–85
pedagogical methods, infiltration of, by feminist rhetorical theory, 184–87
pedagogical practices of universal design, 26
people of color, theorizing by, 115
performance and performative writing, 112–13
performance paradigm, 115
performance studies, 110
personal experiences, in methodological approach, 104–5
personal liberation, rhetorical identification and, 59
personal narrative, and performance, 112–13
perspective, shaping of, 75
Phelps, Louise Wetherbee, 136, 137
phenomenological research, 144
phenomenon, context of, in critical interpretation, 138
philosophers, 126–27
philosophy of science, contextualism in, 138
physical movement, 78–79, 82, 84
Piaget, Jean, 123
place, metaphoric approach to, 72
place/space distinction, 75
play, and writing pedagogy, 181–83
play, as element in feminist writing projects, 174

postmodern feminists, and Jung, 129
primate research, 138–39
privacy expectations, in online forums, 157–58
Progressive Era, 119–20, 124, 130
public sphere, 61, 193n2
Purvis, June, 128

qualitative research, 5–6, 133–34
queer, as strategy, 46
queering feminist rhetorical canonization, 45–51
Queer Race (Barnard), 46
queer theory, 41–42
questioning, as heuristic for theorizing, 98–99
questions, in knowledge building, 176
Quiet American, The (film), 74–75
Quiet American, The (Green), 73
"Quilting for My Life" (Berlo), 132–33

race, as debatable category, 50
random sampling, 145
Ratcliffe, Krista, 49–50, 191n8
Ray, Ruth, 118, 132–33
"Recasting Recovery and Gender Critique as Inventive Arts" (Ryan), 91–92, 96
Reclaiming Rhetorica (Lunsford), 1
recovered women rhetors, anthologies of, 45
recovery and gender critique, as textual research methods, 91, 103
recovery projects in feminist rhetorical scholarship, 10–11, 13, 40, 45–47
redefinition, as means of theorizing, 100
Remote Sensing (Biemann), 63–66
Rensselaer Poltechnic Institute (RPI), 1
researchers: ethical, qualities of, 155–57, 170; online, 158; as participant observers, 160, 165–66
research interactions with participants, 164–68
research methodologies, objective, 32
research methods, 2, 102
research subjects, as agents, 140
Reynolds, Nedra, 177
Rhetorica, historical image of, 1, 189n1 (Introduction)
rhetorical analysis, critical writing as, 96
rhetorical arrangement, 93
rhetorical canons, synergistic relationship of, 93

rhetorical criticism, 109, 114
rhetorical fitness, redefining, 27–29
rhetorical history, as normative text, 27
rhetorical identification, 57–59
Rhetorical Listening (Ratcliffe), 49
rhetorical process of imagin-activation, 131
rhetorical scholarship, lack of attention to
  everyday life in, 110
rhetoric and composition, as contextualized human sciences discipline, 136
rhetoric and rhetorics: affirmative action
  approach to history of, 44; of cyberspace, 170; of emancipation, 37; of genders, 49; gender-sensitive history of, 13;
  of listening, 191n8; patriarchal traditions
  of, 23; of silence, 51, 191n8; as social construction at work on itself, 127. *See also*
  feminist rhetorics
rhetoric as *techne,* aim of, 90
Ritchie, Joy, 11, 15–16, 44–45, 77–78, 95–96,
  173–75
Romain, Dianne, 122–23
Ronald, Kate, 2, 11, 15–16, 44–45, 77–78,
  95–96, 173–75
Royster, Jacqueline Jones, 4, 14–15, 180–81

science, and rational subject-observer, 29
scientific gaze, 31–32
Seko, Yukari, 153, 161–64, 167–68, 196n9
self-invisibility, 191n5
self-reflexivity, 58, 155
sensory metaphors, 37
Sex Changes (Califia), 47–48
sex industry, global, 63–68
sexual abuse victims, survivor discourse
  of, 127–28
sexual normativities in feminist rhetorical
  studies, 45–46
sexual violations against women, 56
sex workers, lured-and-tricked narrative
  of, 64–65
shaping, 75, 94, 99
Showalter, Elaine, 43
signals of difference, 82
silence, as conceptual category of analysis,
  49
silence, rhetoric of, 51, 191n8
Simpkins, Ann Marie Mann, 14–15
sites of critical regard, 4
situated knowledge, 140
Skype chat, 85
Slagle, Anthony, 107

Sloop, John M., 114
Smith, Dorothy, 143
Smoller, Jordan, 184
social arrangements, role in disablement,
  35
social difference, intersectionality of categories, 14
social justice, commitment to, as quality of
  ethical feminist researcher, 155
social science feminist research principles,
  7–8
space/place distinction, 75
speech communication, linguistic and
  textual bias of, 114–15
Spelman, Elizabeth, 60
Stamps, Judy, 138–39
standpoint theorists, 180–81, 195n2 (Researching Literacy). *See also* feminist
  standpoint theory
Stern, Susannah, 162
stigma, labels of, 37
Stoics, 54
strong objectivity, 142–43
subversive thought generation, 179
suicidal bloggers, study of, 167–68
Sullivan, Patricia, 9–10
support groups, 153
surrealist ethnography, 84
synergistic relationship of rhetorical canons, 93

Teaching Rhetorica (Ronald and Ritchie),
  11, 175
Tenepal, Malintzin, 104
textual bias, paradigm shift away from, 115
textual research methods, recovery and
  gender critique as, 91
theories of the flesh, 105, 110–13
theorizing, 98–99, 102–3, 115
theory, 96–98
theory of movement, 76
This Bridge Called My Back (Moraga and
  Anzaldúa), 105
Thi Thu Chung Le, 84
Thuan Vu, 72
Tomm, Winnie, 126
topoi, 72
transgender critique, 42
transgendered people, identity options
  for, 50
transgender rhetors, 48
TransLiberation (Feinberg), 48

transnational feminism, 55, 60–62, 84
transnational feminist methods, 65
transnational feminist rhetorical analytic, 69
transnational movement, methodological challenges of, 61–62
transnational publics, as arenas of struggle, 61
transparency, as quality of ethical feminist researcher, 156, 170
transsexuality, 50
travel, 53, 58–59, 76. *See also* journey narrative
Trent, James, 35

"Under the Burqa" (Ensler), 58–59
universal design concept, in pedagogical practices, 26
University of Colorado at Denver and Health Sciences Center (UCDHSC), 146
Unspoken (Glenn), 49–51

V-Day foundation, 57
vernacular discourse, critique of, 114
victim/agent binary, 63–64
victimization, challenges in documenting, 65
Vietnam, 71–72, 76–77
Vietnamese women, 83
Vietnam War, as cultural trauma, 73–74
virgin market, 66–67
virgin/whore dichotomy, 111
visual rhetoric of identification, 53
voice and voices, 104, 106–7, 110, 114, 123

Walther, Joseph, 158–59
Warner, Michael, 41
"*We Are Coming*" (Logan), 11
Weil, Simone, 126

whiteness of college experience, 108–9
Wilkerson, Abby, 34
With Pen and Voice (Logan), 11
woman: as category, 11–12; and category of disability, 23; defined in feminist rhetorics, 41; naturalized category of, in feminist rhetorical recovery, 45–46
women: academic, in virtual environments, 141–42; African American, 11, 32; in global sex industry, rhetorical competence and strategies of, 67–68; human rights violations against, 56; as language stealers, 179; Vietnamese, 83
women of color, testimony of, 106
women rhetors, 11, 45, 174
women's groups online, 152
women's rhetorical practices, 175
women's writing as theory, 96
wonder, 186, 188
Woolf, Virginia, 180
word-work, 178–79
World Wide Web, 152
Worsham, Lynn, 177, 189n4
writing: as caring, 180; as feminist machinery, 181; history of, as male province, 178; to make sense of the world, 112; as means for invention, 179; as play, 182; and sense of defamiliarization, 177; standards focus in teaching, 191n11; women's, as theory, 96
writing courses, ways of doing feminist rhetorics in, 184–87
Writing Desire (Biemann), 63–64, 66–69
writing theory, 174
writing vs. writing about, 83–84

"Yellow Wallpaper, The" (Gilman), 178

Zen Buddhist ethics, 135